Grain Markets in Europe, 1500–1900

Karl Gunnar Persson surveys a broad sweep of economic history, examining one of the most crucial markets – grain. His analysis allows him to draw more general lessons – for example, that liberalisation of markets was linked to political authoritarianism. *Grain Markets in Europe, 1500–1900* traces early regulation to poor performance and frequent market failures. Price volatility caused by harvest shocks was of major concern for central and local government because of the unrest it caused. Regulation became obsolete when markets became more integrated and performed better through trade triggered by falling transport costs. Karl Gunnar Persson, a specialist in economic history, uses insights from development economics, explores contemporary economic thought on the advantages of free trade and measures the extent of market integration using state-of-the-art econometric methods. *Grain Markets in Europe, 1500–1900* will be of value to scholars and students in economic history, social history and agricultural and institutional economics.

KARL GUNNAR PERSSON is Reader at the Institute of Economics, the University of Copenhagen. A former President of the European Historical Economics Society, and current editor of the *European Review of Econonic History*, he has lectured widely on economic history. He is the author of *Pre-Industrial Economic Growth* (1988) and editor of *Economic Development of Denmark and Norway since 1870* (1993).

Cambridge Studies in Modern Economic History 7

Grain Markets in Europe, 1500–1900

CAMBRIDGE STUDIES IN MODERN ECONOMIC HISTORY

Series editors

Cambridge Studies in Modern Economic History is a major new initiative in economic history publishing, and a flagship series for Cambridge University Press in an area of scholarly activity in which it has long been active. Books in this series will primarily be concerned with the history of economic performance, output and productivity, assessing the characteristics, causes and consequences of economic growth (and stagnation) in the western world. This range of enquiry, rather than any one methodological or analytic approach, will be the defining characteristic of volumes in the series.

The first titles in the series are:
1 *Central and Eastern Europe 1944–1993: detour from the periphery to the periphery*
Ivan Berend
ISBN 0 521 55066 1
2 *Spanish agriculture: the long Siesta 1765–1965*
James Simpson
ISBN 0 521 49630 6
3 *Democratic socialism and economic policy: the Attlee Years 1945–1951*
Jim Tomlinson
ISBN 0 521 55095 5
4 *Productivity and performance in the paper industry: labour, capital and technology, 1860–1914*
Gary Bryan Magee
ISBN 0 521 58197 4
5 *An economic history of the silk industry, 1830–1930*
Giovanni Federico
ISBN 0 521 58198 2
6 *The Balkan Economies c. 1800–1914*
Michael Palairet
ISBN 0 521 58051 X
7 *Grain markets in Europe, 1500–1900: integration and deregulation*
Karl Gunnar Persson
ISBN 0 521 65096 8

To my sons Mårten and Hannes

Grain Markets in Europe, 1500–1900

Integration and Deregulation

Karl Gunnar Persson

University of Copenhagen

CAMBRIDGE
UNIVERSITY PRESS

CAMBRIDGE UNIVERSITY PRESS
Cambridge, New York, Melbourne, Madrid, Cape Town, Singapore, São Paulo

Cambridge University Press
The Edinburgh Building, Cambridge CB2 2RU, UK

Published in the United States of America by Cambridge University Press, New York

www.cambridge.org
Information on this title: www.cambridge.org/9780521650960

First published 1999
This digitally printed first paperback version 2005

A catalogue record for this publication is available from the British Library

Library of Congress Cataloguing in Publication data

Persson, Karl Gunnar, 1943–
Grain markets in Europe, 1500–1900 : integration and deregulation
/ Karl Gunnar Persson.
 p. cm.
Includes bibliographical references and index.
ISBN 0-521-65096-8 (hbk.)
1. Grain trade–Europe. 2. Grain trade–Government policy–
Europe. 3. Grain trade–Deregulation–Europe. I. Title.
HD9045.A2P47 1999
381′.4131′094–dc21 99-12834 CIP

ISBN-13 978-0-521-65096-0 hardback
ISBN-10 0-521-65096-8 hardback

ISBN-13 978-0-521-02388-7 paperback
ISBN-10 0-521-02388-2 paperback

Contents

List of figures   *page* xi
List of tables   xiii
Preface   xv
Acknowledgements   xviii
List of abbreviations   xx

1   Bread and Enlightenment: the quest for price stability and
    free trade in eighteenth-century Europe   1
        The baker of last resort and his critics
        A theory of price stabilisation
        Market integration, profits and incentives
        Uncertainty and effort
        A short digression on Turgot

2   Markets, mortality and human capabilities   23
        Who suffers from price instability?
        Consumption, capabilities and survival
        Deprivation and the moral economy
        Appendix

3   Harvest fluctuations, storage and grain-price responses   47
        The political economy of harvest failures
        The new estimates
        The extent of early modern grain storage
        The 'seven lean years'
        Appendix: notes and sources to table 3.2

4   Market failures and the regulation of grain markets: a
    new interpretation   65
        Technological constraints, risk and price volatility
        The political economy of grain market intervention
        Bread and grain
        Public granaries
        International disorder and autarchy
        Public crowding out of private virtues?

5   Market integration and the stabilisation of grain prices in
    Europe, 1500–1900   91
        The measurement of market integration
        An equilibrium error-correction model
        The decline in price volatility
        Appendix
        METTE EJRNÆS

6   Authoritarian liberalism and the decline of grain market
    regulation in Europe, 1760–1860   131
        Institutional change, welfare and efficiency
        Royals, élites and liberals
        Swedish ambiguity and Tuscan robustness
        France: the fraility of reform
        Two latecomers: the Habsburg monarchy and Prussia
        The changing mood of bureaucracies and their subjects
        The campaign for a free market in early nineteenth-century France and Sweden
        The decline of the food riot
        The Continent in the English mirror

    Sources   156
    Bibliography   160
    Index   170

List of figures

1.1.	Total revenue of a representative farmer	*page* 15
2.1.	Nominal income and grain consumption of a representative small-holder	26
2.2	Food consumption and individual survival probability	33
2.3	Crude death rates and infant deaths, 1750–1914	36
2.4	A shift in the survival function	38
2A.1	Health, consumption and personal constitution	43
2A.2	A rectangular distribution of personal constitution	44
2A.3	A strictly concave survival function	45
2A.4	A single-peaked distribution of personal constitution	45
2A.5	A shift in the distribution of personal constitution	46
4.1	Expected gross return and its standard deviation from storage of wheat, Siena, Cologne and Pisa, 1550–1700	69
4.2	Residual variation of bread prices as a percentage of the residual variation in rye price, Cologne, 1660–1760	80
5.1	Monthly observations of wheat prices, Pisa and Siena, 1560–1580	94
5.2	Monthly observations of wheat prices, Arras and Rouen, 1867–1886	95
5.3	Location of market towns analysed in this chapter	97
5.4	Adjustment of a 'follower' market to a price shock in a dominating market	104
5.5	Mutual adjustment in pairs of European markets, eighteenth and nineteenth centuries	105
5.6	Price of wheat, Toulouse, 1490–1590 and 1825–1913	107
5.7	Standard deviation of the residual in a random-walk model of monthly wheat prices, Toulouse, 1500–1900	109
5.8	Standard deviation of the residual in a random-walk model of monthly wheat prices, Pisa, 1560–1820	110
5A.1	The level of the wheat price, Pisa, 1633–1682	116
5A.2	The log of the wheat price, Pisa, 1633–1682	116
5A.3	The differences of the wheat price, Pisa, 1633–1682	117

5A.4 The monthly average of the differences of the wheat price,
      Pisa, 1633–1682   118
5A.5 The monthly variance of the differences of the wheat price,
      Pisa, 1633–1682   118
5A.6 The autocorrelation of the wheat price, Pisa, 1633–1682   119
5A.7 The standard deviation of the error term in the recursive
      analysis of the autoregressive model   120
5A.8 The standard deviation of the error term in the recursive
      analysis of a random-walk model   122
5A.9 The log price of wheat, Lyon, 1855–1872   127
5A.10 The log price of wheat, Bordeaux, 1855–1872   128
5A.11 The stationary relation between Lyon and Bordeaux,
      1855–1872   129

Tables

1.1 Effects on total revenue of output shocks under different market conditions *page* 17

2.1 Effects of an increase in grain output on a representative farmer in two types of markets 28

2.2 Correlation coefficients between price changes for different agrarian products, Pisa 1632–1663 29

3.1 Elasticities and prices implied by examples from Davenant, Quesnay and Turgot 52

3.2 Estimates of elasticities, grain, Europe, sixteenth–nineteenth centuries 53

3.3 Parameter values for a trend-stationary model of English wheat prices, 1540–1699 57

3.4 Analysis of the residuals, 1540–1699 58

3.5 Variance of future price as a function of present price, English wheat prices, 1540–1699 59

3.6 Statistical indicators for the prices of wheat, potatoes and buttter, Sweden, 1830–1900 62

4.1 Standard deviation of the residuals in a random-walk model of grain price 66

4.2 A typology of grain market institutions 74

4.3 Price volatility in regulated and non-regulated markets, 1685–1801 89

5.1 Results from equilibrium error-correction tests, European cities, sixteenth and seventeenth centuries 99

5.2 Results from equilibrium error-correction tests, European cities, eighteenth century 100

5.3 Results from equilibrium error-correction tests, European cities, nineteenth century 101

5.4 Results from equilibrium error-correction tests, French cities, nineteenth century 102

5.5 Standard deviation of the residual in a random-walk model of monthly prices, European markets, *c.* 1500–*c.* 1913 112

5A.1 Results from the cointegration tests, Lyon and Bordeaux, 1855–1872 130

Preface

This study began as an inquiry into the historical roots, causes and effects of individualism and economic liberalism. The motivating idea was simplistic, but instrumental in getting the project ahead. I believed that institutions thrive to the extent that they are useful and decay when a viable and better alternative emerges. This familiar idea has often been abused or trivialised, or both, so I decided to confront it by analysing an important case of institutional change: the demise of the system of grain market regulation that developed in medieval and early modern Europe. The uniformity of the European experience is striking, as is the subsequent integration *and* deregulation of grain markets during a century or so of reform, which began with the Enlightenment in continental Europe (though earlier in England). The logic was this: the integration of markets can do what regulated markets are supposed to accomplish and sometimes do accomplish – make markets perform better. Improved performance refers to the waning of market power and, more importantly, the suppression of price volatility. Prohibitively high transport costs ruled out market integration but when technological progress in the transport of goods and information lowered costs the integration of markets was stimulated. As a consequence, we should expect both market power and volatility to decline and centuries of price-stabilising regulation to come to an end.

In a previous book, *Pre-Industrial Economic Growth* (1988), I conjectured that the size of an economy – or, better perhaps, the number of people participating in an economy – fostered economic freedom. The reason for this presumption was that as the number of agents increased the opportunities for, and adverse effects of, collusion and market power dwindled. The alleged use or abuse of market power was a repeated complaint against markets and unrestrained individual economic freedom in the medieval and early modern periods. It also provided the motive and excuse for regulating markets, grain markets in particular. It was the specific *combination* of market power and self-seeking behaviour that was opposed because of its detrimental effects on the welfare of others. In this historical context, the connection between integration and deregulation became paramount. One important aspect of integration was that the size of the economy increased from a regional to a national and finally an international network. The number of agents therefore also increased and the impact of purely local events – such as a local harvest failure – on local outcomes – prices – was weakened. (If there are economies of scale internal to firms the size of the firms might increase when markets are integrated. Consequently the number of agents or firms might not change at all. The risks of market power will therefore remain a threat in the modern economy, and that is why there is still regulation out there.)

That market integration effectively halted collusion was one of the favoured themes of the eighteenth-century critique of the prevailing market regulation. This is the focus of chapter 1 of the present book. While contemporaries often identified *any* price increase as the result of monopolistic price-rigging, reformers vigorously asserted that an increase in the number of merchants was antithetical to market power. However, the evidence suggests the *combination* of harvest shocks and poor integration as the immediate and most important cause of price rises. The free trade which the eighteenth-century political economists favoured was a solution – provided transport costs fell – because harvest shocks were local and independent. Trade could therefore cancel out excess supply and demand between regions and nations and exploit the advantages of largeness. A good harvest in one region was usually matched by a shortage somewhere else, a poor harvest in one year was followed by bumper harvests in the near future. Free trade and arbitrage between high and low price regions consequently contributed to price stability and inventory adjustments, or carry-over, would stabilise prices over time.

The advantage of price and consumption stability – which was a permanent and important theme in pre-industrial political economy – has attracted renewed interest from the modern analysis of poverty and famines in underdeveloped nations. This line of thought is discussed in chapter 2, in which it is argued that the quest for price stability was a quest for consumption stability which had welfare-increasing effects. Consumption stability was a central theme in popular agitation as an integral part of the 'moral economy of the crowd'.

However, it is argued – we are now in chapter 3 – that local supply shocks were substantial and had a great impact on local prices when markets were poorly integrated and because grain storage was not great enough to smooth variations in harvests. The obvious question, then, is why markets could not do the job by means of inter-regional trade and intertemporal inventory adjustments. High transport costs, as has already been mentioned, prevented an adequate level of trade and the extremely risky nature of carry-over speculation made inventories of grain storage too low. Chapter 4 continues the argument by suggesting that *ancien régime* markets were performing inadequately because of the negative *externalities* generated by price instability. Price shocks threatened the entire fabric of early modern society, by leading to an increase in crime and contributing to the spread of epidemics when dearth triggered off waves of migrants. Although private trade and storage led to some price-stabilising effects, the private economic incentives and rewards for merchants were not incorporating the social gains from price and consumption stability. This discrepancy between private and social gains revealed an externality which provoked a market failure: the market outcome was not the desired outcome.

But market integration steadily improved over the centuries, as shown in chapter 5. Markets can be said to be integrated, it is argued, if there is some stable price ratio between the price of identical goods in different markets. If the price differential is stable it can be interpreted as the transport cost between the two markets, the market with the lower price being the net exporter. But it is also rewarding to analyse the *extent* of market integration by studying the speed of adjustment back to that stable price ratio between markets after a shock in one market experiencing, say, a harvest failure. It turns out that we can document increasing European market integration from the seventeenth century and a very dramatic transformation in the nineteenth century. The Enlightenment intuition suggesting the price-stabilising effects of market integration can also be corroborated.

Did the improved performance of integrated markets bring down regulation when markets could deliver price stability? In a way it did, though perhaps not in the straightforward way I had imagined when I embarked upon this project. Exactly how regulation was dismantled is discussed in chapter 6. The title of that chapter reveals an interesting paradox, and perhaps one with wider implications: liberalism needed authoritarian rule to get established and a long experience and acknowledgement of well behaved markets to become widely accepted.

Acknowledgements

It has been a real pleasure writing this book. It has taken me to the research centres and cities I like most: the British Library and Goldsmith Library in London, Bibliothèque Nationale and Archives Nationales in Paris and Biblioteca Nazionale in Florence. Again and again I had the privilege of being accommodated by Centre Culturel Suèdois while in Paris. The economic support from the Danish Social Science Research Foundation made the research for the book, the processing of vast amounts of data and the accompanying travel possible. The financial and moral support of the Institute of Economics, University of Copenhagen, has been of great help. I have enjoyed the hospitality of London School of Economics, Katholieke Universiteit in Leuven, European University Institute in Florence and the Research School of Social Science at the Australian National University. Bill Kennedy, Herman van der Wee, Albert Carreras and Graeme Snooks not only arranged these visits but had time for stimulating discussions.

An informal network of scholars working in the field of market integration has been exposed to my attempts to come to grips with the complexities of my subject over the years. If it had not been for the pleasant surroundings of Lerici and other conference spots life would have been harder. I have also learnt a lot from participants in economic history seminars at the universities of Aalborg, British Columbia, California–Davis, Copenhagen, Gothenburg, Leuven, Lund, Stockholm, Sydney, Utrecht, Australian National University in Canberra, Carlos III in Madrid, European University Institute in Florence, Harvard University and Northwestern University.

Early on in my research I was introduced to co-integration and equilibrium error-correction modelling by the best of guides, Katarina Juselius, who also helped my first assistant Karsten Strøbæk with the econometric software. Later Mette Ejrnæs took over as research assistant and has since become a researcher in her own right. She is the author of the technical appendix to chapter 5. Librarian Vibeke Ring has helped me in researching and organising the bibliography.

Paolo Malanima and Jan Tore Klovland have generously supplied me with their unpublished price data. The editors of *Economic History Review* and *Scandinavian Economic History Review* have permitted me to use previously published material.

Stanley Engerman, the late Lennart Jörberg and Cormac Ó Gráda read the entire manuscript. Giovanni Federico, Lars Herlitz, Betrand Roehner and Peter Skott read parts of it. I am indebted to all of them and to two anonymous referees for their comments and suggestions which have improved the quality of the product considerably.

Writing a book in your second language, Swedish being my mother tongue, gives the English an unmistakably Scandinavian accent which could be painful for the native reader. Friend and colleague Cormac Ó Gráda conveniently intervened, however, worked his way through the entire manuscript and suggested innumerable stylistic improvements.

This book has taken a long time to complete. I have sacrificed neither extended holidays on land and sea, nor the Sunday sauna by the Sound. My family has coped with my company and has probably felt relieved when I returned to work. My two sons Mårten and Hannes – now grown-ups and to whom this book is dedicated – even earned a buck when they helped me transfer the price data from Gutenberg to microchips, while I was cooking dinner.

Malmö and Copenhagen, October 1998.
Karl Gunnar Persson

List of Abbreviations

The abbreviations used in citations in footnotes are as follows (roman capitals, as in Ed C 1768: XI, refer to volume or '*tome*'):

EdC   *Ephémérides du citoyen ou Bibliothèque raisonnée des Sciences morales et politiques*

GdC   *Gazette du Commerce*

JdA   *Journal de l'Agriculture, du Commerce et des Finances*

JE   *Journal Economique*

TO Gustave Schelle (ed.), *Oeuvres de Turgot*, 5 vols., Paris: Felix Alcan, 1913–23

1 Bread and Enlightenment: the quest for price stability and free trade in eighteenth-century Europe

The baker of last resort and his critics

Provisioning food was a concern for most local and central governments in pre-industrial Europe. Public granaries sought to stabilise prices by strategic purchases when prices were low and by disbursements to urban and rural wage-earners when prices soared. Most governments were also involved in the regulation of foreign trade, imposing export bans and/or stimulating imports of grain when it was in short supply. These ad hoc bans were usually lifted when harvest outcomes and prices returned to normal. Price volatility caused by disruptions in the grain supply imposed large temporary changes in consumption on urban and rural wage-earners and therefore posed a threat to the political order. Those advocating grain supply regulation were aware of the fact that they were continuing a tradition that reached back to antiquity.[1]

Attempts at stabilising grain supply were given a new lease of life with urban growth in medieval Europe. Those attempts grew out of local concerns, but gradually became identified with the nation-state. The most ambitious centralised systems of food provisioning developed in France under Colbert and in Prussia under Frederick the Great. In England these policies were gradually disbanded from the end of the seventeenth century on, but on the Continent they continued in full force well into the eighteenth century. The remark – made by a historian (Steven Kaplan) of the *ancien régime* – that the king was 'the baker of last resort' was not far off the mark.

However, these traditional grain policies began to be challenged, both

---

[1] See N. Delamare, *Traité de la police*, Paris: P. Cot, 1710–29. Delamare was a contemporary with an impressive knowledge of the 'police' in general and bread and subsistence problems in particular. In his monumental work, book V is devoted to subsistence policies. For France he traces it back to Charlemagne who in 809 banned peasants selling 'en vert' that is, before harvest. Delamare sides with the customary intepretation, arguing that the king's concern was for the peasants who would otherwise be exploited, having no means to support themselves and therefore in a weak bargaining position before harvest. Vol 2, p. 682.

politically and theoretically, from the mid-eighteenth century. The idea that price and consumption stability was a desirable state of affairs was not at stake. It was now argued, however, that price stability was best accomplished by free trade in a world where supply shocks were local but cancelled out globally. Barriers to internal and international trade and the restrictions on entry into the trading professions fostered administrative abuse and obstructed the forces of competition. International and inter-regional trade were seen as the best means of attaining equilibrium between local excess supplies and deficits. A coherent system of liberal ideas, with a strong but not exclusive focus on grain markets, first developed in mid-eighteenth century France, within a few years it had spread to almost every corner of Europe. In nations such as England, where grain markets were already fairly liberalised, debate on the merits of free trade also unfolded, because the advocates of regulation tried to revive the old legislation when grain prices soared in the final decades of the eighteenth century. The advocacy of free internal and external trade, respect for private property, including that in stocks of grain, and the belief in the unrestrained forces of competition, were all ideas associated with the Physiocratic school of economics in France. Yet apart from a shared passionate concern for agriculture, upholders of these ideas had no conceptual or logical connection with other aspects of that body of thought. Nor did Physiocratic thinking much influence them. Indeed, important elements of the new liberal ideology were carried over to the Physiocrats by the 'proto-liberalism' developing in Europe in the eighteenth century. In Prussia – which in other respects was open to Enlightenment – the new ideas gained momentum a little later and by then Physiocratic liberalism had been replaced by the 'Smithian' variety. In England the defence of deregulated grain markets was only marginally influenced by Physiocratic thought, though it was anticipated by another Smith: the English pamphleteer Charles Smith.[2]

This chapter reviews some of the outstanding contributions of the French Enlightenment and its forerunners inside and outside France and then draws attention to similar intellectual currents in other parts of Europe. The political impact of this intellectual assault on the old régime will be discussed in the concluding chapter 6.

One swallow does not bring the summer. But half a century or more before the mid-century assault, Pierre de Boisguilbert, a local official

[2] Charles Smith was an early free-trader and it is clear from his later writing that he was familiar with Physiocratic ideas: see, for example, his *Three tracts on the Corn Trade*, published in 1766. Smith had already developed and published his main ideas in the late 1750s, and he was certainly not alone in voicing a belief in the merits of a free grain trade at that time. See, for example, Anon., *Sentiments of a corn-factor on the present situation of the corn trade*, London, 1758.

based in Normandy, mounted an isolated though intellectually quite innovative and influential criticism of the grain policies perfected by Jean-Baptiste Colbert, minister under *le Roi-Soleil*.[3] In France, the traditional concern for regional self-sufficiency had bred an intricate system of barriers to inter-regional trade. It was this state of affairs that became one of the main targets of Boisguilbert's critique. Systematic criticism, however, gained momentum by the middle of the eighteenth century and dominated the intellectual scene in Paris in the 1760s with its discussion societies, its pamphleteers and its reform-minded journals. However, Boisguilbert's *Le detail de la France, ou la France ruinée sous la règne de Louis XIV*, first printed in Cologne in 1696, introduced themes later to be picked up by the Physiocrats and other liberals. These included radical opposition to market regulation, the idea that grain prices in France were too low because of the isolation of the French market and that price volatility stemmed from a segmentation of the French market which ultimately imposed disincentive effects on producers' efforts.[4] Boisguilbert's booklet is remarkable for its stringent analysis and modernity. A little later, in the 1730s, and under Boisguilbert's influence, the Tuscan writer Salustio Bandini produced another liberal manifesto, *Discorso sopra la Maremma di Siena*, but the *Discorso* circulated only privately until it was published in 1775, fifteen years after its author's death.[5] However, Bandini's influence outlived him and his text later influenced the reform of the grain trade in Tuscany when local reformers popularised his ideas. Although Bandini belonged to the élite, as did most reform-minded activists in these years, his was a dissident voice defending a neglected part of Tuscany, *la Maremma*, the coastal region zone of Siena and around Grosseto, whose potential as a grain-exporting region was stifled, he argued, by rulers who wished to secure an exclusive and stable supply of cheap grain for Florence and Siena. That political intervention in grain markets led to artificially low prices and accompanying disincentive effects later became the standard liberal argument.

The deregulation debate gained momentum both in Tuscany and France in the 1760s, and the pathbreaking role played by Bandini in Tuscany was fulfilled by Claude-Jacques Herbert in France. Herbert

[3] It is possible that Boisguilbert represented an undercurrent of popular anti-mercantilism. Personal communication by Lars Herlitz. See also L.Rothkrug, *Opposition to Louis XIV: The Political and Social Origins of the French Enlightenment*, Princeton: Princeton University Press, 1965.

[4] The isolation of a market can, of course, make the local price higher as well as lower than the world market price. Isolation was generally believed to depress prices, however. A generous interpretation could be that illicit export is easier to control than import, since the public was keen on reporting any grain getting out of the region or country.

[5] A modern edition edited by Lucia Conenna Bonelli was published by Leo S.Olschki Editore (Florence, 1968).

wrote two influential booklets *Essai sur la police générale des grains, sur leur prix et sur les effets de l'agriculture* (Berlin, 1755) and *Observations sur la liberté du commerce des grains* (Amsterdam, 1759). He introduced a series of themes that would be refined – and sometimes vulgarised – in the following decade. The main theme was that only free grain trade can achieve price stability. Local price stability required exports in times of abundant harvests, moderating the decline in prices. In lean years imports would make price increases less violent than if a region had to rely exclusively on its own supplies. Free entry to the grain trade was vital because with many merchants excess profits in the grain trade would not prevail: they would be arbitraged away by competing merchants.[6] The administrative tradition of giving exclusive rights to some merchants – *les marchands accrédités* – only caused monopoly profits, corruption and high prices.[7]

The coherent articulation of the advantages of free intra- and international trade in grain was developed by the Physiocrats. Widely known at the time as *les économistes*, a term which had a derogatory ring to it in some quarters, these influential critics of intervention were close to, or part of, the ruling élite.[8] I will refer to them as *les économistes* for two reasons. The first is that the aspects of their intellectual universe discussed here are *not* those themes uniquely associated with Physiocratic thought, such as the idea of the 'sterility' of the non-agrarian classes. The second is that I wish to stress the collective character of the critique, even while singling out the outstanding individual accomplishment of the Frenchman A.R.J. Turgot. Furthermore I will concentrate on the laissez-faire policies advocated by *les économistes*, and the highly original rationale for these policies. That rationale was not conceptually or theoretically tied to Physiocratic ideology. In fact, a liberal position concerning grain trade was held else-

---

[6] The risk for collusion became minimal with free entry into the grain trade, as *Ephémérides du citoyen* confidently asserts: 'La liberté multipliérá les Marchands.' EdC 1768: XI, p.24.

[7] JE, February 1760, pp. 60–4. The absence of free entry into the profession favours unsound business methods, see EdC, 1768: I, p.221. See also EdC 1769: I, p.91 and JE, April 1769, pp. 173–4.

[8] The group included François Quesnay (1694–1774), Anne Robert Jacques Turgot (1727–81), Abbé Baudeau (1730–92) editor of *Ephémérides du citoyen* until replaced by Pierre Samuel Dupont de Nemours (1713–1817), Guillaume-François le Trosne (1728–80), Mercier de la Rivière (c. 1720–94), among others. Although they were part of the Enlightenment, not all intellectuals associated with that current shared their views on the liberalisation of the grain trade. Voltaire ridiculed some of them for being narrow-minded and flattered the contemporary critic of liberalisation, Ferdinando Galiani, as combining the minds of Plato and Molière. Diderot, the encyclopedian, was instrumental in getting Galiani's work published. Some of them – for example, Quesnay – as a physician at the Royal court, was at the very centre of power, and Turgot worked as an 'intendent' in the regional administration responsible for, among other things, tax collection and the administration of food supply. L. Rothkrug defended the view that the Enlightenment radicalism can be traced back to seventeenth-century opposition to 'Colbertism', see his *Opposition to Louis XIV* (1965).

where in Europe and by people outside that school in France, such as Claude-Jacques Herbert. Nor was Turgot a dogmatic Physiocrat. Some even claim he paid only lip-service to physiocracy.[9] Be that as it may, Turgot and his associates made lasting contributions which were independent of their Physiocracy.

Most important, *les économistes* shifted the concern of economic policy from consumer protection to that of creating incentives for producers to increase production, which would – in the end – benefit consumers as well. The reason given for this optimistic conclusion was that the larger the normal harvest, the less devastating a future poor harvest – defined as a given proportional deviation from a normal harvest – would be.[10] Despite the radicalism of their project – a complete liberalisation of a hitherto tightly regulated grain trade – they influenced legislation inside and outside France from the 1760s onwards. Hitherto, France had been a country of segmented regional markets, but in 1763 and 1764 internal barriers to trade were abolished – although Paris was still granted privileged access to its hinterland – and foreign trade was partly liberalised. Alas for this experiment, it coincided with a period of bad harvests, which produced the expected popular unrest, and paved the way for a return to the old regulative policies in the early 1770s. There were frequent allegations from *les économistes* that local administrations had sabotaged the liberal legislation and thus contributed to the defeat of grain trade liberalisation.[11] The intellectual scene changed by the end of the 1760s, exhibiting an increasing hostility towards *les économistes*; but the liberal intelligentsia was not purged from the highest levels of administration. In

---

[9] Joseph Schumpeter, who suggested that Turgot had a more original mind than Adam Smith, conjectured that the Physiocratic orthodoxy in Turgot's work might have been inserted by Dupont de Nemours, with or without Turgot's consent. See Schumpeter, *History of Economic Analysis*, Oxford: Oxford University Press, 1954, pp. 243–4. It is true that Dupont added paragraphs to some of Turgot's controversial writings when editing them. Turgot had an unorthodox view on the origin and the rationale of proprietary rents on land. The customary right to the land was simply a historical fact turned a cultural convention and upheld by the force of the law, see para. XVII in *Réflexions sur la formation et la distribution des richesses*, written in 1766, TO: 2. Furthermore land-ownership was originally acquired through violent expropriation. Turgot traced the origin of the rental charges to a commutation of servitude, see paras. XXIV–XXVI in *Réflexions*. Slavery originated from the fact that a class which once in history possessed means of coercion enslaved those that otherwise would have preferred to till the abundant factor, land, on their own. The EdC version edited by Dupont added several arguments which considerably softened this verdict on the origin and rationale of land-ownership.

[10] There is one way of evading dearth: 'c'est l'abondance habituelle des récoltes'. EdC 1769: XI, p.72.

[11] See for example a complaint by a reader in JE, September 1766, pp. 387–9. Turgot, as an 'intendent' in Limoges was certainly aware of the problem of local negligence or sabotage and issued a 'Circulaire aux officiers de police des villes' which not only explained the content of the legislative texts of the 1763 and 1764 grain trade liberalisation but also tried to persuade his subordinates of the wisdom in the new laws, TO: II, pp. 471–5.

the mid-1770s Turgot moved from the provincial administration that he had served from the early 1760s, Limoges, to the centre. As *Controlleur Général* he reintroduced free trade, though again without much luck in the face of natural calamities. Turgot was soon ousted and the liberal legislation was not revived – and then, again, only for a short spell – until the French Revolution.[12]

The debate in these turbulent years provoked a response from adherents of the traditional management of food supply, and the dispute was in a sense a very modern one. On the one hand, there was the elegant and sometimes arrogant abstraction of *les économistes* and, on the other hand, the down-to-earth reasoning of their adversaries. While the former discussed how markets worked in principle and showed the force of deductive reasoning, the latter concentrated on the many imperfections and the problems of a 'big bang' transition to a market economy when much of the needed infrastructure was lacking.[13] Faced with these problems *les économistes* were not entirely at a loss, however. First of all, they blamed poor harvests rather than middlemen; secondly, they blamed the reluctance of many regional parliaments and local authorities to follow the new liberal instruction. Finally, they stressed the ambiguities of the 1763–64 legislation, specifically the legal uncertainties surrounding international trade.[14] This problem was admitted by Jacques Necker, a spokesman for the opposing camp (see n. 13), who replaced Turgot as *Controlleur Général*. As an administrator Turgot, the most brilliant thinker among *les économistes*, had shown great skill and compassion in handling the subsistence crisis in Limoges. He was in no way insensitive to the distress caused by a bad harvest, but nonetheless true to his liberal convictions when he bombarded the royal court with demands for support for his poverty-stricken region.[15] Rather than working against the market he

---

[12] See Steven Kaplan's *Bread, Politics and Political Economy in the Reign of Louis XV*, 2 vols., The Hague: Martinus Nijhoff, 1976, for a penetrating history of this period.

[13] This point is made explicitly by F. Galiani in *Dialogues sur le commerce des blés*, London, 1770, which was a widely read critique of *les économistes*. Turgot admitted it was simply the best defence that could be made for a bad cause. One of Galiani's points is echoed in recent French historiography by Jean Meuvret, see chapter 5 below. Both argue that market integration might destroy well functioning local market networks (Meuvret, *Le problème* . . ., Paris, 1977, pp. 259–64). A more restrained type of grain trade regulation is proposed by Jacques Necker in *Sur la legislation et le commerce des grains*, Paris, 1775. Some of those which were in favour of deregulation of the grain trade still advocated a gradual – allons pas à pas – transition, see GdC 1764: XVII, p. 141.

[14] See Dupont de Nemours, Observations sur les effets de la liberté du commerce des grains, EdC 1770: 6, pp. 36–136, specifically pp. 61–3 and 86–7. Le Trosne vigorously defended the rights of foreign ships to engage in the export–import trade, which aroused much opposition from his contemporaries. GdC 1765: XVI and XVIII.

[15] See 'Lettre au Controlleur Général 16 decembre 1769' and letter of 27 February 1770, TO: III, pp. 111–28 and 132–6, and letter of 25 October 1770, TO: III, pp. 141–53, in which Turgot advocates income maintenance through public works and subsidies to mer-

advocated what modern studies of poverty and famines call 'entitlement protection' – that is, income creation by means of public works or income support.[16]

Although *les économistes* only temporarily influenced legislation in their intellectual heyday, they had a lasting impact. As a consequence of their penetrating critique the adherents of regulation moderated their policy proposals and abandoned their belief in a strict and comprehensive regulation of markets. They ended up advocating a mixed-economy approach with a balance of state regulation and market principles. However this effort was based more on common sense and pragmatic thinking, and did not stimulate the intellectual rigour and theoretical innovations for which *les économistes* should rightly be remembered.

A theory of price stabilisation

The contribution of *les économistes* to the analysis of the process of price formation in grain markets had several original features which have not as yet been sufficiently appreciated. One of these accomplishments was the claim that price volatility created not only welfare losses for consumers, which was part of the traditional motive for the management of food supply, but also had disincentive effects on investment and effort in agriculture. The critics made price volatility a prime cause for the distressed state of agriculture. But their theory of price formation boldly suggested that the volatility was unnecessary. Price fluctuations could be tempered provided that an adequate institutional innovation was permitted.[17] Their best and favoured remedy against price fluctuations was market integration, and its prerequisite was free trade in grain.[18]

The arguments developed to underpin these strong and, for contemporaries, unconventional views formed a fairly consistent set of propositions. Deviations from normal price reflected uncontrollable supply or output shocks. The key issue was how markets might mitigate the effect of

chants to encourage them to open up new supply lines. See also Emma Rothschild's 'Commerce and the state: Turgot, Condorcet, and Smith', *Economic Journal*, 102, 1992, pp. 197–210, in which it is argued that these early economists were less hostile to state intervention than usually believed.

[16] See Jean Drèze and Amartya Sen, *Hunger and Public Action*, part 2, Oxford: Clarendon Press, 1989.

[17] L.-P. Abeille makes that point most explicitly by asserting that famines were actually products of institutional failures, including misconceived governmental regulation, rather than a lack of grain. See his *Faits qui ont influencé sur la cherté des grains en France & Angleterre*, 1768, also in JE, July and August 1768.

[18] *Les économistes* also adhered to a natural right argument against governmental infringements on private access to own property. That included the right to trade grain at any price.

such shocks on prices. The explanation offered focused on supply rather than demand shocks – rightly so, given the income and price inelasticity of demand. However, it was assumed that these supply shocks were local, in the sense that if one nation or region had a disastrous harvest there was always some other nation or region that had a bumper one. The idea was made quite explicit and amounted to the argument, using modern jargon, that natural shocks – *accidents* – to local harvests were independent, normally distributed and with a zero mean. For example, it was stressed that a similar natural shock, such as an increase in humidity, might cause very different responses – some favourable, some deficient – in different parts of Europe, because of differing soil conditions. So even in the unlikely event that the whole of Europe was experiencing a similar change in weather conditions, the impact on the aggregate harvest need not be great because local effects would cancel out. The general belief was that harvest disturbances were caused by a multitude of factors – *par milles raisons de tout genre* – which differed locally. As a consequence, in a large area such as Europe the aggregate harvest did not change much from one year to the next.[19] This being the case, the local dearth was an institutional failure caused by inadequate trade. The point made was not only an abstract idea that *les économistes* pursued. There were frequent references to different outcomes at any one time in Tuscany, in France or in parts of it and in the Baltic area to the effect that '*les accidents se compensent entre les Royaumes*'. The merits of free grain trade were often evoked by the example of Holland, which had a reputation for stable prices.[20] This line of thought was also present in the economic debates in other countries, of course, although it was developed with more rigour in France.[21] It should come as no surprise that Adam Smith later dwelt upon the peculiarities of local harvest shocks cancelling out in a large nation, in the digression on the corn trade in *The Wealth of Nations*. More interestingly, however, the argument also crops up almost a century earlier in the English economist, C. Davenant. Davenant observed that 'we enjoy the benefits of such different soils, viz. High Lands and Low Lands, where one hits when the other fails'[22] and a stable price would reign if these markets were permit-

---

[19] See, for example, Abbé Baudeau, 'De l'entière et parfaite liberté du commerce des bleds', EdC 1768: I, pp. 81–224, but specifically pp. 96–105.

[20] See for example JE, June 1768, pp. 260–2. But this is not an isolated case. In fact the peculiarity of the conditions in Holland had been stressed half a century earlier by C. Davenant, suggesting that the stable prices had to do with the stocks held by Amsterdam merchants.

[21] Nothing is new under the sun. A similar observation was made – for the Mediterranean world – by Aristotle as quoted by P. Garnsey, *Famine and Food Supply in the Graeco-Roman World: Response to Risk and Crisis*, Cambridge: Cambridge University Press, 1988, p. 8.

[22] See Davenant, *An essay upon the probable methods of making people gainers in the balance of trade*, London, 1699, p. 82.

ted to trade since price differences would make traders move grain from surplus to deficit regions or nations. In other words, the law of one price applied – i.e. the price difference between two markets would not exceed the transport costs between them, since larger price differentials would invite profit-seeking merchants to trade.[23] The arbitrage establishing the law of one price also secured price stability.

A spatial cancelling out of harvest disturbances was not the only result. This process also applied over time within a single locality, although, as Turgot remarked, 'les vicissitudes ne se compensent que dans une assez longue suite d'années'.[24] Les économistes generally believed that spatial redistribution was preferable to intertemporal redistribution because the former was less risky, although they were concerned with creating favourable conditions for both.[25] They advanced the argument that intertemporal redistribution – i.e. inventory adjustments, positive or negative – should be left to merchants, since if they were handled by the state or the local authorities their very size might easily foster panic-inducing rumours. Rumours, it was repeatedly stressed, fostered speculative bubbles, causing prices to over-react.[26] However, seasonal price differences would have been even greater if it had not been for merchants buying when prices were low and selling when prices were high. For that reason intertemporal arbitrage was defended as a socially beneficial activity.[27] This argument had to be advanced with considerable care because grain merchants were a favourite target in popular agitation in lean years.

The English debate in the last decades of the eighteenth century

---

[23] EdC, 1768: 8, p. 146 contains an admirably clear statement:
> Il est egalement manifeste que quand la difference du prix surpasse la depense des frais de transport, il y a du profit à porter du lieu ou'est l'abondance dans celui ou est la disette.

See also Herbert, C.-J., *Observations sur la liberté du commerce des grains*, Amsterdam, 1759, pp. 8–9, 50.   [24] TO: II, p. 125.

[25] There were frequent references to the fact that the surplus grain in the North (of Europe) was distilled – which was a sort of intertemporal redistribution of calories in grain – rather than exported to southern Europe. *Les économistes* believed that a more rational international division of labour would have been attained if eau-de-vie made of grapes from grain-deficient regions in France was exchanged with Northern grain. See, for example, EdC 1767: II, p. 45.

[26] On this issue, as in many other cases, Herbert had outlined the argument already in the 1750s. See *Essai sur la police générale des grains, sur leurs-prix et sur les effets de l'agriculture*, Berlin, 1755, pp. 23–5, 51.

[27] That argument has had a renaissance in the modern analysis of famines. Since intertemporal redistribution of food halts the fall of prices at harvest time it also reduces the risk of excessive consumption – at too low prices – in the early autumn and scarcity – at too high prices – before next harvest. There are welfare gains in a stable level of consumption compared to oscillations between high and low intake of food. See M.Ravallion, *Markets and Famines*, Oxford: Clarendon Press, 1987 and chapter 2 below for an elaboration of this point.

reflects the inertia of tradition. What was at stake here was not the deregulation of grain markets but rather the defence of a reasonably liberal status quo from attempts to revive the old legislation against 'regrating, engrossing and forestalling'. There was, however, in England as on the Continent a widespread sentiment that 'the present dearness must be owing to the wicked combination of the forestallers'.[28] Others pointed out that the number of sellers was so great that *combination* could not persist for long periods.[29] But there were also the numerous pamphlets by liberals such as Charles Smith and Arthur Young. The former opposed public intervention in much the same way as his French contemporaries did. He believed in the price-stabilising effect of intertemporal 'transport' of grain and therefore defended the private hoarding of large farmers because it served 'at their own private Expence the same purpose as public Magazines, and without ill Consequences which might attain such Magazines'.[30] A similar argument had been anticipated by Davenant, who was in favour of publicly subsidised private granaries to stabilise prices. The private gains were motivated by the services rendered by private granaries, in his view.[31] On both sides of *la Manche* a much more positive assessment of the merits of markets and competition had developed during the eighteenth century, especially its latter half. The simultaneous existence of deficit and surplus regions provided the rationale for trade and the multitude of merchants involved in gainful arbitrage effectively arrested the abuse of market power. Market regulation was not necessary for price stability to obtain, in fact it could be counter-productive. This in a nutshell was the new ideology, and it was repeated, rephrased, and reinterpreted to suit local audiences all over Europe by the likes of a Verri in Milan or a Kryger in Stockholm.[32]

---

[28] Quoted from Anon., *Considerations on the present dearness of corn*, London, 1757, pp. 4–5. See also S.Browne, *The laws against ingrossing, forestalling, regrating and monopolizing*, London, 1765 and Anon., *A compendium of the corn trade*, London, 1757. There are also arguments for establishing, in the continental tradition, public 'magazines' to stabilise prices. See, for example, Anon., *A letter from Richard in the Country to Dick in the City on the Subject of Publick Granaries*, Dublin, 1766.

[29] A. Dickson, *An essay on the causes of the present high prices of provisions*, London, 1773, pp. 17–18.

[30] See Smith, *A short essay on the corn trade and the corn laws*, London, 1758, p. 12.

[31] See Davenant, *An essay upon the probable methods ...* , London, 1699, pp. 85–7.

[32] Both authors were familiar with the French debate and were explicitly referring to it without adding much originality. Intellectual currents travelled as fast as the books and journals and the cosmopolitan élite toured Europe. From the number of references given in their works Pietro Verri seems to be the most well read of the two but interestingly most of the references in his *Riflessioni sulle Leggi vincolanti principalmente nel commercio de'-grani*, written in 1769 but not published until 1797, were available in Stockholm at that date as revealed by lists of books auctioned publicly. Cf. *Förteckning på en samling af wäl conditionerade fransyska, ängelska och andra böcker*, Stockholm, 1765; *Förteckning på en samling af wackra och wälconditionerade böcker, mest om handel*, Stockholm, 1765; and

Market integration, profits and incentives

After centuries of mercantilist protection and subsidies to the manufacturing sectors *les économistes* suggested a new agenda for economic policy
in which a prosperous agriculture evolved as the main goal. They were
preoccupied with what they believed to be an under-utilisation of land
and labour in French agriculture – amidst poverty. The output restraint
stemmed, they argued, from the isolation of the national market from the
rest of Europe, which kept grain prices and farming profits at an artificially low level, but also from the detrimental effects of price volatility.
Price volatility created uncertainty, it blurred the link between effort and
profitability and it activated governments and angry crowds often to the
disadvantage of farmers and the landed interests.[33] Sallustio Bandini, in
la Maremma di Siena, had articulated a similar diagnosis several decades
earlier and in the English debate Arthur Young, among others, argued
that low prices discouraged the farmer from sowing, while high prices
activated governments into making life hard for the farmer: 'Thus a great
crop or a bad one operates equally against him.'[34] In a speech to the Royal
Swedish Academy of Science, which in these years was a tribune for
enlightened thought, Carl Carleson, like many of his contemporaries
across Europe, also stressed the disincentive effects of good harvests. But
his diagnosis of the effects of a poor harvest did not mention the dangers
of political pricing. The main problem in his view was that in a year of a
poor harvest peasants, lacking in grain, had to buy seedcorn at inflated
prices. The implication was that peasants could not exploit the potential
merits of the high prices because they did not possess a marketable
surplus, in fact they did not even have enough for their own consumption.[35] In the pamphlets and journals of *les économistes* there were also
repeated references to this peculiarity of grain markets – i.e. that agrarian
producers and labourers lost out in times of both dearth and plenty.[36]

Förteckning på en samling af medicinska, oeconomiska och diverse andra böcker, Stockholm,
1765, Royal Library collection. There is more about Kryger and Verri in chapter 6.

[33] It was a widely held view that the general level of grain prices were below international
prices, often assumed to be reflected in Amsterdam prices. You can trace the idea back to
Boisguilbert and find it later with Herbert, Quesnay and Turgot. See also GdC 1764: VI,
p. 45; Dupont de Nemours in EdC 1770: VI, pp. 51–8. Sallustio Bandini also had an
intellectual debt to Boisguilbert and transferred the validity of the argument to *La
Maremma di Siena*. See his *Discorso Sopra la Maremma di Siena* (L.C. Bonelli edn),
Florence: Leo S. Olschki Editore, 1968.

[34] See his *Political arithmetic*, London, 1775, p 195.

[35] *Tal om spannemålsbristens afhjelpande*, Stockholm, 1759.

[36] Supplement to EdC 1768: XI, pp. 72–89. See also the critical review of F. Galiani,
Dialogues sur la commerce des blés, in EdC 1769: XII, pp. 193–247, and Abbé Baudeau, 'De
l'entière et parfaite liberté du commerce des bleds', published in EdC 1768: I, pp.
81–224, see pp. 91–2.

The contemporary discussion about the peculiarities of grain markets reveals two distinct explanations. In the first, the *politics* of grain market intervention were singled out as the main cause, while in the second, the emphasis was on the *economics* of price formation. Let us start with the former. In the absence of regular export markets an abundant harvest drove prices down to the extent that total revenue for the typical cultivator actually decreased. As a consequence labourers were laid off when cultivators did not even bother to harvest, process or market all their grain. But there was an asymmetry because, it was argued, when poor harvests drove prices up cultivators were denied the profits from the sales by arbitrary requisitions and price controls imposed by the authorities and *taxations populaires* by angry crowds. Urban crowds often dictated the ruling price with or without the consent of the city councils. These actions did not last long because supply dried up as a response. Nonetheless rural employment suffered because there was less need for day-labourers in lean years. The thrust of the argument was that the combined effect of export prohibitions and price controls lowered the price level to the extent that production suffered, which made temporary harvest failures even more damaging. In the French – and, for that matter, Swedish – debate the English bounty on grain export, introduced late in the seventeenth century, was often looked upon with admiration and as worth imitating for exactly the same reason as Arthur Young and others defended it: it made England less vulnerable to famines because it stimulated the general or normal level of production. The bounty was, however, not uncontroversial. It was in fact opposed on perfectly liberal grounds: there was no reason to reverse the direction of mercantilist subsidies and give export subsidies to agrarian producers; these subsidies would only penalise the manufacturing sector through higher subsistence costs or real wages.[37]

The argument referred to so far is based on the observation that the demand for grain is price-inelastic. Furthermore in a segmented market an increase in local output would generate a proportionate decline in prices *larger* than the output shock. A representative farmer who experienced an increase in output would consequently see his total revenue decline, total revenue being equal to price times quantity. But if demand was inelastic a local decline in output should have the reverse effect – that is, it should *increase* total revenue, had it not been for the political interventions in price formation. However, it is highly doubtful whether the incidence of the *taxations populaires* – i.e. politically dictated prices – were frequent and long-lived enough to explain Arthur Young's observation

---

[37] See Anon., *Considerations on the exportation of corn*, London, 1770, pp. 40–3.

that 'a great crop or a bad one operates equally against . . . [the farmer]'.

Turgot offered a more ingenious explanation for Young's paradox that good and bad harvests were equally harmful. It is economic rather than political because, implicitly, it makes use of the plausible idea that point elasticities *change* along a downward-sloping demand curve for grain. He thereby transcended the ad hoc explanations used by his contemporaries. The argument identified price volatility as a barrier to a prosperous agriculture because it reduced average long-term profits – and, as a consequence, investment – which was assumed to be proportional to profits. Turgot presented this persuasive and innovative interpretation of the perennial problem why cultivators were helped neither by good nor by bad harvests in a letter to Abbé Terray, then *Controlleur Général*.[38] The letter was one in a series written when the first period of liberal grain trade was about to be halted after only a few years of existence. Turgot and many local parliaments lobbied for a continuation of the liberal experiment but in the end they failed to keep the liberal spirit alive. Not surprisingly, Turgot identified the root of the problem as the continued segmentation of markets and the half-hearted implementation of liberal legislation.

Turgot's interesting results appear in two tables which try to estimate the effects of harvest fluctuations on total earnings or revenue of identical output shocks in two different market regimes. On the one hand, there was England, illustrating the favourable consequences of relatively stable prices typical of an open economy integrated into the European market. On the other, there was France, considered a segmented and isolated market with larger price fluctuations. No doubt Turgot was indebted to Quesnay on this particular point, but a closer look at Turgot's examples shows that the implications of the latter's were radically different and anticipated modern economic analysis. These insights have, however, so far been neglected in the rich secondary literature on Turgot's economics.

[38] Turgot developed his view in a series of letters from his provincial office to Abbé Terray, then Minister of Finance, during the autumn of 1770. The fourth of these letters is of particular interest: 'Quatrième lettre', in G. Schelle (ed.), *Oeuvres de Turgot*, vol. 3, Paris: Felix Alcan, 1919, pp. 277–85. The original of this letter has not been found but there was a summary in Dupont de Nemours' first edition of Turgot's work published in the early nineteenth century, and that summary was reproduced in the Schelle edition. To my knowledge no doubts as to the authenticity of Turgot's tables have been voiced. Dupont was primarily a vulgariser of Physiocratic thought, a devoted disciple but not an original thinker. When he independently reflected on these matters in *De l'exportation et de l'importation des grains*, Paris 1764 he merely reproduced Quesnay's tables, which are quite different in content and implication from Turgot's. However, he later adopted Turgot's views, see EdC, 6, 1770, pp. 114–15. This is part of the correspondence already referred to, see n. 15 above, from the autumn and early winter of 1770. Not all of these letters remain in their original state but have been reconstructed, probably by Dupont de Nemours, first editor of Turgot's collected work and a close friend. The fourth and the fifth letters, TO: III, have particular interest to us here.

Both Quesnay and Turgot elaborated examples involving a representative cultivator who had chosen a target production per *arpent (arpent* being a unit of land). Exactly how that target production was determined was left unexplained: we are told only about the total costs at that particular level of production. Turgot – as is pointed out on p. 21 – was one of the first to formulate what we now call the law of diminishing returns. The fact that production is expressed in output per unit of the fixed factor of production – land – is noteworthy. It provides a basis for the conjecture that the particular level of production chosen in his example was a level where marginal cost equalled price. Be that as it may, Turgot nonetheless offers some new and interesting insights into a mechanism that might have had detrimental effects on profits, investments and production.

The actual output varied from year to year around the target output because of local uncontrollable climatic events and other natural '*accidents*'. These events, being local, affected all producers' output more or less equally. If markets were segmented the price would be influenced by these output shocks because they were large relative to the size of the (local) market demand. A small aggregate local output would increase price, and vice versa. While consumers' demand curve for food will always be downward-sloping – buying more the cheaper it is – it is only in a segmented market that producers can affect the price they get by regulating the output sold. In an integrated market the price is exogenously given, but in a segmented market it is endogenously given by the slope of the demand curve and the output that farmers have available, or want to sell. Turgot's important, although implicit, insight was that point elasticities change along a downward-sloping demand curve from being very inelastic at abundant harvests to becoming less so when grain is in short supply. The reason for this was not discussed explicitly by Turgot, and he did not, of course, refer to a demand curve or elasticities as such. His observation is consistent with basic economic principles, however. We are accustomed to associate necessities with low price elasticity: we have to have them irrespective of their price. The inelasticity stems from the lack of suitable substitutes; it implies that a change in price will not affect demand much. Since demand was very inelastic when grain was in abundant supply, prices fell more than the increase in output and total revenue declined. When wheat became scarce prices soared and there was an intensified search for substitutes such as rye or chestnuts. That would necessarily generate a change in the price elasticities of demand: demand can be expected to become less inelastic when prices are high. The important implication was that the increase in total revenue from a harvest failure would not fully compensate the farmer for the losses incurred in a year with a good harvest. The producers' total revenue curve across a

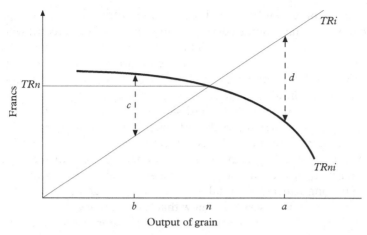

Figure 1.1 Total revenue of a representative farmer in an integrated and a non-integrated market with unexpected changes in output of grain

sequence from bad to good harvests would be concave, like an inverted U in a non-integrated market (the *TRni* schedule in figure 1.1), and total revenue would be smaller than if prices remained stable over a sequence of bad and good harvests. It should be pointed out that Turgot's example implied that the demand actually became elastic when grain was scarce and expensive. However, his argument does not require this strong assumption; it suffices that demand becomes *less* inelastic when the price soars.

Turgot then continued his exposition by exemplifying the advantages of market integration, a state of affairs characterised by stable prices. In other words, the local community was small relative to the market so that a local supply shock would not affect prices at all, or very little. Consequently the total revenue curve would be an upward-sloping straight line, the *TRi* schedule in figure 1.1. A deviation in output would produce a proportional change in total revenue. The implications of different degrees of market integration for the shape of the total revenue schedules are demonstrated in figure 1.1.

But why should long-run profits be greater if the local economy was integrated into a larger one, so that prices remained stable? Turgot assumed that production costs were tied to planned output and not to realised output, the latter being influenced by unforseen natural *accidents*. (The plausibility of that assumption will be discussed on p. 20 below). He then showed that total revenue increased through integration. If price remained stable while output varied stochastically from year to year, producers' income would vary directly with output along a straight upward-sloping total revenue curve, implying an increase in income when harvests were good, and vice versa. This is the *TRi* schedule in figure 1.1, which reflects the fact that in an integrated market the price is exogenously given and not influenced at all by local supply shocks. The total revenue schedule in a non-integrated market is concave because point elasticities change along a downward-sloping demand curve for grain, being less inelastic at high prices than at low prices.

If we consider a producer who is subject to output shocks such as *b* from a bad harvest, and *a* from an abundant one, and faces an average or normal harvest, *n*, then the long-run average total revenue will be at *TRn*.[39] The long-run average total revenue for a cultivator in a non- integrated market will necessarily be below that level. An easy way to see this is to investigate what a cultivator gains from being in a non-integrated market – i.e. along the *TRni* schedule, in a bad harvest rather than in a perfectly integrated environment. That gain is the vertical distance, the dotted line *c*, in figure 1.1. The income forgone will always be greater from an abundant harvest however, equal to the vertical distance, the dotted line *d*.[40]

A series of numerical examples in table 1.1 illustrate the point just made. What we have here are the effects on total revenue, measured as proportional changes from the revenue accruing from a normal harvest, of identical changes in output of (say) wheat, but with different assumptions regarding the price elasticity of demand. In column *A* we have the case of a perfectly integrated market for which changes in total revenue are proportional to changes in output, this being so because local output shocks do not affect prices at all. That means that the above-average revenue from a good harvest is exactly offset by the below-average revenue from a bad harvest. Next, in column *B*, a case is reproduced which is the case Turgot had in mind, where demand actually becomes elastic at high grain prices. The total revenue is lower than the revenue

---

[39] If price is constant, changes in total revenue, *TR*, will be determined by changes in output only. Since $TR = PQ$, with *P* being the price per unit and *Q* units of output, the proportional change in total revenue is $TR^\star = P^\star + Q^\star$, with $\star$ denoting a proportional change in a variable. If price remains constant $TR^\star = Q^\star$. Perfect market integration has the property of making the total revenue change strictly proportional to the output deviation. Over an extended period of output deviations the summation of yearly total revenues would yield the same sum as if output did not deviate from mean output.

[40] I have for expositional reasons simplified Turgot's argument by assuming that market integration implies constant prices, despite the local output shock, while Turgot just assumed much less volatility in prices. However, the same qualitative implications hold if the implied total revenue schedule converges – as market integration proceeds – symmetrically towards the total revenue schedule in the perfectly integrated market – that is the straight upward-sloping schedule in figure 1.1.

Table 1.1 *Effects on total revenue of output shocks under different market conditions*

	A Integrated market	B The Turgot case	C 'The plausible case'
Percentage change in total revenue at a 10 per cent decline in wheat output	−10	−5[a]	2.5[b]
Percentage change in total revenue at a 10 per cent increase in wheat output	10	−10[c]	−10[c]

Notes:
[a] Assuming an elasticity of −2.
[b] Assuming an elasticity of −0.8.
[c] Assuming an elasticity of −0.5.

from a normal harvest, irrespective of whether the harvest is above or below average. The more plausible characterisation of a segmented market is that of decreasing but still inelastic demand when grain becomes scarce, and that case is demonstrated in column C. Column A displays the fact that perfect integration would make long-run total revenue constant – including profits if total costs were fixed – over a sequence of bad and good harvests. The segmented market with price volatility is less successful in this respect. The difference between the original Turgot case (column B), and C is that the story told in column C admits an increase in total revenue when a harvest fails, but an increase too small to offset the losses in total revenue during an abundant harvest.

While total revenue and profits – assuming fixed production costs – would be higher in an integrated market, nominal income *volatility* would actually increase. Would that condition not undermine the general thrust of the argument stressing the advantages of market integration? It would not – as will be shown below – because the majority of peasants will be able to increase their consumption of food in years of bumper harvests, *without* being worse in years of failure than they would have been in a segmented market. For the majority of peasants, for whom a normal harvest was just about sufficient to pay rents and taxes and to afford a small expenditure on manufactured goods after deductions for own consumption and seedcorn, the decisive advantages of integrated markets were that they could benefit from a good harvest. Contemporaries both in and outside France described the typical consequences of a poor harvest as a decline in urban employment and the accumulation of peasants' arrears in rents and taxes. The obvious interpretation is that in periods of harvest failure peasants had to consume most or all of their shrinking output, having nothing to bring to the market. They would not, in other words, be able to benefit at all from the rise in prices.[41] To the extent that they were forced to buy seedcorn during spring, they were actually victimised by the high prices, as repeatedly pointed out in the contemporary debates. The crucial difference is thus the favourable consequences of a good harvest on consumption possibilities in an integrated as compared to a non-integrated market. Peasants then had a marketable surplus, but with stable rather than declining prices of grain that surplus commanded more manufactured goods, and less output had to be exchanged for rents and taxes. Households would therefore increase both their consumption of food and manufactured goods and be better prepared to get rid of the burden of arrears. The effects of an abundant harvest on the consumption of food when markets are poorly integrated and prices fall are indeterminate.[42]

Uncertainty and effort

The economic debates of the eighteenth century diagnosed the failings in the economy and society and suggested radical remedies which appear familiar to a modern mind. The potential disincentive effects of uncertainty about political interference in market processes and the violation of property rights was, as discussed already, a central theme among the reformers. That theme has had a revival in modern interpretations of the uniqueness of the growth experience of the western world. There is also an extensive discussion about the way in which price volatility disguises the link between effort and reward. This argument associates a reluctance to invest and to increase production with the frequent experience among producers of a coincidence between good harvests and low prices.

One of the reasons why market integration was considered preferable was that it generated a clear relationship between output and total

---

[41] There is the possibility of substitution of the expensive variety of grain for a cheaper nutrient, but in practice that possibility was quite restricted, as will be shown in chapter 2, since prices of all nutrients moved rather closely together.

[42] Technically speaking, an increase in output, prices remaining stable, increases income and therefore consumption of all (normal) goods through what in consumption theory is called the '(positive) income effect'. If, on the other hand, markets are poorly integrated and grain prices decrease proportionally more than the increase in output then income declines and there will be a negative income effect on the consumption of all normal goods. There will also be a negative effect on the consumption of manufactured goods via the so-called 'substitution effect', because manufactured goods have become relatively more expensive in terms of grain. The same substitution effect will consequently boost grain consumption. It cannot be determined a priori whether or not the positive substitution effect will dominate the negative income effect for grain, however.

revenue. A decrease in output implied a proportional decrease in revenue, while an increase in output caused a proportional increase in revenue. There was an urgent need, it was argued, to establish a direct link between effort and reward. The contemporary literature contained colourful descriptions of the idleness generated by abundant harvests and desperation when harvest failed. Did these complexities foster a sort of effort illusion to the effect that little effort was believed to be preferable to greater?[43] It would be too facile to dismiss this argument as a fallacy of composition. The fact that an increase in output, when experienced by all producers and due to a natural *accident*, will cause prices to fall does not imply that a good harvest experienced by a single cultivator produces the same result. All other things being equal, it would always be advantageous for a single producer to have a larger product. It is my impression that most of *les économistes* understood that. What they wished to highlight, admittedly in a vague way, was the demoralising effect of an excessively risky and uncertain environment. However, there is a series of hints of a more precise economic interpretation of the effects of risk and uncertainty. A plausible clarification is that the frequently depressed price and profit levels made cultivators react in an overly short-sighted manner.[44] The structure of the argument is clear. Low profits and uncertainty about future prices and earnings discouraged producers from fixed investments in improvements of land, implements and buildings and thus caused the allegedly depressed output. The most obvious link between harvest outcomes and disincentive effects on investment was of course that the relative price of investment goods increased on those rare occasions when peasants had a marketable surplus – that is, when good harvests depressed prices of grain. If on top of that nominal incomes decreased, there is an additional cause for restrained investments. This interpretation gains additional strength from the fact that it is reasonable to expect the short-run marginal cost curve to be steeper than the long-run marginal cost curve. The implication would be that output would be lower if short-term adjustments predominated. In the short run, adaptations will mainly consist of increased input of labour to land and implements already in use, and the law of diminishing returns will immediately be

[43] Dupont de Nemours also refers to this idea, but without the detailed and consistent argument found in Turgot, cf. EdC 1770: VI, p. 114–15.

[44] See, for example, EdC 1769: I, pp. 73–9. In these years, when there was a mounting opposition to free grain trade, some regional parliaments wrote petitions in support of the existing legislation presenting the supply-side advantages. See, for example, 'Lettre du Parlement de Provence au Roi sur le commerce des bleds' in EdC 1769: II. It was also repeatedly asserted that the new legislation stimulated long-term adaptations such as clearing of new land. See EdC 1770: IV, pp. 72–6; EdC 1770: VIII, pp. 41–52. EdC 1770: XII, pp. 39–41.

effective. The very characteristics of *ancien régime* agriculture, so often and vividly described by *les économistes* inside and outside France as a state of under-utilisation of land, low investments, misuse of land and neglect of maintenance, lend support to the idea that short-run adaptations prevailed. And for good reason: facing great uncertainty as to future prices, risk-averse producers would not dare to invest in land improvements and new equipment. Output variability remained, of course, but integration might in fact stimulate diversification. If different products were not greatly correlated in output shocks diversification was a means of stabilising income, as will be discussed in chapter 2. Here, then, we have additional arguments for price stability, which furthermore explains why market performance was made the pivotal case of economic reform at the end of the *ancien régime*. In chapter 2 we will scrutinise the robustness of the analysis provided by the Enlightenment economists, although our main interest will be in the welfare implications of price instability and improved market performance. Before that, however, a digression on some of the finer points in Turgot's economics is in order.

A short digression on Turgot

In order to derive the result that long-run profits would increase in an integrated market with stable prices Turgot argued that total costs were fixed – i.e. they did not vary, for example, in anticipation of a bad harvest. The rent and interest component can reasonably be seen as fixed in nominal terms irrespective of the real value, at least within the year. Here Turgot was on solid ground. Wage costs vary somewhat, but the weight attached to this argument has to do with the importance of hired labour for cultivators, which might not have been very great for most of them. Part of the wage bill is rightly seen as a fixed cost, at least until the quality and quantity of the coming harvest is known. But after that date, it is plausible that nominal wages were affected. However, taking that into consideration the outcome need not be damaging for the argument. Turgot, like many of *les économistes,* subscribed to the theory of a backward-bending supply curve as an adequate description of labour-supply responses to real wage changes. So as corn prices drop labour supply also drops because real wages increase. This decline in the supply of labour halts the fall in nominal wages; when prices rise and real wages decline the expected catching-up of nominal wages is arrested by the increase in labour supply.[45]

The intuition behind the claim that higher prices for agricultural goods would boost production is self-evident, but Turgot's comments were far

---

[45] Letter to the *Controlleur Général*, 2 December, TO: III, p. 336.

from trivial. His was a world of idle labour and under-utilised land. He furthermore pointed out that increased expenses on a piece of land would ultimately yield smaller and smaller increases in output. In other words, the law of diminishing returns, as it is now called, would apply. But as he was keen on pointing out, as long as there was a net marginal gain (*produit net*) it was worth increasing outlays on land.[46] From that perspective it is easy to see that an increase in the price of grain would increase effort, expenses and production. That the desired effect actually occurred as a response to the grain trade liberalisation was also repeatedly and triumphantly reported in the reform-minded press following the reforms in France and Tuscany in the 1760s.[47]

The increase in the price level of necessities admittedly affected real wages negatively but, since under-employment was endemic, this effect was compensated – partly, at least – by increasing employment prospects in rural areas. The rural under-employed were correctly identified as most vulnerable to price increases: if employment improved they would be much better off.[48]

So much for short-term effects. But what about the long-run effects on production, employment and investments of higher prices for agrarian goods? The question whether higher prices would permanently increase profits for cultivators or not was explicitly addressed. It was admitted that cultivators faced the risk of both higher agricultural wages and rents. Wages, it was generally believed, adapted in the long run to the prices of necessities. That implied that costs increased, though admittedly with a delay. Unless the increase in grain prices did not permanently affect the terms of trade in favour of agriculture relative to urban trades there need not be much long-term effect on agrarian output since the French price level increased relative to other European nations. If, however, prices on manufactured goods lagged behind then real wages in agriculture could be restored by a nominally smaller proportionate increase in wages than in prices, since part – although a small part – of rural consumption consisted of manufactured goods.[49] This was a desirable outcome from the point of view of *les économistes*. They did not hide their dislike of the favours and subsidies given to urban trades which inflated urban income and distracted resources from agriculture.[50] But it was also argued that

---

[46] TO: II, pp. 644–6.
[47] See for example JdA, October 1768, pp. 10–12; JE, June 1768, pp. 260–2.; EdC 1770: V, pp. 22– 3 and 1770: VI, p. 50.   [48] EdC, 1768: XI, p.11. Cf. also GdC 1764: XXVI.
[49] That there actually was a change in the rural–urban terms of trade in favour of agriculture is sometimes argued. See EdC 1771: VIII, pp. 39–42.
[50] Sometimes, but not always, authors were frank about this. Paris – cette grande et opulente ville – had to accept somewhat higher prices, it was argued. That was, after all a slight disadvantage compared to the gains for the rest of the country. GdC 1764: IV, p. 29.

increased agrarian demand for manufactured goods when agriculture prospered would stimulate urban employment.

This supply-side vision of economic regeneration also included a detailed discussion on whether cultivators could actually resist attempts from owners of land to increase rents when earnings for cultivators were augmented. Turgot here developed an ingenious argument for the assertion that cultivators could permanently boost earnings but it presupposed that they increased their investments.[51] First, Turgot noted, there was an asymmetry of information. The cultivator was better informed than the owner about actual or potential earnings, and would benefit from that informational advantage when renegotiating the rent. Other cultivators were, of course, equally well informed, Turgot conceded, and they would therefore be able to bid down excess earnings to the particular peasant now cultivating the land. But there was a lower limit to this bidding process. Turgot argued that even a temporary increase in profits – before wages caught up – increased investments so that capital per cultivator, and hence output and income, increased. Turgot's second point was that an equally endowed cultivator would not under-bid the original tenant because there was an opportunity cost in capital endowment. Turgot estimated the opportunity cost to the prevailing rent at 10 per cent. Of course an even better endowed (i.e. more productive) cultivator might offer the owner of land a higher rent but that would only be in the interest of economic progress, as the ousted tenant replaced someone else further down the productivity ladder.

[51] See the sixth of these letters, TO: III, pp. 301–10.

2   Markets, mortality and human capabilities

Who suffers from price instability?

In chapter 1 we met *les économistes* within and outside France who reflected on the prevailing policy-induced uncertainty and its alleged discouraging effect on cultivators' effort. They believed that profitability could be increased in the agrarian sector by price-stabilising market integration through free trade. This chapter examines the *welfare* implications of price instability for the main classes in pre-industrial economies. The social disruptions caused by price instability made its welfare impact a central issue in contemporary political discourse.

The most appropriate analytical framework for the analysis of welfare effects of price instability in pre-industrial economies is provided by modern inquiries into famines and poverty, which assert that price volatility destabilises food consumption and therefore has adverse effects on human capabilities. That approach also demonstrates that stabilisation of consumption over time and redistribution from rich to poor will enhance welfare. The welfare improvements generated by price stability are expressed in terms of human capabilities and functionings. More precisely, it is asserted that price stability will enhance the survival chances of a population and increase the *steady-state* proportion of a population in a capability condition that permits normal 'doings and beings'.[1] It is argued that the quest for and defence of customary living standards, at a level which permitted normal 'doings and beings', were expressed in the 'moral economy of the crowd'. Often seen as an expression of contempt towards markets in general, it is suggested here that the 'moral economy' targeted market *failures* and poor market performance. The provisioning

---

[1] Among contemporary economists and philosophers, Amartya Sen has most vigorously advocated the view that welfare is best seen as capabilities to achieve 'doings and beings'. The idea is that income- and entitlement-related welfare is but a means to an end, the end being to be able to have a capability to function and to fulfil personal goals and also to participate in social life. See A. Sen, 'Poor relatively speaking', *Oxford Economic Papers*, 35, 1983, pp. 153–69 and numerous other publications, most recently in *Inequality Reexamined*, Cambridge, Mass., Harvard University Press, 1992, and in J. Drèze and A. Sen *Hunger and Public Action*, Oxford: Clarendon Press, 1989, chapters 1, 3.

policies so typical of the *ancien régime* and discussed in chapter 4 will illustrate this point succinctly.

Traditional grain policies in pre-industrial societies were motivated by a concern for consumers, wage-earners, and the urban self-employed. Although these policies invited a mounting critique by the middle of the eighteenth century there was nonetheless a consensus around the favourable consequences of price stability as such. *Les économistes* focused primarily on rural producers and the disincentive effects of price instability on their production, but we will now turn our attention towards such producers as consumers. While it is quite easy to establish the disruptive effect of price instability for wage-earners experiencing nominal wage rigidities, we want to know whether agrarian producers were also adversely affected as *consumers* by price instability.

So far, it has been taken for granted that price fluctuations generate consumption instability. Before exploring the consequences of consumption instability further the connection between price and consumption variability must be corroborated. The impact of price instability on three major classes will be discussed: urban wage-earners and self-employed, rural wage-earners and small-holders and finally rich peasants and land-owners. The direct link between price variability and consumption instability is most evident for the urban population. Price fluctuations of food affected the real consumption of the urban population because for most of them savings were small, access to credit difficult or prohibitively expensive and nominal wages and income rigid in the short run. Furthermore, as will be demonstrated below, there was little scope for substituting expensive nutrients for cheaper ones. While prices could fluctuate violently, wages – as observed by most contemporaries, including Adam Smith in *The Wealth of Nations* – responded sluggishly, if at all. However, a large section of the rural population was also adversely affected by increases in the price of food. Those who were marginal farmers and/or rural wage-earners were net demanders of food in normal times and thus suffered from declining consumption opportunities when their own output dropped and real wages declined owing to higher food prices. The preferences for a stable level of consumption were revealed by the inelastic demand with regard to the price of food. The ability of households to retain a customary living standard when prices increased therefore depended on the proportion of income spent on food in normal years. The vast majority of the population, urban and rural wage-earners in particular, used the greater part of their income on food. In a context in which prices often doubled and on some occasions tripled, it may be worth noting the truism that the share of income spent on food could not double if it exceeded 50 per cent in an average year. Although rural wages sometimes responded more quickly than urban wages to changes in the cost of subsistence, employment often contracted when a poor harvest diminished the demand for farm-hands. So there is no doubt that large sections of the urban and rural population were victims of periodic and severe destabilisation of their customary standard of living. Only a smaller variance in prices, and/or a general increase in real income, so that a smaller proportion of income had to be spent on food, could liberate the masses from shocks in the price of food.

Rural producers were in an ambiguous position, however. For rich peasants and landlords the effect was different than for small-holders. When the demand for food was inelastic and output shocks – shared by all local producers – had an inverse effect on price nominal income would also be *inversely* related to output – that is, the smaller the output the larger the nominal income, and the larger the output the smaller the income. If we apply the idea introduced by Turgot that demand is less inelastic at higher prices for food – because point elasticities change along a downward-sloping demand curve for food – the nominal income schedule of a representative farmer along a sequence of bad to abundant harvests would look like the concave curve d in figure 2.1. However, consumption of food may or may not be affected by a decline in output, depending on how large a proportion of normal output was consumed by the household. Small-holders would have to consume their output when the harvest failed and would have little or nothing to gain from the high prices and high nominal income caused by the local harvest failure. The advantages that increasing prices opened for land-holders with a surplus of grain were not open to the vast majority of the rural population. Although it is true that the inverse relationship between output and price movements smoothed income variability, that was no comfort for small-holders; the small farmer would be forced to the often usurous credit market to be able to buy seedcorn at inflated prices and more often than not rental arrears were accumulated. Only in normal – and, specifically, in abundant – years would they have a sizeable surplus to bring to the market. But in the latter case they would be hit by the decline in food prices following a bumper harvest. These stylised facts help to describe the relationship between the nominal income and the consumption of grain, the single most important item in consumption of a representative small-holder over a sequence of bad, b, and good, a, harvests that affect all farmers equally in a specific region

In figure 2.1 the 45° line, e, represents the nominal income – that is, output times price per unit, on the vertical axis when price per unit of output is set to unity and with output on the horizontal axis. It can also be interpreted as the hypothetical consumption (vertical axis) of grain *if* all

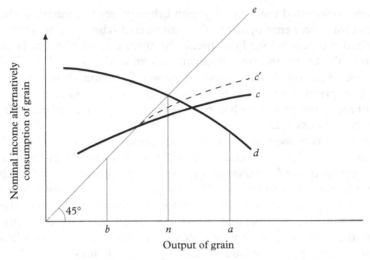

Figure 2.1 Nominal income and grain consumption of a representative small-holder.
Note: At first sight, it might look confusing to have both consumption and nominal income on the vertical axis, but see the text for explanation. Note that the *d* schedule indicates nominal income only in a segmented market. The *e* schedule illustrates the hypothetical case in which consumption equals production, irrespective of whether the market is segmented or integrated. Only in an integrated market is it also the nominal income schedule. *c* is actual consumption.

own output (horizontal axis) is consumed by the household. In that respect, it is the production constraint for consumption – i.e. consumption equals production. Operating with a constant price, as we do when the *e* schedule represents nominal income, presupposes a perfectly integrated market, in which local output shocks do not affect prices at all and nominal income is strictly proportional to output. In this respect the *e* schedule is just the *TRi* schedule in figure 1.1. By contrast, output shocks affect prices in a segmented market and nominal income is depicted by the concave schedule *d* along *b*ad over *n*ormal to *a*bundant harvests. You recall this schedule from figure 1.1 as the *TRni* schedule. Although nominal income is now inversely related to output, the actual nominal income variability is smaller in the non-integrated market. But, as we will soon see, nominal income variability is of limited importance when we discuss consumption variability for poor peasants.

What can we say about consumption? We may safely argue that the actual consumption of grain, the *c* schedule, increases with the production constraint, *e*, irrespective of whether we are in an integrated or in a non-integrated market when output increases from *b* to *a*, but at a decreasing rate. That condition generates the actual grain-consumption schedule, *c*, which might lie above the production constraint, *e*, at *b*, a harvest failure. The reason for this could be that the household is becoming indebted or selling off some property (say) cattle, in order to maintain customary living standards.

We are now interested in knowing the effect, if any, on the consumption of food for small-holders of a shift from a segmented market regime to an integrated market. We will compare two extreme cases, perfect integration and non-integration, but the qualitative conclusions will hold for movements towards integration. The question asked is this: will small-holders be better or worse off in terms of *consumption* when markets get more integrated – that is, when local prices are becoming increasingly insulated from local supply shocks that affect all local producers? To the left of *n* in figure 2.1 consumption, *c*, is dominated by the production constraint rather than by nominal income, irrespective of the level of nominal income. In a segmented market the behaviour of nominal income over various harvest outcomes are illustrated by the *d* schedule. The increasing nominal income associated with falling output just matches the increase in the price of subsistence grain and cannot therefore boost consumption, being constrained by actual production along *e*. Would not a small-holder in a segmented market be able to exploit the high nominal income by substituting out of the type of grain that fails to some other grain? Might he not sell what little there was left of the crop that failed (e.g. wheat) and buy a cheaper nutrient (e.g. rye)? It turns out that prices of all substitutes move closely together – that is, relative prices remained practically unaffected by a supply shock that affected the major staple good. So only to the extent that price differentials just reflect tastes, rather than quality or nutritional content, is there some scope for substitution. But more about this issue below.

Let us now shift our attention to a larger than normal harvest – i.e. to the right of *n* in figure 2.1. At point *a* nominal income in an integrated market (the *e* schedule can now be interpreted either as nominal income or a production constraint for consumption), is much higher than in a segmented market in which output and price is inversely related (on the *d* schedule). It turns out that not only is nominal income higher in an integrated market at *a*, but real income as well. Since relative prices remain constant nominal and real income changes are identical in an integrated market. It is true that the difference in nominal income between the two regimes is due to the difference in price of grain only. However, in the non-integrated market a bumper harvest triggers off a fall in price and this fall in price of the producer's own good will always *decrease the real*

Table 2.1 *Effects of an increase in grain output on a representative farmer in two types of markets*

	Integrated market	Non-integrated market
Income	Increase	Decrease
Consumption of food	Increase (owing to positive income effects)	Indeterminate (owing to negative income effects and positive substitution effects)
Purchases of investment goods and durable goods	Increase (owing to positive income effects)	Decrease (owing to negative income and substitution effects)

income, relative to the case of an integrated market, when the share of own goods in consumption is less than 1. Higher real income for the integrated farmer means that the household can consume more grain *and* more of other goods relative to the alternative non- integrated case. If the choice is not *either/or* but some of both, there is a reasonable presumption in favour of the latter alternative. This conjecture is illustrated in figure 2.1 by an upward shift of the c schedule to c', with c representing consumption in an integrated market. This shift implies that average consumption over a sequence of harvests will be higher in an integrated market.

The argument discussed so far can be neatly summarised as a comparison of the effect of an unanticipated increase in local output on nominal and real income, consumption and purchases of investment or durable goods for a representative farmer in an integrated and non-integrated market, respectively. The concepts 'income' and 'substitution effects' refer to the familiar results from consumption theory that if income increases (decreases) consumption of all normal goods will increase (decrease). The substitution effect implies that an increase (decrease) in the relative price of a good will cause consumption of that good to decrease (increase). There will not be any substitution effects in an integrated market because relative prices remain constant while a non-integrated market will experience a relative increase in prices of manufactured goods – i.e. durables and investment goods – because of the fall in food prices caused by the increased output (table 2.1).

The logic of this argument is that when harvests failed in locally segmented markets small farmers were ruled by the production or output constraint, and when harvests were abundant they had to cope with a fall in income: they faced the worst of both worlds. Could substitution in consumption and diversification in production help them out of this predicament? Although harvest outcomes for different crops, such as wheat and rye, were only weakly but positively correlated, price movements were

Table 2.2 *Correlation coefficients between price changes for different agrarian products, Pisa 1632–1663*

	Wheat	Rye	Beans	Olive oil
Wheat	1			
Rye	0.92	1		
Beans	0.85	0.89	1	
Olive oil	0.21	0.26	0.27	1

Sources: Archivio di Stato di Pisa, Opera del Duomo; the Malanima manuscript (see Sources, p. 156).

strongly and positively correlated. That also goes for other types of food as long as they were close substitutes. Beans and meat are two important examples. Only for products that were complementary from a nutritional point of view, such as olive oil and beans, did correlations weaken, as is clear from the correlation matrix in table 2.2.

Since those most at risk already in normal times primarily consumed nutrients at the cheaper end of the scale there was not much scope for defending customary living standards when one crop failed through substitution in consumption – i.e. by selling dear and buying cheaper food. The substitution that occurred could be for low-quality food. It is a well known fact that during famines the incidence of food poisoning increased, suggesting that price differentials reflected differences in quality. This underlines the elusive nature of higher nominal incomes for farmers during years of harvest failures.

Diversification of production would insure farmers if one crop (say, wheat) failed and others did not. In such a case, the price of all close substitutes would increase while production was affected negatively only in one – i.e. wheat. But diversification offered mixed blessings for peasants in poorly integrated markets. If there was a bumper harvest of wheat only, rye and bean prices would also decline but the peasant would not be compensated by a larger than normal harvest of the latter crops. Income might in fact become lower than if the peasant produced just the crop which experienced the bumper harvest. So diversification helps stabilise actual consumption of food in bad years but affects nominal and real income adversely if one of the main crops is abundantly produced. However, market integration might stimulate diversification because the adverse price effects from (say) a bumper harvest of wheat, disappear not only on wheat but on substitutes as well. A diversified output of products which were not, or only weakly, correlated in harvest outcomes would help peasants to stabilise income in an integrated market.

The customary although paradoxical complaint, repeatedly referred to by contemporaries as shown in chapter 1, that good harvests in segmented markets often offered little to cheer about, was certainly not without foundation. Part of the problem was that poor peasants had been drawn into the money economy but could not always exploit its advantages. If all transactions were made in kind – i.e. if their debts incurred in years of poor harvests to buy seedcorn or to pay rents could be repaid in grain – then peasants would have been insured against some of the adverse effects of harvest outcomes on prices and income. Consider a small-holder in a poor harvest year who has to borrow money in February to feed the family or to buy seedcorn. Assume furthermore that the price of grain is 1, and the nominal interest rate is 10 per cent for half a year. If the loan runs to next harvest, in August, this particular small-holder has to pay back 1.1 per unit of grain bought. But the price in August can be much below the February price (say, at a price of 0.7). The grain rate of interest – that is, the grain it takes to pay back the nominal sum of 1.1 – will be $1.1/0.7 = 1.57$, that is almost 60 per cent on a six months' basis. It is not difficult to understand the reluctant integration of peasants into the money economy under these circumstances. Instead of looking at this resistance as an expression of peasant conservatism we should look at it as a rational response of a class which could not reap the benefits of market pricing. Contemporary sources indicate that it was commonplace for peasants to postpone payments of nominal charges from years of harvest failures to years of abundant harvests and low nominal incomes. Had these arrears been paid in kind peasants would have been better off. There is a peculiar Swedish institution which developed alongside increased market integration, which is worth considering in this context. From the latter half of the eighteenth century a decentralised and fairly spontaneous system of village based co-operative savings banks, the so-called *sockenmagasin*, developed and remained vigourous throughout the first quarter of the nineteenth century. But these savings banks accepted deposits, granted loans, and charged interest in kind (i.e grain) only. Even non-members could take up a loan, even if the interest rate was slightly higher and a collateral was demanded. The grain rate of interest was much lower than in the example above, only some 5–10 per cent – that is, farmers did not have to pay dear for the seedcorn, only to sell cheap when it was time to pay back the loan. Second, these peculiar savings banks also constituted a technological breakthrough for more advanced storage methods – imported from the Continent and England – since the deposited grain was stored in purpose-built premises, and considerable care was taken to control for excessive humidity, rot and rats.[2]

It seems as if both the urban and large sections of the rural population had an interest in stable prices – the urban wage-earners and self-employed because consumption instability was reduced, and the rural small-holders because average consumption of food could be increased, see table 2.1. Consequently they would be better prepared for the bad years to come owing to higher income in good years. Consumption smoothing owing to increased opportunities for savings in the years of good harvest and high income cannot be ruled out. For the richer peasants and the land-owners price volatility in a non-integrated market might not have had any adverse effects on consumption. But it is worth noting that a poor harvest is a real output decline and in the end no one will actually win. Cormac Ó Gráda has made a detailed analysis of the economic impact of the effects of the severe disturbances of the Great Irish Famine, and concludes that practically all groups lost, even money-lenders and landlords because they could not collect their rents.[3] So the difference in market integration lies in the improved opportunities to exploit the advantages in a good harvest.

Consumption, capabilities and survival

Let us now return to the welfare implications of consumption instability provoked by price fluctuations of food. It can be shown in a rigorous way that a stable consumption is welfare-enhancing in the following sense: if consumption is stable at a given level the survival chances of an individual is greater than if consumption fluctuates around that level.[4] The analysis on p. 28 was ambiguous about whether price stabilisation actually stabilised consumption of small-holders but suggested that stabilisation increased the scope for savings in the good years – and hence made consumption-smoothing possible. However, we were confident that stabilisation would tend to increase mean consumption for small-holders. An extension of the argument is that consumption stabilisation will reduce crude death rates and fluctuations in these rates, so-called 'crisis mortality'. These important results will be more fully elaborated in the appendix to this chapter (pp. 42–6), while an intuitive approach will be

---

[2] See *Handlingar rörande inrättandet av sockenmagasiner*, Kungliga remisser, Riksarkivet, series D: aa (National Archives, Stockholm).

[3] C.Ó Gráda, *Black '47 and Beyond: The Great Irish Famine in History, Economy and Memory*, Princeton: Princeton University Press, 1999.

[4] M. Ravallion, *Markets and Famines*, Oxford: Clarendon Press, 1988. The model is developed in Ravallion's chapter 2 and an appendix to that chapter, see also pp. 42–6 in this volume.

offered now. The easiest way would perhaps be to extend, by analogy, the familiar concept of decreasing marginal productivity applied to the effects of consumption on survival chances, being positive but decreasing. While this is the main proposition on which the argument is based it would, however, be unsatisfactory just to postulate it. It turns out that the idea of decreasing returns to consumption in terms of survival chances will need a rather ingenious set of arguments. First, we have to make use of the idea that a given level of health is 'produced' by inputs, food and the personal constitution of individuals, and that these inputs can to some extent be substituted for each other. That means that an individual with a good personal constitution will have a higher probability of surviving to the next period than an individual with a poor constitution, consumption held constant. The former might furthermore have an equal survival chance as the latter with less consumption. We may talk about different levels of health say, the level of health that permits survival in the literal sense of the word, or the level of health necessary to perform normal 'doings and beings.' Of the inputs into the production of health only consumption can be observed with some certainty so the latter, the personal constitution, will be considered a continous stochastic variable with a single-peaked distribution. The personal constitution is related to physiological characteristics in man – energy needs, metabolism, caloric storage and immunocompetence – and might, as we will soon see, become the subject of changes owing to events affecting an individual.

The health 'production function' is strictly convex in the relevant domain. 'Convexity' means that each unit decline in food consumption is associated with an increasingly greater claim on the personal constitution to attain a given level of health. The level of health chosen for analysis can be the level required for mere physical survival or a level that permits normal or customary functionings. The trade-off between food and personal constitution produces a survival probability function, as depicted in figure 2.2, with decreasing returns of food in terms of survival chances. Note, however, that at very low levels of consumption there is a section of the survival function with increasing returns. As explained in the appendix, this is caused by the assumption of personal constitution having a single-peaked distribution.[5]

What are the implications of this survival function? The most obvious one is that the survival probability over a sequence of periods is larger, with stable consumption at its mean $c\#$ than if it fluctuated between c' and $c^\star$. The reason is that the decline of survival probability associated with a decline in consumption from $c\#$ to $c^\star$ would be greater (in absolute

---

[5] If, instead, personal constitution had been assumed to have a rectangular distribution the survival function would exhibit decreasing returns over its entire domain.

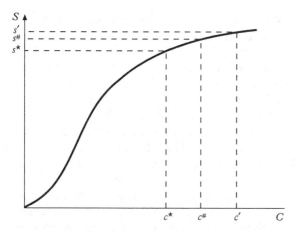

Figure 2.2 The survival function suggests that food consumption has decreasing returns in terms of individual survival probability

terms), from $s\#$ to $s^\star$, than the subsequent increase in survival probability when consumption increases from $c\#$ to c', causing survival chances to increase from $s\#$ to s'.[6] The other implication is that crude death rates – that is, $1 - s$, s being survival probability – and the fluctuations in these rates will decline as income or consumption increases and we move to the right into the flat part of the survival function. This seems to capture quite well the observed patterns of declining crude death rates and their variability as we enter the nineteenth century. However, we should be careful not to rush to strong conclusions. Both crude death rates and crisis mortality – that is, short-term mortality responses to consumption fluctuations – began to decline before clear, recognisable improvements in income or consumption. In the eighteenth and nineteenth centuries most European countries experienced a decline in both crisis mortality and crude mortality rates although there were considerable differences in the start of that decline. Mortality was not as high in the eighteenth century in England as in France, although there is some controversy as to when it began to decline.[7] However, other demographic variables such as

---

[6] There is a formal derivation of the results presented here in M. Ravallion, *Markets*, chapter 2, although there is little discussion of how the nutritional 'history' of a population affects the distribution of personal constitutions.

[7] R. Lee, 'Short-term variations in vital rates, prices, and weather', in E.A. Wrigley and R. Schofield, *The Population History of England, 1541–1871: A Reconstruction*, London: Edward Arnold, 1981, pp. 356–410, argues that deviations from normal mortality attributable to price variance started its decline in the seventeenth century and had almost disappeared in England by the end of the eighteenth century. The timing is not corroborated by P.R. Galloway, 'Annual variations in deaths by age, deaths by cause, prices, and

nuptuality and fertility continued to respond significantly to price fluctuations well into the nineteenth century. Some of these effects were behav-
ioural – that is, human adaptations to hard times – others were
physiological responses such as increases in spontaneous abortions.[8]

Looking at figures 2.3a and 2.3b, which illustrate the evolution of
crude death rates and infant mortality in Sweden and France, the decline
seems to set in around the turn to the nineteenth century. This is most
evident for infant mortality in Sweden and a little later for crude death
rates in both Sweden and France. The other interesting property in the
series is the decline in year-to-year fluctuations. It is also clear that the
decline in mortality is stimulated by the increase in income from the end
of the nineteenth century but that the continued improvements in living
standards cease to have an effect on these rates after the Second World
War. By then, we are obviously in the flat part of the survival function, s.

Crisis mortality in the narrow sense – i.e. as a deviation from normal
mortality – was never a dominant proportion of total mortality, but an
'important determinant of the timing of deaths'.[9] It was, as we have seen,

footnote 7 (*cont.*)
weather in London 1670–1830', *Population Studies*, 39, 1985, pp. 487–505, who detects
continued impact on mortality from economic variables well into the eighteenth century,
but notes that it was very weak in the sixteenth century. British results are quite problematic since price series are based on a geographically very limited area while demographic figures are not. For Sweden, T. Bengtsson and R. Ohlsson, 'The standard of
living and mortality response in different ages', *European Journal of Population 1*, 1985,
investigated real wage effects on mortality which turned out to be strong but weaker in
the nineteenth century compared to the last half of the eighteenth century. D. Weir, in
'Markets and mortality in France 1600–1789', in J.Walter and R.Schofield (eds), *Famine,
Disease and the Social Order in Early Modern Society*, Cambridge: Cambridge University
Press, 1989, pp. 201–34, reports a weakening impact from wheat prices on French mortality from the eighteenth century and by the start of the nineteenth century the effect is
very weak S. Drame *et al Un siècle de commerce du blé en France 1825–1913*, Paris:
Economica, 1991, pp. 41–2 reports similar results for France. Crude death rates also
varied from some 35–40 per 1,000 in mid-eighteenth-century France to about 30 in
England. It declined to around 25–27 per 1,000 in both countries 100 years later.
[8]   P.R. Galloway, 'Basic patterns in annual variations in fertility, nuptuality, mortality and
prices in pre-industrial Europe', *Population Studies*, 42, 1988, pp. 275–304.
[9]   There is some controversy around these claims, depending on author, country, method
and period, although there is general agreement on the declining importance of famine-
related mortality in western Europe from the eighteenth century, and much earlier in
England. The role of crisis mortality – narrowly defined – was downplayed by the publication of the detailed population data on England presented and analysed by W.A
Wrigley and R. Schofield, *Population History*. Estimates of the proportion of total mortality owing to crisis mortality – in the narrow sense defined above – differ. Weir, in 'Markets
and mortality', detects a larger impact, some 20 per cent of total mortality, for France up
to the middle of the eighteenth century. Galloway, in 'Annual variations', found that
between 20 and 40 per cent of the variance in non-infant mortality was a response to
price fluctuations, but generally the impact was smaller the higher the *per capita* income.
This result is implied in the model discussed above. He also confirmed continued effects
on mortality from prices in the nineteenth century in poor parts of Europe.

to a large extent a delayed response to economic hardship since nutritional deficiencies seldom caused death by outright starvation but rather through a decline in resistance to and an increase in the incidence of diseases. That would suggest that, at least in part, the observed development in both death rates and crisis mortality were caused by an upward shift and a lower slope of the survival probability function as demonstrated in figure 2.4. At this higher survival schedule, not only would a consumption at $c\#$ be associated with higher survival chances, and consequently lower crude death rates, but consumption fluctuations in the interval $c^\star$ and c' would generate lower crisis mortality. Is it possible to reconcile such a shift with the health production approach?

There are two modifications of the argument which actually generate an upward shift of the survival functions. J. Mokyr and R. Stein have proposed a slightly different health production framework in which improved knowledge of the relationship between consumption, hygiene and health plays a major role.[10] Until the late eighteenth century the popular knowledge of health maintenance and disease control were so limited that the idea that individual optimising behaviour played a role in health production is misguided. But as time passes, and certainly by the nineteenth century, the stock of knowledge increases and hence individuals were able to improve health by changing their behaviour and consumption patterns. In the framework discussed here this is equivalent to saying that there is a shift in the health production function, or more precisely improved knowledge implies technological change. That means that a given level of health could be produced with fewer inputs, which would in turn imply an upward shift of the s function, other things being equal.

But this is not the only way by which such a shift can occur. The other problem is the way we represent the personal constitution as a continuous single-peaked stochastic variable. This might seem an elusive strategy but is in fact quite helpful when we cannot observe personal constitution directly, although the idea that personal constitution matters seems too obvious to dispute. We can, however, make qualified statements about whether personal constitution is improved or not, and that is enough to generate further interesting implications.

It can be argued – and there is ample nutritional and medical evidence to support the argument – that the personal constitution is itself influenced by chronic malnutrition or short spells of severe deficiencies of food intake as well as the derived effects thereof, such as the incidence of diseases. The effects on personal constitution can be either irreversible or

---

[10] J. Mokyr and R. Stein, 'Science, Health and Household Technology: The Effect of the Pasteur Revolution on Consumer Demand in the US 1850–1941', National Bureau of Economic Research, mimeographed conference report, 1994.

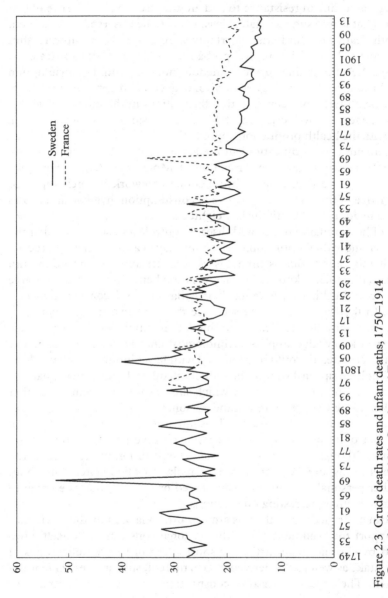

Figure 2.3 Crude death rates and infant deaths, 1750–1914
a Crude deaths per 1,000 in Sweden and France
Source: R.B. Mitchell, *International Historical Statistics, Europe 1750–1988*, London: Macmillan, 1992, tables A6, A7.

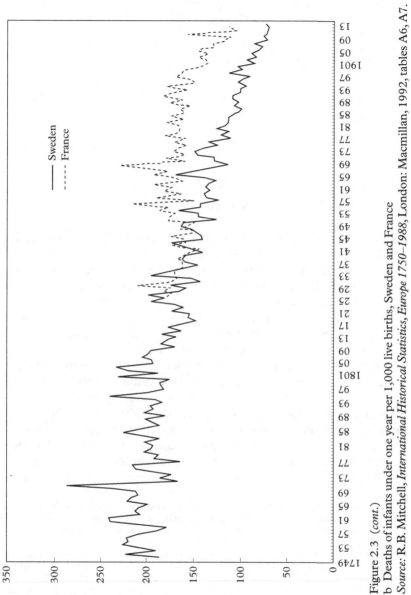

Figure 2.3 (cont.)
b Deaths of infants under one year per 1,000 live births, Sweden and France
Source: R.B. Mitchell, International Historical Statistics, Europe 1750–1988, London: Macmillan, 1992, tables A6, A7.

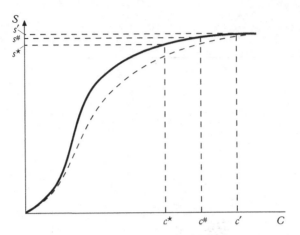

Figure 2.4 A shift in the survival function

transitory, depending on whether nutritional deficiencies can be compensated for later or not. This claim finds support in recent research which
indicates *irreversible* negative effects on human physical and mental
capacities and life expectancy arising from malnutrition.[11] But such
effects are not necessarily caused by chronic malnutrition but also of
shorter spells, for example during pregnancy. Foetal growth seems to be
particularly sensitive to imbalances in nutritional composition. Also in
the post-natal period stunting that appears in early childhood cannot be
wholly compensated at later stages. The mechanism here seems to be that
some diseases cause malabsorption of food, others affect appetite and
that fever increases the energy losses. Compensatory nutritional intake
necessary for a catch-up will not erase the scars of the past. Since (temporary) malnutrition increases the risk of infections it can constitute the
beginning of a vicious circle through the energy losses imposed by infections. It also seems as if the severity of communicable diseases is greater
for the under-nourished, which has consequences for physical stature

[11] There is a vast literature on this subject. For irreversible effects of (early) malnutrition on
the development of the brain and mental capacities, see for example *Early Malnutrition
and Mental Development*, XII Symposia of the Swedish Nutrition Foundation, Uppsala:
Almqvist & Wiksell, 1974, and M. Winnick, *Malnutrition and Brain Development*, New
York: Oxford University Press, 1976. The effects of nutritional defects on immunocompetence is reviewed by P.G. Lunn, 'Nutrition, immunity and infection', in R. Schofield,
D. Reher and A. Bideau (eds.), *The Decline of Mortality in Europe*, Oxford: Clarendon
Press, 1991, pp. 131–45 and in R.R. Watson (ed.), *Nutrition, Disease Resistance and
Immune Function*, New York: M. Decker, 1984. The role of micronutrient deficiency –
e.g. iron and vitamins – on immunocompetence and probable irreversible effects on per-
formance is surveyed in K.Pietrzik (ed.), *Modern Lifestyles, Lower Energy Intake and
Micronutrient Status*, Berlin: Springer Verlag, 1991.

and, possibly, life expectancy.[12] The height of an individual reflects the incidence of stunting as a consequence of previous diseases, and has been associated with life expectancy in the sense that higher mortality risks were associated with lower stature.[13]

The fact that there are irreversible effects of short spells of poverty is in itself an argument for consumption stabilisation. To the extent that decreasing consumption instability affected the incidence of malnutrition and the spread of diseases it would contribute to an improvement in the personal constitution. This is consistent with the observed decline in crude death rates interpreted as the consequence of an upward shift in the survival probability function as shown in figure 2.4. It should be pointed out, however, that we cannot say much about the slope of the new higher survival probability function without knowing more about the distribution of personal constitution. The fact that it has been drawn as having a smaller slope than the old between $c^\star$ and c' is a conjecture.

There is a third way in which market integration, with or without higher consumption stability, might cause a shift in the survival probability function, and that is the 'endemicisation' of communicable diseases. Some diseases, such as tuberculosis, pneumonia, influenza, cholera and scarlet fever, had a higher incidence among the malnourished. Dearth also forced people to abandon their homes and they therefore became exposed to, or exposed others to, communicable diseases. But if that was the case, would not market integration with the supposed increased human mobility also contribute to the prevalence of infectious (i.e.communicable) diseases? John Walter and Roger Schofield address this problem and suggest that market integration increased regular and permanent contacts between hitherto separated regions.[14] What matters here is the regularity of contacts as opposed to the erratic and massive contacts caused by dearth and famines. Regular contacts generated, in Schofield's words, an 'endemicisation' of a disease and therefore diminished the number of people who in a given locality and at a given time were susceptible. Needless to say, it is difficult to detect the possibly benign effects of market integration in a period which saw other and simultaneous effects of early industrialisation – for example, worsening sanitation and hygiene in the rapidly growing urban centres.

[12] G. Alter and J.C. Riley argue that present health is heavily dependent on past health. See 'Fraility, sickness and death: models of morbidity in historical populations', *Population Studies*, 43, 1989, pp. 25–46.
[13] See for example R.W. Fogel, 'Second thoughts on the European escape from hunger: famines, chronic malnutrition, and mortality rates', in S.R.Osmani(ed.), *Nutrition and Poverty*, Oxford: Clarendon Press, 1992, pp. 243–86.
[14] J. Walter and R. Schofield, 'Famine, disease and crisis mortality in early modern society', in J. Walter and R. Schofield, *Famine, Disease and the Social Order*, pp. 59–61.

Deprivation and the moral economy

Premature death, by its irrevocability rather than through its incidence, was the most dramatic but by no means the only effect of permanent or transitory malnutrition caused by strong price increases at constant wages. Political, physiological and demographic responses other than mortality were more sensitive to sudden changes in the standard of living, and revealed that price shocks had a profound impact on all vital aspects of human functionings, since they restrained freedom to act and achieve. The disruptions of customary human functionings erupted in social unrest well into the nineteenth century. Without loss of generality, the level of health that we want to discuss in this context is not the minimum necessary for 'survival' in the literal sense of the word. More rewarding for an analysis of the conditions for political and social stability would be to focus on the level necessary for a social and economic functioning, a level at which human beings can develop a basic capability to work and participate in society. The main results from the preceding analysis still holds – the steady-state proportion of the population that can remain in a state permitting them to perform basic functionings will be higher over an extended period if prices (and consumption) are preserved at their mean rather than fluctuating around that mean. And the rationale for a transfer of purchasing power from the rich to the poor remains – in other words, price stability and equitable redistribution were enhancing human capabilities. It will be suggested here that consumption stabilisation will also breed political stability. The concept of 'capability' underlines the importance of abilities for human welfare, the idea being that recurrent deprivation of customary functionings for large segments of the population acts as a powerful catalyst for political action.

Riots and political unrest were endemic in societies with unstable prices and found expression in hostile attitudes towards engrossers, forestallers, millers and their kind. What mattered here was the fact that the customary living standard was repeatedly disturbed. Popular attitudes towards markets were, not surprisingly, affected by the poor performance of food markets. Economic hardships and deviations from *expectations* of what life should be like were seen as market failures or failings of those operating in the market. As a consequence the market as an institution was repeatedly challenged when the moral economy of the crowd was violated by the threat of abnormal – and what often amounted to the same thing, *unfair* – prices.

When it comes to explaining demographic responses and the effects on health and human capabilities, we have to deal with a complicated interplay of physiological and nutritional properties in man and epidemiological processes. Mentalities and their morphology are not as easy to analyse. Riots were not simply 'rebellions of the belly', as E.P. Thompson expresses it. They were not only related to material conditions but also to *expectations* of what a just society should look like. In fact, those whose lives were literally threatened by severe and prolonged starvation seldom rebelled at all.

E.P. Thompson's influential article, 'The moral economy of the English crowd in the eighteenth century' (1971), is often interpreted as saying that the moral economy was antithetical to markets in general. I am not so sure about that. It can, without much violation to the original, be interpreted as saying that the moral economy and furore of the crowd was aroused by poor market performance and periodic market *failures*.[15] While the evolution of political culture has its own logic it will be affected by the welfare impact associated with a particular institution, such as the market. If market failures recurrently obstructed people from living a decent life we would expect this experience to be represented in political demands for market reform or regulation. It is a fact that rioting was often effective in inciting authorities to act on behalf of the crowd. To the extent that such policies were efficient they would affirm the prevailing political culture, which advocated regulation of markets when prices exploded. Only an improvement in living standards and a better performance of food markets could stop these political protests.

I have quoted E.P. Thompson as saying that riots, and even food riots, were not simply 'rebellions of the belly'. The important point here is that expectations not only of consumption stability – the concept 'customary' is vital to Thompson's analysis – but also of what ought to be a good life are powerful determinants in mass protests. Expectations of a good society or a decent life are, in part at least, products of human imagination fuelled by myths and dreams and ideology, both religious and secular in origin. But these expectations are also based on experience of life such as it once was, and on knowledge about others. Those chronically deprived might be less prone to imagine what a decent life should be like, or what basic capabilities were like because they never had a chance to exercise these capabilities and were practically excluded from the communicative action with those of their fellow citizens, who were a little better off. In most countries there was a history of government intervention with the

---

[15] *Past and Present*, 50, 1971. The literature on the topic has developed into an academic sub-discipline, and E.P. Thompson commented upon it, with little generosity, in 'The moral economy reviewed', in his *Customs in Common*, London: Merlin Press 1991. For an innovative study in this tradition, see J. Bohstedt, *Riots and Community Politics in England and Wales*, Cambridge, Mass.: Harvard University Press, 1983, which points out that riots were often deliberate negotiations over prices, but ultimately based on a widely shared conviction of fairness. Rioters expected the élite to 'understand' their grievances.

aim of stabilising prices and even when these policies were abandoned they survived in the memories of the crowd. One possible interpretation of E.P. Thompson's thesis of the moral economy of the crowd as being made up of a legitimising notion would be that it is related to the concept of relative deprivation. That concept is usually understood as a normative concept – that is, that absolute standards are less interesting than the standard of living relative to that of others – or relative to a norm or a custom which is cultural and historical rather than purely nutritional. We can broaden the concept by introducing a relativity into historical time: that is, relative deprivation might be a powerful motivational force when income and consumption fall below what has been the expected historical norm for an individual or a group of people. For example, habits slowly changed so that white bread gradually replaced brown bread, a coarser mixture, and a return to the former habits were not made without protest.

The structure of political protests can now be related to the nature of markets. Those who were thrown into the ranks of the poor by recurrent price and real wage shocks brought with them memories of a better life and sometimes stories about the policies of authorities in defence of stable prices. They became relatively deprived in two respects: relative to the 'jobbers', the millers, the 'interlopers' whose riches were seen as rising at least relatively and sometimes absolutely. 'Plenty amidst poverty' is a common theme in popular agitation in times of dearth. But equally important was the deprivation relative to the customary way of life. As a consequence, the common people could not fulfil their basic human capabilities. This is why fluctuations in prices might be more destabilising politically, more dangerous to the rulers, than constant deprivation of a significant, but stable, part of the population.

The political vulnerability of rulers made them, or forced them, to adapt to popular demands. As long as price and consumption volatility had an impact not only on the quality of life but on life itself, the problem must be tackled, or so rulers were repeatedly told by rioters. But were the policies which were designed accurate and efficient? That question will be explored in chapter 4. But first we will dwell on the question why markets performed so poorly, and what ultimately made them perform better, paving the way for a deregulation of grain markets.

APPENDIX

This appendix extends but also draws heavily on chapter 2 in Martin Ravallion's *Markets and Famines* (1988). The reader interested in the precise mathematical properties of the model is referred to the original formulation.

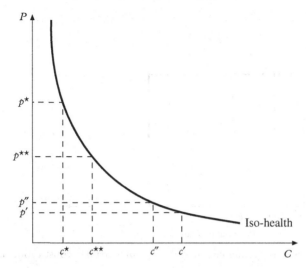

Figure 2A.1 A given level of health in an individual is produced by consumption, c, and personal constitution, p

Let us first introduce the idea of health as produced in a production function with two arguments, food consumption, c, and the individual's personal constitution, p. This can generate an iso-health contour such as the one in figure 2A.1, although the precise contour will depend on the elasticities of substitution in the production function. The level of health corresponding to the iso-health contour in figure 2A.1 can be the one permitting the individual to survive to the next period. If we had wanted to show a level of health compatible not only with survival, but with normal 'doings and beings', it would have been situated outside the present contour. In Figure 2A.1 p' is the minimum personal constitution necessary for survival with consumption at c', p'' at c'', etc. With the convex iso-health contour it can easily be seen that a sequence of equally large reductions in consumption will generate larger and larger claims on personal constitution. This is illustrated by comparing the increase in claims on the minimum personal constitution necessary from a reduction of consumption from c' to c'' – i.e from p' to p'' – with a decline in consumption from $c^{\star\star}$ to $c^{\star}$, which increases the minimum personal constitution from $p^{\star\star}$ to $p^{\star}$.

We have admitted that personal constitution, although important, cannot be directly observed and we therefore treat it as a stochastic variable. Mostly for expositional reasons we start by just assuming personal constitution to be uniformly distributed, and such a distribution is

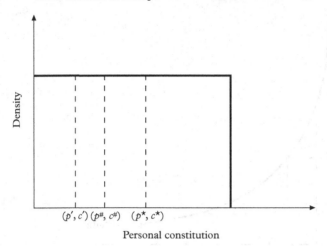

Figure 2A.2 A rectangular distribution of personal constitution is a special case

illustrated by the rectangular density in figure 2A.2, which indicates that the levels of personal constitution are equally probable.

We can now look at the survival probabilities for this individual at different levels of consumption, starting at a high level, c', and reducing it stepwise to $c^{\star}$. We have already learned that there is a unique minimum level of personal constitution necessary for survival associated with each level of consumption. The minimum personal constitution necessary for survival associated with consumption, c', is p', and in figure 2A.2 the survival probability is the area of the rectangle with a personal constitution above (higher than) p' – i.e. to the right of (p', c'). Since unit reductions in consumption requires increasing claims on the minimum personal constitution the reduction in survival chances becomes larger and larger, illustrated by successive reductions in consumption from c' to c*. The survival function emerging from this example is found in figure 2A.3, and it is strictly concave.

However, what generates the particular shape of the survival function used in the text (see figures 2.2 and 2.4) is the unimodal or single-peaked distribution. Let us therefore repeat the argument with a more general distribution, a log-normal, shown in figure 2A.4. Reductions in consumption will make the decline in survival chances larger and larger for a while, as in the previous case. At some stage, further reductions in consumption will get you into the right-hand tail of the distribution where each successive segment might represent a smaller area. Although the increased claim on personal constitution with each reduction in con-

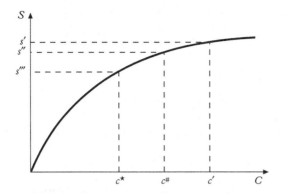

Figure 2A.3 A strictly concave survival function is associated with a rectangular distribution of personal constitution

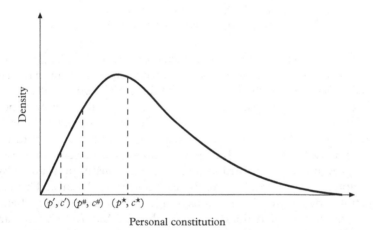

Personal constitution

Figure 2A.4 A single-peaked distribution of personal constitution generates the survival function in figure 2.2

sumption will still make the width of the segment (along the p axis) larger and larger, the area might actually decrease owing to the downward slope of the distribution. That means that survival chances decrease with further reductions, but at a slower rate at very low levels of consumption. This is the underlying argument for figure 2.2 above, which showed increasing returns at low levels of consumption.

Finally, a few words on how we can introduce the changes in consumption technology and personal constitution referred to in the interpretation of figure 2.4 (p. 35). Technological progress can be represented by an inward shift of the iso-health contour in figure 2A.1, which means that the given health could be produced with fewer resources. Let us take an

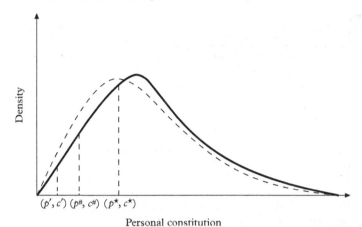

Figure 2A.5 A shift in the distribution of personal constitution generates a shift in the survival function as in figure 2.4

example. Assume resources spent on consumption to be given, but with
the difference that it can now be associated with a lower minimum level of
personal constitution for survival because the consumption pattern has
been improved (say, because of a healthier diet). If the distribution of personal constitution is constant, the survival chances increase for the individual. (It is equivalent to moving to the left on the personal constitution
axis in figures 2A.2 or 2A.4.) But survival chances can also be increased
by an improvement in the distribution of personal constitution caused by,
for example, the absence of severe diseases during adolescence. This can
be illustrated by the two distributions in figure 2A.5, the solid line being
the new distribution and the dotted line the old. Survival chances are
higher in the new distribution at each of the different levels of consumption (p', c') to $(p^\star, c^\star)$, implying that an upward shift in the survival function has occurred, as illustrated in figure 2.4.

3   Harvest fluctuations, storage and grain-price responses

The political economy of harvest failures

That the price fluctuations discussed in earlier chapters were triggered by output shocks is too obvious to dispute. But how big were these harvest shocks, and could stocks not smooth supply? Did market imperfections and changes in income distribution also play a part in the severe political repercussions and adverse welfare impact of harvest failures? This and chapter 4 will answer these questions.

Research on modern famines has shown that they can be provoked by a small decrease in the supply of food, and the important policy implication is that the food shortage is manageable, provided there is good government and in the absence of speculative bubbles. This has inspired some economic historians to similar conclusions regarding the extent of harvest failures in early modern Europe. Paradoxically, this view seems to revive the contemporary popular mistrust of markets, viewing the price movements as caused by man rather than nature. That merchants sometimes succeeded in cornering markets does not mean that collusion and insider trading were the main or even *the* pervasive element in markets – for one thing, because trade was closely monitored, especially during subsistence crises, by the public authorities.[1] But markets still failed, for two distinct reasons. Although not much could be done by man to calm output shocks they were aggravated because inventories – that is, grain carried over from one harvest to the next – were small. But it will also be shown in chapter 4 that market incentives for trade and carry-over did not adequately reflect the social gains from price stability. Trade and inventory adjustments can be expected to be price-stabilising. However, there is a positive externality in price stability because epidemics and petty crime decline. These social gains are not reflected in the private gains from trade and storage.

---

[1] John Chartres suggests that in early modern England the share of major traders in grain markets was usually compatible with competition, with London providing a possible exception. Competitive conditions varied across product markets, though. Dealers in dairy products and meat, for example, seem to have exercised market power. See 'The marketing of agricultural produce, 1640–1750', in J.Chartres(ed.), *Agricultural markets and trade 1500–1740*, Cambridge: Cambridge University Press, 1990, pp. 227–8, 237.

In what follows, we will first look into the conflicting views held by contemporary authors regarding the magnitude of output variations, and then present a series of new empirical assessments of those variations. Finally, we will discuss the nature and extent of storage. Charles Davenant was one of many contemporaries who commented upon the relationship between output and price variations, which he also expressed in numerical terms, thereby continuing to attract interest among historians and economists. Davenant's comments have often, rightly or wrongly, been attributed to Gregory King, although there is no documentary evidence that King was the first to draft the particular example, or anything similar to what Davenant later published.

Davenant's *An essay upon the probable methods of making people gainers in the balance of trade*[2] uses an example of the proportionate 'defect' of the grain harvest and its consequent effect on price, again measured as the proportionate increase from the 'common rate'. The underlying cause is what in modern parlance is characterised as a very inelastic demand with regard to price – that is, an increase (decrease) in price generates a much smaller decrease (increase) in demand. This is a property normally associated with necessities: you have to have them irrespective of their price. However, strictly speaking, the price elasticity of demand measures the response of demand to a price change, and it is only under special circumstances that it is also a good guide to the response of price to a change in the local quantity harvested. In the case of Davenant and his contemporaries, the focus has been on the price response to a deficient harvest. Modern scholars have reversed the order and made attempts to estimate harvest outcomes from observed price changes. As long as the economy was little affected by international trade and changes in stocks, the price elasticity of demand – properly estimated – can be used as an appropriate indicator of local output changes. In other words, the elasticity of demand with regard to price predicts reasonably well the change in output from an observed price change. In an open economy, however, the price variance is only remotely related to the local harvest because local production is small relative to aggregate supply and the integration of markets cancel out local harvest shocks. This ambiguity is worth having in mind when we discuss the differing estimates of the elasticities reported below. Only when pointed out explicitly can the reported elasticities be interpreted as price elasticities of demand. In this chapter, I have chosen to estimate harvest outcomes from yields and then tried to make inferences about the price elasticity of demand. However, yield series must be adjusted for inventory changes and trade to be used for that purpose (see table 3.2, p. 53).

---

[2] London, 1699; Also in *The Political and Commercial Works of Charles D'Avenant*, vol. 2, London, 1771, ed. Charles Whitworth.

Davenant's particular example is of dubious value but survived him well and was transformed to something of an economic law, which is in fact what Stanley Jevons called it in his *Theory of Political Economy*, where he developed a precise formula based on the alleged empirical relations found in Davenant's example.[3] Jevons' interest lay primarily in exploring the utility attached to the 'necessaries of life', but he did not hesitate to express his confidence in the actual numbers suggested by Davenant. He implicitly neglected both inventory changes and trade in his estimate of supply. That procedure has been repeated among economic historians who have used slightly modified formulas *à la* Jevons to infer unobservable yields or output series from observed grain prices.[4] However, the accuracy of Davenant's quantified relation between supply or harvest and price has too often been taken for granted. The elasticities inferred from Davenant's figures are in the order of -0.4, and, indeed, there are modern scholars, the most prolific being R.W.Fogel, who consider that this is an over-estimate of the response of quantities to prices, arguing that the appropriate figure would rather be between -0.1 and -0.2 for the early modern period.[5] It is clear that with elasticities of the order implied by Davenant, or even lower as tentatively suggested by Fogel, the severity of the 'defects' in the harvests have been grossly over-stated by both contemporaries and modern historical research. An elasticity of demand with regard to price of (say) -0.5 would imply that a 10 per cent increase in price was triggered off by a 5 per cent quantity defect, while an elasticity of -0.1 implies a defect of only 1 per cent. So the magnitudes of the estimated elasticities matter a lot. However, the large swings in prices remain both a fact and a problem for many of those with inadequate entitlement, irrespective of how great the underlying disturbance in harvests proved to

[3] London: Macmillan, 1879, pp. 165–71. Jevons, like other, later commentators, was preoccupied with whether Davenant here spoke his own mind or if he was just echoing Gregory King, whose work Davenant quoted at length in his *Essay*. In the particular section of Davenant's *Essay* where he discussed the vital example there are no references to Gregory King. Jevons had every reason to suggest that the 'law' bears Davenant's imprint.

[4] E.A. Wrigley has critically examined these attempts, which included Thorold Rogers (*Six Centuries of Work and Wages*, London, 1908) and Slicher van Bath, in 'Reflections on corn yields and prices in pre-industrial economies', in *People, Cities and Wealth*, Oxford: Basil Blackwell, 1987, pp. 92–130. W.G. Hoskins adopts a more cautious strategy when he infers wheat harvests from wheat price variations in England. He does not quantify the harvests precisely but establishes an ordering from 'abundant' to 'dearth', the latter being the case if the wheat price deviated more than 50 per cent from a moving average. See Hoskins, 'Harvest fluctuations and English economic history, 1480–1690', *Agricultural History Review*, 12, 1964, pp. 28–46 and 'Harvest fluctuations and English economic history, 1620–1759', *Agricultural History Review*, 16, 1968, pp. 15–31.

[5] R.W. Fogel, 'Second thoughts on the European escape from hunger: famines, chronic malnutrition, and mortality rates', in S.R. Osmani (ed.), *Nutrition and Poverty*, Oxford: Clarendon Press, 1992, pp. 243–86.

be. Inspired by modern research on poverty and famines, focus has now turned, and rightly so, to the effects of an unequal income distribution and the loss of entitlement experienced by marginal farmers and day-labourers hit by unemployment in the wake of a local harvest failure.[6] Important as these findings are, they must not conceal the fact that in early modern Europe the magnitude of harvest 'defects' was very large indeed. The severity of national harvest failures typically referred to by contemporaries were in the order of magnitude of 30–40 per cent of a normal harvest. As shown below, the standard deviation of regional yield series for agriculture is between 20 and 25 per cent and there were occasional outliers around 50 per cent. Given the fact that harvest disturbances were local the variation of (say) European grain output can be expected to be much smaller, but that was little consolation for deficit regions cut off from trade by high transport costs. In this context, the question of whether the harvest failures were 'manageable' will be addressed – that is, whether a feasible set of institutions could be and were designed to handle the consequences of harvest failures by stimulating international trade and management of inventories.

Fogel has been in the forefront among those playing down the magnitude in supply variations in early modern agriculture. He relies partly on the information handed over by Davenant – although he neglects the fact that Davenant typically (as most of his contemporaries) refers to harvest failures in the order of magnitude of a 30 per cent decline. Fogel also uses very optimistic assessments of the stocks available. However, neither of these arguments are robust, as will be shown shortly. The resolution of the issues sketched above carries implications far beyond the history of economic ideas. In fact, the way we analyse early modern grain markets will depend on it, in particular in regard to whether inventories were large enough to evade grave social consequences in a sequence of below-average harvests. Before investigating the empirical basis for these claims, it is worth examining what some of Davenant's illustrious contemporaries were saying.

Half a century after the publication of Davenant's *Essay*, François Quesnay wrote an article for Diderot's *Encyclopédie*, in which he constructed an example similar in structure but different in content to Davenant's.[7] It set out to demonstrate the effects of positive and negative deviations from the mean harvest on prices in France. The irony is,

---

[6] A. Sen, *Poverty and Famines: An Essay on Entitlement and Deprivation*, Oxford: Clarendon Press, 1981.
[7] The discussion referred to here is found under the entry 'Grains' in vol. 7, published in 1757. Also in A. Oncken (ed.), *Oeuvres économiques et philosophiques de F. Quesnay*, Paris: J. Peelman, 1888.

however, that Quesnay argued that the main reason for large swings in prices was that France, as opposed to England, was a closed economy. He then continued by constructing a hypothetical case in which prices varied within a range deemed to be typical of an open economy, specifically mentioning England, but subject to the same local output shocks as France. Price responses to these local shocks were believed to be much smaller because England was open to internal and foreign trade. Small price movements stimulated inter-regional and international flows of grain. The implied elasticities indicated that the proportionate change in price was smaller than the proportionate change in the local harvest in an open economy. Quesnay's purpose was polemical, but so was Davenant's. The former advocated a trade régime similar to England's because he believed that it would stabilise prices, as his second example served to prove. Trade could stabilise prices, he argued, because harvest outcomes among trading partners differed: a bad harvest in one nation was balanced by an abundant harvest in another. The polemical intent would, however, have been strengthened by an example *à la* Davenant since that generated even stronger price volatility from identical harvest outcomes. Davenant's polemical aim was to show that if the English had larger inventories, as he claimed the Hollanders had, then the price fluctuations would be smaller, something both he and Quesnay considered to be desirable.

A third view, that of A.R.J. Turgot, is worth mentioning in this context, because it is an implicit recognition of the fact that point elasticities change along a downward-sloping demand curve. Turgot, a long-serving French civil servant with an intimate knowledge of the grain markets he set out to administer, as we saw in chapter 1, showed in his example that when wheat became scarce and prices soared demand would ultimately become less inelastic and perhaps even elastic. The reason we would now give for such a phenomenon is that as wheat becomes more expensive there is an intensified search for substitutes such as rye or chestnuts. Turgot, like Quesnay, was a fervent advocate of free trade. His aim was to convince his contemporaries that stable prices were good for consumers because consumption was stabilised, and good for producers because average total revenue increased over an extended period of output variations. If the point elasticities along the demand curve became less inelastic when a bad harvest drove prices up, income did not increase enough to offset the decline in income from a good harvest. Since demand was more inelastic when bumper harvests occurred and grain was abundant, prices fell more than the increase in output and income declined. The producers' total revenue curve across a sequence from bad to good harvests would be concave, like an inverted U. Producers, as pointed out in chapters 1 and 2, were caught in a sort of 'elasticity trap'; they were

Table 3.1 *Elasticities and prices implied by examples from Davenant, Quesnay and Turgot*

	Davenant	Quesnay		Turgot	
	Price	France Price	England Price	France Price	England Price
Normal harvest	1.0	1.0	1.0	1.0	1.0
Bad harvest	2.6	1.6	1.09	1.26	1.1
Elasticity	−0.37	−0.76	−4.14	−1.54	−3.74

Sources: C. Davenant, F. Quesnay, 'Grains', in A. Oncken (ed.), *Oeuvres économiques et philosophiques de F. Quesnay*, 1888; A.R.J. Turgot, 'Quatrième lettre', in G. Schelle, *Oeuvres de Turgot*, vol. 3, 1919.

helped neither by harvest failures nor by bumper harvests. If we now look more closely at the elasticities implied by these three authors, it turns out that Davenant's example gave rise to much lower elasticities than either Turgot's or Quesnay's. Note, however, that the elasticities cannot be interpreted as the price elasticity of demand in the case of England. This is because the variation in harvest outcome differed from domestic demand, given England's status as an open economy with considerable trade. From the other side of *la Manche,* England seemed to be in a more favourable position than Davenant would have us believe it was. Table 3.1 presents hypothetical examples, which were thought to be applicable if France had been as open to trade as England. The elasticities have been derived from prices proposed by the three authors to reflect a bad harvest, meaning sometimes 60 and sometimes 70 per cent of a normal harvest. The prices in the table are implied by the elasticities thus derived, but a bad harvest has been normalised to a harvest of 70 per cent of the average. 'France' and 'England' refer to the examples Quesnay and Turgot constructed to reflect French and English conditions – i.e. a closed and an open economy, respectively.

That these three examples should imply such widely different estimates is a reminder that the views of contemporaries, even very talented ones, should not be taken at face value.

The new estimates

Let us now turn to the empirical evidence available for estimating the price elasticity of demand for grain. I shall proceed by using a simplified formula suggested by R.W. Fogel and then present a series of estimates.

Table 3.2 *Estimates of elasticities, grain, Europe, sixteenth–nineteenth centuries*

	I	II	**III**	IV	V	VI	VII
σ_q	0.04	0.25	**0.16**	0.15	0.19	0.13	0.19
σ_p	0.22	0.25	**0.25**	0.27	0.21	0.22	0.22
ϵ	−0.18	−1.0	**−0.64**	−0.55	−0.90	−0.59	−0.86

Formally, the elasticity of demand with regard to price is expressed as

$$Q^\star = -\varepsilon P^\star \tag{3.1}$$

where ε is elasticity, Q is quantity, P is price and an asterisk ($\star$) denotes the proportional change of the variable. Assuming that the correlation between the two variables is negative and perfect, the elasticity can be expressed as the ratio of the standard deviation of $Q^\star$, σ_q, over the standard deviation of $P^\star$, σ_p – that is

$$\varepsilon = -\sigma_q/\sigma_p. \tag{3.2}$$

Data on either prices or quantity deviations for a given region in the early modern period are scarce. In fact, there are no available series on aggregate output, trade or inventories at all for the early modern period. What we do have are yields – i.e. output per unit of land or seedcorn. Treating variations in yields as an approximation of output variations presupposes that the short term changes in planned output are negligible – i.e. changes in yields and output are both driven by natural accidents. If producers made short-term compensatory adaptations of planned output – for example, by varying the area under the plough – as a response to unanticipated shocks in yields the standard deviation of output would be greater than that of yields. That implies that estimates of elasticities based on yields will have a downward bias – i.e. the degree of inelasticity is exaggerated. However, there is an implicit assumption here that the demand curve does not shift inwards when the supply curve does. If it does, there is an upward bias in the estimates. In table 3.2 I present a menu of different estimates. The way they have been obtained is explained in the appendix (p. 64), where there is also reference to the periods and regions to which the data apply.

Columns I, II and IV–VII are comparable and share the characteristic that the quantity variations are not corrected for trade and inventory adjustments, and we cannot therefore directly interpret the implied elasticities as elasticities of demand with regard to price. In column III, the bold figures have been corrected for the impact of trade and inventory adjustment, albeit in a rather mechanical way. The effect of inventories is, as will be argued below, negligible, but the impact of trade is not. A comparison between columns IV and V illustrates this point. The reason why the implied number in column V reveals less inelasticity is that the Bordeaux region is more open to trade than Central France, which means that the yield variations are less adequate as an indicator of demand and supply variations than for Central France. If we want to infer the elasticity of demand with regard to price we have to adjust the output figures with respect to trade, which would imply that quantity variance is smaller than yield variance. The elasticities would then be adjusted in a downward direction. In column III, which relates to Southern Scandinavia, quantities have been adjusted for trade and carry-over and should be compared with column II. The difference between the standard deviation of the quantities in columns II and III is generated by an assumed export (import) of 25 per cent of the output above (below) average. If we also add carry-over so that stocks knock off 10 per cent of the yield variations the elasticity will be −0.64. Had the other output series been adjusted accordingly, the relative order of the different elasticities would have remained, of course, and the likely interval, if we ignore column I, would be between −0.6 and −0.4, that is, about 65 per cent of the quoted figures.[8] The odd result in table 3.2 is clearly the one from column I, with an elasticity below −0.2. This is the value suggested by R.W. Fogel as an absolute maximum for England in the early modern period. The odd number doing the trick is the estimate of the standard deviation of output, which differs markedly from all other quantity deviations. Price variance is more uniform across time and regions. The yield data in column I stem from a period and region characterised by fairly advanced farming methods (1884–1913), and there is no reason for using that data set when there are yield statistics available from the very period under consideration. It is important to note that yield fluctuations were very large (cf. σ_q) well into the nineteenth century. If we combine σ_p from column I with the highest and lowest estimate of σ_q found in the rich French data set, we would have a more likely range of values of ϵ, which are reported in columns VI and VII, respectively. A plausible elasticity is around −0.6, which implies that the burden of proof has shifted to those claiming that price volatility was caused by small changes in supply and very inelastic demand (say, in the order of −0.2).

---

[8] If output shocks are local and independent, deviations from trend in output will diminish the larger the area from which output data are collected. That might explain part of the large gap between the estimates used by Fogel and myself.

The extent of early modern grain storage[9]

Underlying the conclusion in the preceding section was the presumption that the quantity of grain carried over from one harvest to the next was not substantial. This is a controversial issue and must be discussed at some length. Lacking conclusive direct evidence, scholars have turned to indirect evidence and inference from prices as first suggested by Tony Wrigley. He observed that while harvest outcomes from year to year were uncorrelated the prices of grain in different years were not. Grain prices typically exhibited so-called 'runs' – that is, serial correlation or autocorrelation.[10] The supposed mechanism was that a bumper harvest would not only depress prices that year but would spill over to the next because stored grain increased future supply. The mechanism also worked at the other end of the price spectrum: when a harvest failed stocks were depleted, which would keep prices up next year because of smaller supply and greater demand if granaries were restocked. Randall Nielsen has developed Wrigley's argument by suggesting additional implications for the nature of price structure of systematic, in fact 'profit-maximizing storage'.[11] There are three distinguishing implications for the price structure of grain storage:

- First, given the fact – which is not disputed – that the underlying harvest shocks are uncorrelated, the existence of autocorrelation in prices is caused by inventory changes.
- Second, a sudden price increase is generated by poor harvests and indicates that granaries are depleted, reducing the capability to smooth a future harvest shock. Variance in future price will consequently depend on present price. High (low) price this year implies higher (lower) variance in price next year.
- Third, since storage cannot be negative, the price-stabilising property of storage is most pronounced when prices are low and granaries are full. The distribution of prices will as a consequence be positively skewed.

While the Wrigley–Nielsen reading of the data might well indicate inventory status and changes, it contains no testable implication that discriminates between profit-maximising storage[12] as opposed to (say) a mechanical storage rule. Nielsen asserts that all three implications are corroborated for two English yearly prices series – notably the Exeter

[9] This section is based on a joint paper by Mette Ejrnœs and myself (1999), 'Grain storage in early modern Europe', *Journal of Economic History*, 59(3).

[10] E.A.Wrigley, *People, Cities and Wealth*, Oxford: Basil Blackwell 1987, pp. 100–1.

[11] R.Nielsen, 'Storage and English government intervention in early modern grain markets', *Journal of Economic History*, 57, (March 1997), pp. 1–33.

[12] It must be added that Wrigley never made such an extravagant claim.

wheat series which is used for the Medieval period and an early modern wheat series, 1540–1699.[13] Wrigley's analysis is primarily based on the long Exeter series.

Unlike Wrigley, who restricted his analysis to the autocorrelation properties of the series Nielsen's results depend crucially on a peculiar transformation of the original data. Prices are expressed as ratios of either a 31-year or 15-year moving average. The 31-year moving average in the early modern series was not chosen for some intrinsic econometric or economic properties but is due to Lord Beveridge, collector of the data, who invoked it because it represented the average of a human generation in the early modern period. It is not the ideal way of removing inflation, for example.

While a supply shock at a high price level will have a larger absolute effect on prices than if the price level was deflated, it is reasonable to believe that a given supply shock will have the same *proportional* effect on price irrespective of price levels if the underlying demand function is stable. It is standard practice to perform analysis of price series after transforming them into logarithms when variance increases with the level of prices. It is important to do so because the price level was affected by inflationary monetary policies shocks and shifts in tariff regimes, and more generally because the price level is a *nominal* variable. The 1540–1699 period, for example, experienced debasements and recoinage of the currency and rapid inflation, especially in the sixteenth century, but monetary shocks and sudden trade restrictions were quite common in the earlier period as well.[14] Introducing a 31- (or 15-) year moving average and expressing prices as ratios to that average does not adequately control for shifts in the price level. Not surprisingly, it turns out that the second and third implications disappears when the price level is instead transformed by its logarithm. An analysis of the English early modern series (1540–1699) is quite revealing in this respect. Let us first look at some simple statistical indicators. Nielsen found positive skewness in the series with prices expressed as ratios to a 31-year moving average, and it is necessary to investigate whether this is a statistical artefact or if the result remains when the original series is used in levels and in logs. It turns out that skewness was non-significant using the original prices and became

---

[13] William Beveridge, 'A statistical crime of the seventeenth century', *Journal of Economic and Business History*, 1, 1929, pp. 503–33, presents the so-called Exeter series of which a portion is used for the Medieval period. W.G. Hoskins, 'Harvest fluctuations and English economic history, 1480–1619', *Agricultural History Review*, 12, (1), 1964, pp. 28–46 and W.G.Hoskins, 'Harvest fluctuations and English economic history, 1620–1759.' *Agricultural History Review*, 16, (1), 1968, pp. 15–31.

[14] R.H.Britnell, *The Commercialisation of English Society 1000–1500*, Cambridge: Cambridge University Press, 1993, pp. 179–85.

Table 3.3 *Parameter values for a trend-stationary*
model of English wheat prices, 1540–1699[a]

	1540–1699	1540–99	1600–99
α	0.660	0.378	0.622
	(0.059)[b]	(0.123)	(0.079)
λ	0.944	1.477	1.289
	(0.164)	(0.293)	(0.280)
γ	0.0024	0.011	0.0005
	(0.0006)	(0.003)	(0.0006)

Notes:
[a] The analysis has been performed using the log of price.
[b] Unless explicitly specified, figures in brackets are
standard deviations.
Sources: Hoskins, 'Harvest fluctuations . . . 1480–1619',
appendix 2; 'Harvest fluctuations 1620–1759', appendix
1.

significantly *negative* using a log transformation of the original series.
These results might seem paradoxical but typically occur in the absence
of explicit modelling. The next step therefore involves finding an appropriate model. Will, for example, a simple trend stationary model be adequate? That turns out to be the case. The following model was estimated:

$$p_t = \lambda + \alpha p_{t-1} + \gamma t + \epsilon_t.$$

The dependent variable p_t is the log price. The error term ϵ_t is assumed
normally distributed with mean 0 and constant variance. λ is a constant,
α is the parameter associated with the lagged value of the log price and γ
is the parameter associated with the time trend, t. If $|\alpha|<1$ the process of
the prices, p, is a stationary mean-reverting (trend-stationary) process.
When analysing the entire period it was found that the negative skewness
(as opposed to the positive skewness which was expected from the 'profit-
maximising storage' model) remained, and this suggests a misspecification of the process. It would be worthwhile to separate the period into two
sub-periods, making the (approximate) end of the high-inflationary
Tudor era the dividing line. The second period (from 1600 on) corre-
sponds roughly to the period when the *Book of Order* grain market regulation was operative and when inflation slows down. There is some
controversy, admittedly, as to whether or not the *Book of Order* regulation
had become a dead letter by the end of the period. The results presented
in tables 3.3 and 3.4 confirm the expectation that the 1540–1699
period consists of two different regimes. The first period was one of high

Table 3.4 *Analysis of the residuals, 1540–1699*

	1540–1699	1540–99	1600–99
Mean	0	0	0
Variance	0.0526	0.061	0.0338
Skewness	−0.509	0.091	0.051
Autocorrelation	0.06	0.13	0.068
ARCH *t*-statistics[a] (*p*-value)	−1.17	−1.73	1.159
	(0.241)[b]	(0.088)	(0.115)

Notes:
[a] The ARCH-test is performed on the residuals as a Lagrange multiplier-test.
[b] Unless explicitly specified, figures in brackets are standard deviations.
Sources: As for table 3.3.

inflation (the third row in table 3.3) and high and constant variance of the residual (the second row in table 3.4). The second period was one of virtually static prices but with lower and constant variance. The findings concerning skewness and variance are documented in table 3.4.

Analysis of the residuals shows that the variance of the error term was twice as large in the first as in the second period. Furthermore the ARCH-test indicates that the variance within each period was constant. Finally, the analysis of the residuals shows that the skewness of the residuals disappears in both cases. This indicates that the previous result about the skewness is the product of a misspecified model.

The third implication referred to above suggested a positive association between the variance of future price and the level of price. Granaries are typically depleted when prices are momentarily high, making prices more volatile in the face of future supply shocks – high prices this year would generate high variance in price next year. That proposition has been investigated in the early modern series, but when the logarithmic transformation of the series is used the positive association disappears, which should be clear from table 3.5. Price levels at time t are grouped in five categories, the first column in table 3.5, with reference to the mean price. The results clearly reject any positive association between variance at time $t+1$ and price level at t.

Finally, what about autocorrelation, the first of the three implications suggested to reveal grain storage? High autocorrelation persists in the logarithmically transformed series – and, more importantly, when we introduced an explicit model, as demonstrated in the first row of table 3.3. However, significant autocorrelation is present in almost all price series. The conclusion that it indicates 'profit-maximising grain storage'

Table 3.5 *Variance of future price as a function of present price, English wheat prices, 1540–1699*

Log price	Number of obs.	Variance in year t	Variance in year $t+1$
Log $p < m - 2s$	9	0.026	0.104
$m - 2s < \log p < m - s$	18	0.021	0.059
$m - s < \log p < m$	44	0.021	0.100
$m < \log p < m + s$	67	0.013	0.066
$m + s < \log p < m + 2s$	22	0.010	0.049

Note: m = mean of log price; s = standard deviation of log price.
Source: As for table 3.3.

is therefore rather extravagant. In order to say something about profit-maximising storage we need to know what expectations agents held about future price. To assume that agents would adopt the best currently available forecasting model which can be detected by sophisticated econometric packages seems far-fetched. Besides, no single model adequately represents price movements in all periods. Plausible models also have very different implications as to the possibility of profit-maximising storage. Whether agents could discern the differences in even a rudimentary way is, of course, another matter. If prices are expected to revert to an expected mean, that might be compatible with profit-maximising storage if the expected speed and direction of the reversal to the mean is covering storage costs. However, other plausible forecasting models do not generate unambiguous implications regarding storage. Although we have discovered autocorrelation in most series a simple random-walk model usually performs very well in the sense that the size of the error term is usually trivial compared to the very best model which usually incorporates an element of autocorrelation and which would be impossible to reveal without detailed price data and computer support. We cannot know, of course, what particular 'model' a historical person herself made of price movements, but the random-walk model has the learning advantage of being very simple: price tomorrow is equal to price today. Or, expressed in another way, the change in price, if any, is random. Since a random-walk model suggests that all available information is expressed in current price, changes in price are caused by new information, which is a random event. Everyday experience must have confirmed the view that price changes were actually brought about by new information. But if people believed that prices actually followed a random walk – something we can only speculate about – then there is not any scope for profit-maximising storage at all, since expected price tomorrow is equal to price today. Storage costs will not be covered.

Consider now this additional problem: if inflation suddenly picks up will agents interpret that as a permanent increase in the rate of inflation or a transitory movement – that is, a movement which will soon revert to its origin or trend? It is not easy to know, because only after some time can one tell whether there was a permanent increase in the rate of inflation. If agents believe the price increase to be transitory the expectation is that price will revert to the old level, which will hamper storage until 'normal' prices have been attained or until agents understand that a structural shift has occurred. Some of the issues involved here might be beyond the comprehension of contemporaries, both now and then, and they might resort to rule-of-thumb reasoning because there is no obvious profit-maximising solution to the problem they face. In fact, even today sophisticated forecasting models often perform worse than naive random-walk forecasting in the face of structural breaks, such as a change in the inflation rate. A rule-of-thumb might in fact be the most rational strategy given the uncertainty of the environment and when the costs of *making* decisions are very high. A storage decision cannot be made once and for all in the harvest year, but must be reconsidered when new information flows in. That the quality of new information, especially early and late in the harvest year, is low does not make decisions easier. There are, furthermore, rule-of-thumb strategies which are compatible with autocorrelation in yearly price data:

(1) Use stored grain when harvest fails, replace it if harvest outcome permits.
(2) Restore the granaries when harvests are plentiful.

Why would this rule cause autocorrelation in prices? When prices soar and granaries are empty prices next year will get an upward push since there is demand for inventories if harvest outcome permits or because empty granaries reduce normal supply if harvest remains poor. When granaries are filled after a good harvest there will be an increased supply and lower demand for stocks next year and prices will be kept a little lower. In fact, any strategy which smooths supply relative to harvest shocks will generate autocorrelation.[15] Autocorrelation alone does not tell you an awful lot about the nature and extent of storage.

The question now arises whether autocorrelation in prices is a distinguishing and unique property of storable goods. Wrigley and Nielsen believe so. As evidence of the importance of inventory changes Nielsen

---

[15] For a formal proof see Ejrnæs and Persson, 'Grain storage' (1999).

looks at butter as a perishable good (i.e. one with no carry-over). In an early modern series which he investigates – after having transformed it into ratios of a 15-year moving average – he finds no autocorrelation. He asserts that this supports his interpretation of autocorrelation as an indicator of inventory changes. The result is surprising. There are strong reasons to believe that butter prices had high autocorrelation even if butter was a non-storable commodity simply because the grain and resources that were inputs into grain production were also potential inputs into butter production. Since butter is produced continuously you would expect that grain price movements therefore influenced butter prices without a considerable lag. Once again, it turns out that the absence of autocorrelation seems to be a property of the transformation of the series to ratios of a moving average. Let us discuss these two points in some detail.

Previous studies seem to agree that high autocorrelation is a property of almost all types of price series. This was exactly what Lennart Jörberg discovered in his careful study of 25 goods in eighteenth-century Sweden.[16] After having eliminated trend in the series the one year autocorrelation coefficients for almost all goods were of the order of 0.3–0.5, and this included non-storable goods like butter and farm-workers' day wages. There was no obvious difference between agrarian goods and goods like charcoal, iron ore and pine wood for which the same pattern of supply shocks and inventory adjustments should not be expected.

We initially had some misgivings about letting butter represent a 'no-carry-over' type of agrarian good since, unlike grain, it is produced continuously. Besides, butter can be made storable for long periods by just adding salt. Long-life salted butter was exported from Sweden in the early modern period and to the American colonies from Ireland in the eighteenth century. Against this background, it would be interesting to see if potatoes, which like grain are produced once a year, but which cannot be carried over from one harvest year to the next, behaved differently. Table 3.6 summarises the results on the basis of Swedish nineteenth-century price data and it is clear that Jörberg's previously reported results hold also for potatoes in the nineteenth century. (The coefficients are generally higher, which is probably due to the fact that trend has not been eliminated in our estimates.) The important implication is that the existence of autocorrelation does not itself distinguish storable from non-storable goods. It is also worth noting, in the light of the previous discussion about skewness, that it is insignificant in all cases except for wheat in levels.

After this glimpse at evidence from non-English data we shall return to

[16] Jörberg, 'A history of prices in Sweden', vol. 1, table III, pp. 12–13.

Table 3.6 *Statistical indicators for the prices of wheat, potatoes and butter, Sweden 1830–1900*

	Wheat		Potatoes		Butter	
	Price	Log price	Price	Log price	Price	Log price
Skewness	0.655	0.214	0.227	−0.294	−0.118	−0.341
Autocorrelation	0.745	0.758	0.759	0.774	0.969	0.971
ARCH t-test	3.50	1.593	2.237	0.277	3.050	1.734
(p-value)	(0.001)	(0.116)	(0.03)	(0.782)	(0.003)	(0.08)

Sources: Myrdal, *The Cost of Living in Sweden, 1830–1930*, London: P.S. King, table B.

the English early modern butter series.[17] It turns out that investigating that series in levels and in logs you get approximately the same result as for the Swedish series reported in table 3.6: autocorrelation coefficients are 0.85 and 0.82, respectively, in contrast with the −0.02 reported by Randall Nielsen when the original series was transformed to ratios of a moving average. Transformation itself has non-trivial effects on autocorrelation. An explicit trend-stationary modelling of the time series reveals that the autocorrelation in butter prices is a robust result.

In both wheat and butter we found a significant drop in variance after the introduction of the *Book of Order* regulation in England. Was regulation responsible for the decline, as R.W. Fogel asserts? Our findings seem to support that interpretation. Nielsen denies it by referring to a similar decline in variance in the rest of Europe, but forgets to note that there is a common drift towards grain market regulation after the turbulent last half of the sixteenth century. However, this is a big issue which will be discussed further in chapter 4. Since none of the distinguishing implications of systematic grain storage can be corroborated for representative price series, one tentative conclusion is that carry-over was not substantial enough to affect prices in the implied direction.

The 'seven lean years'

The principal conclusions from the analysis so far are that the recorded price variations were responses to large, rather than small, variations in

[17] It is to be found in P. Bowden, 'Statistical appendix', in J.Thirsk (ed.), *The Agrarian History of England and Wales*, vol. 4, Cambridge: Cambridge University Press, 1967, pp. 814–70.

supply. The plausible elasticity of demand with regard to price is around
−0.6 (±0.1) when foreign trade exposure and our best guess as to the
extent of inventory adjustments have been taken into account. Does this
imply that the natural accidents that caused harvest failures were unman-
ageable? Not necessarily. In the Southern Scandinavia yield series
referred to in table 3.2, there is one instance in relation to both rye and
barley when the harvest failure wiped out the entire stock if it was
assumed to be 40 per cent – which Fogel suggests optimistically to be a
plausible level of inventories – of a normal harvest, and there are four
instances if the inventories were 20 per cent. For a region with access to
both the Amsterdam and Baltic markets, such disturbances need not be
disastrous. It is more rewarding to look at long sequences of harvest failures. The 'seven lean years' in the period covered by the Southern
Scandinavia series were in the years 1645–51. The rye harvests were all
well below average, varying between 50 and 80 per cent of a normal
harvest, but barley yields performed very well except for a single year. The
prices of both rye and barley increased dramatically. It can be useful to
look at the problem of manageability of the seven lean years by introducing an account of the *stock* of grain accumulated during the period. The
'stock' is defined as the accumulated difference between observed yield
and the average yield of both rye and barley, assuming that the average
yield is consumed each year. Consumption includes seedcorn, animal
fodder and human food. Assumptions regarding the volume of the initial
volume of inventories vary between zero and 40 per cent of the normal
harvest. Assuming first a carry-over of 40 per cent (I use this assumption
not because I find it plausible but because it has been used in the current
literature on the topic) in the initial year will imply that in the *seventh* lean
year the accumulated stock is negative for rye, thus the initial inventories
have been wiped out; but the stock is positive for barley. By converting the
accumulated stock of barley to rye-equivalents, which is done by multi-
plying it by the ratio of barley to rye prices, the aggregate deficit expressed
in rye-equivalents amounts to half a year's consumption of rye. If we
assume zero initial inventories, which is much closer to the plausible
volume of inventories than the previous assumption, this accounting
exercise amounts to the loss of a full year's consumption of rye. From a
purely intertemporal accounting standpoint, the difficulties would seem
manageable, in the sense that adjustments in trade and livestock consumption and an equitable decline in human consumption would not
necessarily generate severe social and demographic consequences.
However, markets reacted quite dramatically to these events, doubling
the prices of rye and barley – which, given the distribution of income, was
bound to have severe consequences. The impact of the decline in human

consumption fell on those who were already living close to subsistence level. There was little point in price controls because experience showed that they would only divert flows of grain to other markets, and income redistribution was not easy to accomplish. What were the options? That is the subject of chapter 4.

APPENDIX: NOTES AND SOURCES TO TABLE 3.2

Column I England, 1540–1914. Wheat. Deviations from trend. Output: yields per acre 1884–1913. See R.W. Fogel, 'Second thoughts', pp. 251–2. Prices 1540–1840, estimated by R. Lee, 'Short-term variations in vital rates, prices, and weather', in E.A. Wrigley and R.S. Schofield (eds.), *The Population History of England, 1541–1871: A Reconstruction*, London Edward Arnold, 1981.

Column II Southern Scandinavia, 1610–62. Barley. Deviations from mean. No significant trend in this period. Yields per seed corn. Data in G. Olsen, 'Studier i Danmarks Kornavl og Kornhandelspolitik i Tiden 1610–60', *Historisk Tidsskrift*, 1942–4, pp. 428–84.

Column III As column II, but the yield series has been adjusted for carry-over and trade. See text for details.

Column IV Central France, 1825–69. Wheat. October price in Bourges. Deviations from trend. Output: hl per ha. Price data in S. Drame *et al. Un siècle de commerce du blé en France 1825– 1913*, Paris: Economica, 1991. Output from Ministère de l'Agriculture et du Commerce, Direction de l'agriculture, Bureau des Subsistances: *Récoltes des céréales et des pommes de terre de 1815 à 1876*, Paris, 1878.

Column V Southwest France, 1825–69. Wheat. October price in Bordeaux. Data as in column IV.

Column VI Price deviation from column I combined with the lowest standard deviation of output found in the French data set, which was in Northwestern France. See columns I and IV for sources.

Column VII Price deviation from column I combined with the highest output deviation found in the French data, which was in Southwestern France. See columns I and IV for sources.

4   Market failures and the regulation of grain markets: a new interpretation

Technological constraints, risk and price volatility

When harvest shocks are independent and local, inter-regional trade and carry-over can be expected to stabilise prices, though not to the extent that makes price fluctuations disappear.[1] It is easy to show that if storage and transport costs are high within a large geographical region, large swings in prices will necessarily occur even though output shocks cancel out. This will also happen over time in a single region. In that respect, technological constraints affect prices, real wages and welfare.

Consider the somewhat stylised case in which there is a stable world market price and a single market small enough *not* to influence world market price. The higher the transport cost to the world market from that single market, the more prices would vary in that market before it would become worthwhile to trade. The export and import points of the single market define the limits of local price volatility. There is a local minimum price which would motivate export to the world market, and that minimum price is the world market price *minus* transport costs. If prices fall below that level exporters in the local market will bid up prices. Likewise, there is a maximum price in the single market, which will attract imports from the world market, and that is the world market price *plus* transport costs. In other words, if the world market price is 100 lire and transport costs 35 lire, then local prices can vary between the export point at 65 lire and the import point at 135 lire before trade occurs. It thus appears that, given these technological constraints, not much can be done to dampen price volatility within the range determined by the export and import points. However, it must also be said that prices will fluctuate even more in the absence of trade and carry-over. Furthermore the historical decline in transport costs also causes price fluctuations to decline. This is what actually happened, as will be shown by reference to results from time-series analysis in chapter 5.

---

[1] This chapter relies on my previously published paper, 'The seven lean years, elasticity traps, and intervention in grain markets in early modern Europe', *Economic History Review*, 49 (November 1996), pp. 692–714.

Table 4.1 *Standard deviation of the residuals in a random-walk model of grain price*

	Pisa 1550–1684 (per cent)	Vienna 1692–1802 (per cent)
Wheat	6.2	5.7
Rye	11.0	7.9
Barley	12.2	9.4

Sources: Pisa prices are from an unpublished source based on prices collected by Pisa's subsistence bureau which I have had the opportunity to use thanks to Paolo Malanima, who originally collected the data. Vienna prices were published by A.F. Pribram, in *Materialien zur Geschichte der Preise und Löhne in Österreich*, Vienna: Carl Überreuters Verlag 1938.

Another way of corroborating the relationship between transport costs and price volatility is to compare, at one point in time, the variability of prices for different types of grain. In this particular study we have chosen to concentrate on wheat, rye and barley. Although nominal transport costs are about the same for different grades of grain the *relative* costs are smaller for the most expensive variety – i.e. wheat – and, then, in descending order, rye and barley. The expectation that price fluctuations were smallest for wheat and highest for barley with the highest relative transport costs is clearly confirmed by table 4.1. The differences are far from trivial, with volatility being almost twice as high for barley with the highest relative transport and storage costs as for wheat, with the lowest. 'Volatility' is measured as the standard deviation of the residual – that is, the prediction error – in a random-walk model with a deterministic seasonal pattern.[2] A random walk supposes that all available information is expressed in the present price. All that is known about future prices is the

[2] Using a random-walk model might seem surprising given the results from chapter 3. It was suggested that there is no one single model which is the best across countries and over time but that there usually is some autocorrelation in prices. This indicates that markets are not – strictly speaking – efficient (as a random-walk model supposes) since future price is not generated by *new* random events only but by present price as well; furthermore, the coefficients on the seasonal dummies were seldom significant. I have nonetheless decided to measure volatility in a random-walk model to enhance comparability. I also conjectured in chapter 3 that the random-walk model, although strictly speaking not the best, had the advantage of being very simple and therefore was plausibly held by contemporaries. There is usually a trivial difference in terms of the size of the residual between the random-walk and the best model; see the appendix to chapter 5 (pp. 121–2) for a detailed account of time-series modelling.

seasonal pattern reflecting storage costs. New information generates the prediction error, the residual, and can itself be considered a random event.

The price data for Pisa and Vienna consist of monthly market prices. The model used in predicting price movements is a random walk – i.e. expected price tomorrow is equal to price today – with seasonal dummies which catch the seasonal price pattern.

In the eighteenth century transport costs were high. The cost of shipping grain from the Baltic ports to Western Europe might constitute 50 per cent of, say, Amsterdam prices, while storage costs were probably around 20–25 per cent from one harvest to the next. In such a context an interesting issue, which will be addressed below, is the extent of carry-over – that is, intertemporal, as opposed to spatial, 'transport' as a means of stabilising prices. I will argue that although carry-over was less costly, other factors militated against it. The distinctive characteristic of carry-over is that the time horizon of such an operation stretches over into the unknown – next year's harvest – and further into the future. Trade, even long-distance trade, primarily concerned intra-year transactions in which uncertainty was less pronounced.

It is well known that the price of grain usually falls to a low at harvest time and that it then tends to increase until next harvest, but that this pattern is subject to large forecasting errors. P.A. Samuelson was the first economist to investigate this empirical fact in a rigorous way.[3] His was a model of perfect foresight and without unexpected disturbances in the size of the harvest from year to year. If, starting with the most simple case, harvests were known to remain the same from year to year, then prices would rise at a constant rate during the harvest year, only to fall to the initial level at the next harvest. This pattern would be repeated year after year. A harvest year normally begins in August calendar year 1 and continues to July calendar year 2. The explanation behind the peculiar seasonal price pattern of grain is that the good is produced only once a year but is consumed throughout the year. Price must increase at a constant rate over the harvest year because in equilibrium the costs of 'transporting' the grain over time – that is, storage costs, waste and deterioration of the grain – must match the interest rate on the value of the stocks. The larger these costs, the higher the rate of price increase over the harvest year. There would be no carry-over from one harvest year to another under the specified assumptions because *harvest* prices were identical from one year to another. Expected future output shocks might make carry-over profitable, but only if next year's shortage was expected to

[3] Samuelson, 'Intertemporal price equilibrium: a prologue to the theory of speculation', *Weltwirtschaftliches Archiv*, 79, 1957, pp. 181–219.

make the price at next year's harvest cover the costs of carrying the grain to the next period. This 'intertemporal arbitrage' would stabilise prices in so far as price in the year with the expected harvest failure would be lower than in the absence of carry-over, while price in the preceding year would be higher, since grain available for consumption that year would diminish when grain was set aside for carry-over. Samuelson conjectured that the uncertainty of the real world would make speculative hoarding and trade very risky. This might favour large-scale merchants with a capital large enough to enable them to endure inevitable periodic losses;[4] the selection bias in favour of the few and wealthy might foster market power.

Samuelson's prediction of no carry-over in the steady-state perfect foresight model was based on the observation that there were positive costs in storage but zero expected returns. Although this conclusion is generated in a model with limiting assumptions, it seems to fit the world as we know it, with all its uncertainties. More precisely, as we will soon discover, the null hypothesis of zero returns from carry-over cannot be rejected empirically.

An ambitious first empirical inquiry into the returns from storage of grain was begun by D.M. McCloskey and J. Nash in an analysis of J.E. Thorold Rogers' English price data.[5] I share their conclusion that carry-over was negligible, say around 5–10 per cent of a normal harvest. In chapter 3 (pp. 55–62) I advanced a series of arguments to the effect that grain storage could not be considered substantial. McCloskey and Nash estimated storage costs by looking at the monthly increase in prices during the harvest year. The number of observations they used was fairly small so I have replicated their approach with a much larger set of observations. My results are reported in figure 4.1. It describes the implied gross returns, which is conceptually identical to what McCloskey and Nash call 'cost of grain storage', from holding (buying) grain in August and holding it through to (or selling it in) September, or from August to October . . . and finally from August to August in the next harvest year. I analysed three markets – Siena, Cologne and Pisa – over a period of 150 years and normalised the results to returns on an annual basis. The gross returns should equal storage costs including the waste of grain, the income forgone by holding stocks (i.e. the prevailing interest rate) and a risk premium.

---

[4] This conjecture is corroborated by S. Kaplan's study of Parisian grain merchants, and it was also much discussed by contemporary commentators such as Jacques Savary. See S. Kaplan, *Provisioning Paris, Merchants and Millers in the Grain and Flour Trade in the Eighteenth Century*, Ithaca: Cornell University Press, 1984, pp. 80–3.

[5] D.M. McCloskey and J. Nash, 'Corn at an interest: the extent and cost of grain storage in Medieval England', *American Economic Review*, 74 (1) (March 1984), pp. 174–87.

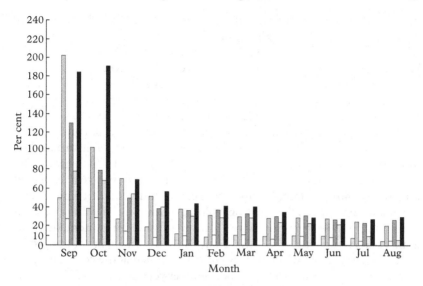

Figure 4.1 Expected gross return and its standard deviation from storage of wheat in Siena, Cologne and Pisa, 1550–1700, per cent per year
Sources: See Sources (pp. 156–8).

The first two bars in each cluster of six refer to Siena, the third and fourth bars to Cologne, the fifth and sixth to Pisa. The first bar for each city shows the expected gross returns and the second exhibits the standard deviation of the gross returns (the returns and standard deviations have been expressed in annual terms). Note that the standard deviation is about twice the expected return which makes a straightforward interpretation of the expected returns impossible. 'Sep' refers to the returns from storage from August to September, 'Oct' indicates returns from August to October, and so on. Thus 'Aug' refers to carry-over from August in year one to August in year two.

As can easily be seen from figure 4.1 the most striking fact is the huge standard deviation of the gross returns, the second, fourth and sixth bar in each cluster of bars, and the disturbing fact that returns and their standard deviation were not uniform over the year. An obvious interpretation would be that the high variance in price reflected the great uncertainty, and perhaps to some extent differing quality of the grain. In this interpretation, flows of new information early in the season about the size and quality of harvests at home and elsewhere change expectations and prices. However, after a couple of months the new information stops coming in, and this stabilises prices and returns. The high expected returns the first months after the harvest also suggest a market imperfection stemming from an asymmetry of wealth. The revealed price pattern is consistent with the view that prices are unnaturally depressed immediately after the harvest because poor peasants sell grain prematurely because they have to pay off their debts to grain merchants, who incidentally also act as creditors. It would be in the interest of the poor to wait and see, but they are locked in by loan contracts which do not permit them to do so.

McCloskey and Nash concluded that an observed decline in the gross returns from medieval to early modern times was attributable to a decline in interest rates, but that conclusion seems fragile and adventurous. The size of the standard deviation – two to three times the average or expected returns for most estimates, somewhat smaller in the case of Pisa – does not make the expected return on holding inventories a robust or even meaningful guide to interest rates. And, returning for a moment to an issue raised in chapter 3: can this analysis shed some light on the profitability of carry-over? We know from other sources that the cost of holding stocks were in the range of 20–30 per cent per year of the initial value consisting of an interest rate of some 5–15 per cent, a rate of wastage of at least 10 per cent and a cost of storage at around 3–5 per cent. A possible, but rare, outcome in a carry-over operation (i.e. from August to next August) can be defined as the sum of the expected gross return *and* its standard deviation and amounts to a mere 23 per cent for Cologne, 28 per cent for Siena and 32 per cent for Pisa, with an average (i.e. expected) return around 3–4 per cent. Even if speculators were rewarded, not by the theoretically speaking zero expected returns, but by optimistic expectations, there was not much of a profit to take home. The rare outcome of gross returns of about 25 per cent just about covered the costs, including the prevailing interest rate and storage, but did not allow for a positive risk premium. We have to allow positive returns of twice the standard deviation to get any potential and sizeable profits at all. In a world of uncertainty, one cannot of course exclude carry-over based on expectations of this sort. But in such a process of carry-over speculation only few will survive since the expectations will only rarely be fulfilled. Survival over longer periods would require a substantial financial reserve *and* exceptional luck, exclusive information, or market power.

Short-term speculation in the immediate post-harvest months – that is, from August to November – leaves scope for much larger potential profits (and losses), as revealed by figure 4.1. It is safe to conclude that exclusive information in these early months after the harvest offered great rewards. Variance also differed between markets. If we transform the returns estimated by McCloskey and Nash into annual returns, the levels they found typical of medieval England are almost identical to the results for early modern Pisa. But Siena differs from Pisa, and so does Cologne, both displaying smaller variance. Two markets like Siena and Pisa, which we know were well integrated already in the sixteenth and seventeenth centuries should not have such large differences in variance.[6] The differences are more apparent than real, however; the reason is probably that the data for Pisa are prices quoted the first market day of each month while Cologne and Siena report monthly averages. The data used by McCloskey and Nash are similar to the Pisa series in that they also rely on single observations each month.

The analysis of the variance of returns in holding inventories of grain does not support the supposition that carry-over was substantial – if we want to believe it to be a rational profit-seeking pursuit. This assertion is consistent with the results discussed on pp. 55–62 but reached on the basis of a different and independent argument, which can only strengthen the general conclusion. The best guess is that inventories were primarily held by households as a sort of insurance against unexpected events, in order to cover private consumption in the current harvest year and that it followed some mechanical rule rather than a purposeful speculative pursuit. If we look at inventory adjustments *within* the year we would expect a deterministic price pattern, as suggested by Samuelson: that is, prices will increase at a steady rate (reflecting uniform storage costs) from harvest to the wake of the next harvest. Not only have we noticed that the increase was not steady at all but subject to large differences over the year. Furthermore, in the econometric analysis we were generally unable to ascertain significant seasonal coefficients – see chapter 5 and the appendix to that chapter (p. 117). The implication is that markets failed to honour the storage for later consumption in the year. That is, the cost of storage from (say) September to May was not systematically covered. Again, this leads us to the conclusion that 'rules-of-thumb' played a great role in household decisions, not only over long- (carry-over) but also in relation to short-term storage.

But there are additional reasons for a sceptical view as to the capacity of *markets* to generate the desired level of carry-over and trade. It can be argued that there are *positive externalities* in price stability. If, for example, the crime rate declines as a consequence of price stability, it falls for all, and in that sense we can talk about a non-exclusive property in price stabilisation.[7] A sharp fall in real wages imposed by price increases has been

---

[6] A formal cointegration test (see chapter 5 for details) has been applied and accepted. It reveals a rather fast convergence to a constant price ratio in between the cities after exogenous disturbances.

[7] That the incidence of petty theft of food was related to price instability is shown by J. Walter and K. Wrightson, 'Dearth and the social order in early modern England', *Past and Present*, 71, 1976, pp. 22–42.

shown to have effects on the state of health because vagrancy increased diffusion of contagious diseases. Nuptuality and mortality were also affected by price volatility, and as an ultimate effect it could cause a breakdown, albeit temporary, in the social order.[8] Price stability would consequently bring a variety of social benefits, but these improvements are non-exclusive and therefore, technically speaking, externalities. While merchants involved in competitive carry-over speculation and trade can be expected to generate price stability as a by-product, they were motivated by the expected *private* gains in these ventures alone. Yet since there also were social gains inherent in price stability, the *efficient* volume of trade and carry-over would not obtain, since these social gains were not internalised as private gains by merchants and corn factors. Even in the unlikely event of a Pareto-efficient state obtaining, the prices and consumption possibilities which characterised that state would not necessarily stop some people from starving: that is, the future price which would make a speculator carry over grain might not be a morally or socially tolerable price. Behind the 'veil of ignorance' of members of society fearing that they might end up among the destitute or because a subsistence crisis posed a threat to the social order, redistributive policies and famine protection might have been considered desirable by all. In that case, the resulting income distribution or distribution of consumption possibilities must be considered a pure public good. But such a desired distribution will not obtain in a market process or through voluntary charities, since the non-exclusive nature of the benefits brought by a given distribution of consumption can be expected to invite free-rider behaviour.[9]

The political economy of grain market intervention

We have just outlined the traditional rationale for public intervention provided by economic theory. But did actual policies stem from a desire to stabilise prices and consumption? And if so, were they good at accomplishing that aim? The view that economic policy makers somehow detect and correct market failures has increasingly come under attack from the modern political economist as a naive viewpoint. We now know that the élites were moved both by ideas and self-interest and sought the support from groups of citizens with particular interests and were sensitive to pressure from others. It cannot be taken for granted that optimal policies

---

[8] See J. Walter and R. Schofield, 'Famine, disease, and crisis mortality in early modern society', in J. Walter and R. Schofield (eds.), *Famine, Disease and the Social Order in Early Modern Society*, Cambridge: Cambridge University Press, 1989, pp. 1–73.
[9] See L.C.Thurow, 'The income distribution as pure public good', *Quarterly Journal of Economics*, 85, 1971, pp. 327–36.

emerge in a world where the ruling élite is keen on remaining in power while balancing conflicting interests. It appears as if the traditional view assumed that there was a benevolent and enlightened dictator, to some extent that was the belief the ruling élite wanted their subjects to have. However, I am not primarily concerned with the political game that generated the observed policies, but if the nature of public intervention conformed to the expectations provided by the economic theory of market failures. To a surprisingly large extent it does, although that fact in itself does not suffice to explain the policies. For example, one would expect public subsidies to be paid to grain merchants as compensation for the social gains they generated, and that the public sector would provide the services, carry-over and trade not adequately provided by the private traders. On the other hand, the potential market power of corn dealers provided a rationale for supervision and control, in order to stop them cornering the market. We would also expect policies that redistributed consumption over time and between income groups. These contradictory claims on public policies will, needless to say, make an interpretation of public institutions difficult. There ought to be both a carrot and a stick, and indeed there were. In the process of tackling these questions, one constantly encounters another: can it be that the political interventions were themselves the *real* cause of the poor performance of the markets? Although that question is finally answered in the negative, it is not one that should be disposed of lightly.

It will be useful at this stage to outline the structure of the argument to be pursued here. It is summarised in table 4.2. This scheme identifies important characteristics of markets, and there is subsequently an attempt to relate specific institutional responses to potential market failures. The specific relation between market characteristics and institutional responses is then developed.

Public intervention in grain markets was practised from the very beginning of urban resurgence in medieval Europe. Although the scale of these operations, and the priority and coherence of specific programmes, differed from city to city and from nation to nation, what is striking is the large similarities across time and within Europe.[10] The following

[10] The medieval origin of regulation and its subsequent development in the early modern period are discussed in a series of monographs covering major nations or regions, – for example, M.-Y. Tits-Dieuaide, *La formation des prix céréaliers en Brabant et en Flandre au XVe siècle*, Brussels: L'Edition de l'Université de Bruxelles, 1975; A.P. Usher, *The History of the Grain Trade in France 1400–1710*, 1913; S. Kaplan, *Bread, Politics and Political Economy in the Reign of Louis XV*, 2 vols., The Hague: Martinus Nijhoff, 1976; D.G. Barnes, *A History of the English Corn Laws from 1660 to 1846*, London: Routledge & Son, 1930; J. Chartres (ed.), *Agricultural Markets and Trade 1500–1750*, vol. 4. of J. Thirsk (general ed.), *Chapters from the Agrarian History of England and Wales*, Cambridge:

Table 4.2 *A typology of grain market institutions*

Possible market failures	Varieties of institutional response
Market power, insider trading (pp. 74–8)	Rules prescribing transparency
	Anti-collusive measures
	Stimulus to competition
External effects of price stability:	Public 'production' of price stability:
Inadequate incentives for private carry-over and trade	• Price-stabilising subsidies financed by redistributive policies
Income distribution is a public good (pp. 78–84)	– over time or across income groups
	Supply and demand management:
	• supply incentives and demand restrictions
	Two-tier prices
	Redistribution
	Public granaries
	Subsidies to private granaries and import
Uncertainty regarding the robustness of the international order and trade (pp. 84–5)	Autarchy
	Risk-sharing between consumers and producers through export–import regulation

discussion concentrates on these similarities and is illustrated with references to the experience of a particular nation or city, but only when that particular example has some general validity. That makes it worthwhile considering whether the interventions can be considered as a common response to a similar set of considerations and perceptions of identical problems.

Let us first look at how cities and nations coped with the presence, perceived or real, of *market power* and *insider trading*. Imperfect integration opened up prospects for large merchants to exploit *insider information* and to corner the market, and this they did if possible and if not deterred by the crowd or the police. In chapter 5 we show that although prices adjust

footnote 10 (*cont.*)
Cambridge University Press, 1990, pp. 160–255; K. Åmark, *Spannmålshandel och spannmålspolitik i Sverige 1719–1830*, Stockholm: I. Marcus Boktryckeri, 1915; H.C. Peyer, *Zur Getreidepolitik Oberitalienischer Städte im 13. Jahrhundert*, Vienna: Universum Verlag, 1949; L. dal Pane, *La questione del commercio dei grani nel settecento in Italia*, vol. 1, Milan: F.lli Temperi, 1932; A.M. Pult Quaglia, *Per provvedere ai popoli. Il sistema annonario della Toscana dei Medici*, Florence: Olschki, 1990; W. Naudé, *Die Getreidehandelspolitik und Kriegsmagazinsverwaltung Brandenburg-Preussens bis 1740*, Berlin: Acta Borussia, 1901. Several monographs were produced early in this century on 'Lebensmittelpolitik' in the major German cities. See for example A. Herzog, *Die Lebensmittelpolitik der Stadt Strassburg im Mittelalter*, Berlin: W. Rothschild, 1909. For a contemporary appraisal of this vast literature see G. Franz, 'Die Geschichte des deutschen Lebensmittelhandels' in G. Franz et al. (eds.), *Der deutsche Landwarenhandel*, Hannover, 1960.

to each other in different markets the speed of that adjustment is very slow. By implication, local monopolies can exert market power. A large variety of public regulations and instructions can be seen as a way of restricting the potential abuse of market power, although some of them probably served as assurances to the urban crowd that something was being done rather than efficient measures in their own right.

There was an ever-present fear of collusion and of insider trading, which is not surprising given the slow and erratic ways in which not only grain but also information flowed. The quest for transparency in transactions and information must be seen in this perspective.[11] The rules for accomplishing transparency and combating collusion were practically identical throughout Europe during the *ancien régime*, and were codified in, for example, the *Book of Order*, worked out in the troubled last decades of sixteenth-century Tudor England. However, the *Book of Order* represented a revival and restatement of rules first codified in the medieval period, specifically as regards sanctions against forestalling and the preferential treatment given to ordinary customers, who did not have to compete with bakers and richer purchasers in the early hours of market days.[12] Some of these rules had little practical significance – or at least diminishing importance – in England from the latter third of the seventeenth century, but rules identical to those in the *Book of Order* survived another century or so in many parts of continental Europe. Authorities always suspected collusion and exploitation of insider information or any other measure to 'enhance the common price'.[13] The quest for 'transparency' implied that dealings should be made not before or outside markets, that markets should be held in public places and at regular hours, publicly known.[14] These rules were strictly adhered to only in periods of restricted supply, and sometimes only when popular protest alarmed the ruling élite.[15] The

[11] Delamare finds the first explicit rules for 'transparency' in 1299 in France, see his *Traité de la police*, vol. 2, Paris: P.Cot, 1710, pp. 653–4.

[12] See Alan Everitt, 'The marketing of agricultural produce, 1500–1640' and John Chartres, 'The marketing of agricultural produce, 1640–1750', in Thirsk (general ed.), vol. 4, pp. 92–3, 174–5. Also R.H. Britnell, *The Commercialisation of English Society 1000–1500*, Cambridge: Cambridge University Press, 1993, pp. 171–3.

[13] S. Browne, *The laws against engrossing, forestalling, regrating and monopolizing*, London, 1765.

[14] The liberal reformers of the eighteenth century tried to convince the public that collusion in the grain market was impossible, implicitly admitting the need for transparency. Collusion would require 'immense purses, and would be visible'. Anon., *An appeal to the public: or consideration on the dearness of corn*, London, 1767.

[15] Everitt, 'The marketing of agricultural produce', in Thirsk (general ed.), pp. 92–101, 128–32. S. Kaplan underlines the pragmatic attitude of regulators to the effect that they refrained from action unless provoked by hard times. See *Provisioning Paris*, Ithaca: Cornell University Press, 1984, pp. 30–9 and 167–9. See also J. Meuvret, *Le problème des subsistances à l'époque Louis XIV. La production des céréales dans la France du XVIIe et du XVIIIe siècle*, Paris: Mouton, 1977, p. 22.

ideal market was supposed to involve a large number of buyers and sellers; farmers should bring their corn to the market individually so that they could not combine. Large-scale dealers and middlemen were not allowed access to the market in the early hours – that is, not until the general public, or the poor, had had the opportunity to make their purchases. However, corn factors increasingly stepped in – much to the relief of peasants, it should be added, who were thus not forced to travel long distances. The size of the city mattered greatly here: small urban centres were serviced by peasants coming in from the nearby villages to the weekly markets, while big cities had to rely on corn merchants.[16] From time to time the activities of large-scale dealers were looked into, however. The type of restriction found in the *Book of Order* was then evoked, always at the height of a crisis, allegedly to halt speculative abuse. But in the public mind the middlemen were never loved, suspected as they were – especially in times of dearth – of masterminding the price increases by collusion and false rumours.[17]

In most continental cities the authorities were keen on controlling and registering the stocks held by their citizens. They sometimes established upper limits on the volume of the stocks that households were permitted to have, and that limit was approximately what the household needed to get through to the next harvest. Some public granaries were open for private deposits, which had the dual effect of increasing transparency and improving the conditions for storage. By diminishing waste, the cost of storage to the public would fall and, all other things being equal, increase the propensity to stock grain. However, in general there was suspicion against large private inventories as long as the authorities had no say in their future use. A plausible interpretation of this paradoxical animosity towards private prudence is that the authorities acknowledged the prohibitively high risks of carry-over and suspected that hoarding was primarily short-term speculation undertaken when prices were already high but in the anticipation of further increases in what could turn out to become a speculative bubble. We have noted that in *monthly* price data we

---

[16] Cf. P. Hertner's comparison between Strassbourg and Marburg, in 'L'approvisionnement des villes et la politique des prix alimentaires des administrations municipales aux 17e et 18e siècles', in M. Flinn (ed.), *Proceedings of the Seventh International Economic History Congress*, Edinburgh: Edinburgh University Press, 1978, pp. 347–59.

[17] This view was increasingly challenged by early liberals. See for example C. Smith, *A short essay on the corn trade and the corn laws*, London, 1758 and A. Dickson, *An essay on the causes of the present high prices of provisions*, London, 1773 for the liberal argument. But others warned of the market power and inside information of the forestallers, engrossers and their like; see for example Anon., *An essay to state some arguments relative to Publick granaries*, Dublin, 1766. J. Chartres argues that on the whole provincial English grain markets were competitive, and perhaps increasingly so. See Thirsk (general ed.), *Chapters*, vol. 4, pp. 226–8.

usually observe a significant first-lag autocorrelation (see appendix to Chapter 5, pp. 117, for details) which implies that prices instead of expressing all available information actually foster expectations about the direction of future price changes. This might induce speculators to over-react in the sense that they stock too much in anticipation of future price increases, and too little when they expect future price decreases. If, however, these expectations are self-fulfilling prophecies the bubble they create will eventually burst. The efficiency of markets can be contested when price changes are dependent on past price.

Even if there was a spirit of suspicion in the way the corn dealers were viewed both by the public and the political authorities, it was not all regulation and control. There were very few attempts to control prices as such by dictating a maximum price, and for good reason. There was a firm reliance on markets to provide most current food needs. To keep prices down by decree was simply counter-productive, since it was known that outside supply dried up immediately. On the contrary, there were attempts to encourage and subsidise corn factors in order to overcome risk-aversion and uncertainty. For example, in the middle of, or in expectation of, a supply crisis, city councils would promise to pay merchants a minimum future price for the grain, and in addition they would give the merchants the right to profit from the ruling market price, if they so wished.[18] In other instances, the city could simply pay the merchant some of the transport and transaction costs. This policy amounts to reducing the import point of grain, referred to in the opening paragraphs of this chapter as the price at which it is profitable to import grain from outside, and thereby it stabilises prices. Given the social gains created by price stability, this policy was well founded, but it also reflected the reluctance of the business community to get involved without some insurance against risks.

The near self-sufficiency of many nations under normal conditions (see pp. 84–5 below) also hampered the development of a suitably large class of merchants, in whose absence the state or a city council had to act as a substitute when unexpected local harvest failures occurred.[19] Cities, however, could not be self-sufficient in food and relied on private traders and developed in the course of history a commercial network, with its members coming out against restrictions on trade. But it was often the case that local governments, as well as representatives of the Crown, were

[18] M. Aymard, *Venise, Raguse et le commerce du blé pendant la seconde moitié du XVIe siècle,* Paris, 1966, pp. 80–1, 100. For the medieval origins of public purchases see, for example, L. Stouff, *Ravitaillement et alimentation en Provence aux XIVe et XVe siècles,* Paris: Mouton, 1970, pp. 73–5.

[19] See, for example, H.C. Johansen, 'Staten som kornhandler, 1783–88', in *Erhvervshistorisk årbog 1969,* Aarhus: Universitetsforlaget, 1969, pp. 62–82.

actively involved in the grain trade, sending their agents to markets far away to contract supplies. This practice emerged in medieval times, when the commercial networks were still unreliable, and survived into the early modern period. It was increasingly a matter of emergency operations when 'normal' trade links were insufficient for the unexpected needs of a specific crisis.

Bread and grain

The argument advanced above was that private rewards were insufficient to induce the desired volume of carry-over and trade, since there were externalities in price stability. There was therefore a rationale for public 'production' of price stability. There is evidence that governing élites were concerned about price stability, that they were aware – or were reminded by angry crowds – of its effect and, finally, that the policies pursued actually achieved stabilisation of consumption over time and across social classes. There was also an element of equitable redistribution. Some of the measures adopted did not target the price of grain, but rather the price of bread as the essential variable. Throughout Europe there was a fairly uniform system in which prices were held constant while the weight of bread varied according to the market price of grain, regulated by the *assize of bread*. Some cities practised a fixed weight/variable price regime for all or some types of bread. However, the point was that the price per weight unit of bread changed with the variations in the price of grain. In some places the price/weight ratio was constantly and automatically changed, permitting bakers a constant proportional mark-up on costs. However, the assize of bread was normally used as a price-stabilising method. In Venice, for example, bakers actually took most of the burden of the price variations of grain through fluctuations in their profit, since the assize of bread was changed only when there were substantial and long-lasting changes in grain prices and to a lesser degree than the changes in grain prices. Ideally this worked both ways, with below-average *proportional* mark-up in periods of high grain prices, for which bakers were compensated by above-average proportional mark-up when grain prices were low. A simple way of accomplishing an inverse variation in the relative share of the mark up was used in Scotland and amounted to having a constant *nominal* mark-up irrespective of the price of grain.[20]

---

[20] I. Mattozzi *et al.*, 'Il politico e il pane a Venezia, 1570–1650: calmieri e governo della sussistenza', *Societa e Storia*, 20, 1983, pp. 271–303. Similar methods were used in, for example, Modena and sometimes in Antwerp, Brussels, and Cologne. Gibson and Smout are quite explicit in their discussion of Scotland: 'baxters' allowance did not vary with the cost of wheat'. For 'allowance' read 'mark-up'. See A.J.G. Gibson and

The idea was to dampen both the seasonal and the stochastic fluctuations.

Another city, which for a long time, and with considerable skill and persistence, practised these policies was Cologne. For a period of about a century we have access to both the grain prices and the bread prices prescribed by the assize of bread. That makes it possible to compare the variability in the latter with the fluctuations in the price of the constituent grain. If these policies were effective we would expect the price variability of bread to be smaller than that of grain. To verify that prediction we must decide on how to measure the price fluctuations in both bread and grain. As pointed out above, price movements in grain markets are well predicted by a random-walk model. Price volatility is defined as the prediction error. I have used monthly observations of the log of price of both wheat and rye prices in Cologne and three types of bread: white, rye and the so-called 'Malter'. The chosen measure of price fluctuations is as previously the standard deviation of the residual, and the results indicate that the volatility of prices of bread in Cologne was about three-quarters of what the fluctuations would have been if bread prices had varied in proportion to grain prices (figure 4.2). In figure 4.2 prices are monthly averages based on weekly observations. The standard deviation of the residual has been obtained in a random-walk model with deterministic seasonality. The estimates are based on overlapping periods of 20 years each, starting in 1659.

Figure 4.2 demonstrates that bread prices persistently fluctuated less than grain prices, when rye bread and Malter are compared to rye grain. The same results apply to white bread as compared to wheat, although this is not explicitly shown in figure 4.2. To the extent that there were fixed production costs we would always expect bread prices to fluctuate less than grain prices. However, fixed costs were small since not only did the raw material consist of grain but wages were also partly paid in kind. In Cologne, this institution not only contributed to a stabilisation of bread prices over time but also to a redistribution between rich and poor consumers. The assize of bread permitted a higher mark-up on the luxury varieties of bread such as *Semmelgin*, while there was little or no profit in

T.C.Smout, *Prices, Food and Wages in Scotland 1550–1780*, Cambridge: Cambridge University Press, 1995, p. 27.

This policy created an endemic friction between city officials and the bakers' guild, with the latter pressing for compensation by delaying an increase in the weight of bread when the price of grain declined, and the former being nervous of the anger of the consumers. See G.L. Basini, *L'uomo e il pane. Risorse, consumi e carenze alimentari della populazione modenese nel cinque e seicento*, Milan: A. Guiffrè, 1960, and J. Craeybeck, '*Brod en levensstandard. Kritische nota betreffende de prijs van het brood te Antwerpen en te Brussel in 17e en de 18e eeuw*', *Cahiers d'Histoire des Prix*, 3, 1958, pp. 133–62.

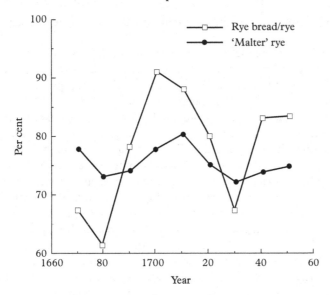

Figure 4.2 Residual variation of bread prices as a percentage of the residual variation in rye price, Cologne, 1660–1760, rye = 100
Sources: See Sources (p. 157).

Malterbrot, the latter being an important element in poor people's diet.[21] The Cologne authorities were known as being efficient in their bread policies: almost alone among European cities of its size, Cologne did not experience a single bread riot in the seventeenth and eighteenth centuries.[22]

Letting the bakers shoulder part of the burden of price stabilisation was not without its problems. Sometimes bakers, or some of the less wealthy in their trade, were forced out of business unless they were provided with grain below market price by the public granary. Public sales of grain at subsidised prices helped bakers keep to the prices ascribed by the assize of bread and countervail sudden price increases. The way the state or the city council funded these tasks contained an element of intertemporal stabilisation of real income, or redistribution from rich to poor, or both. Taxes could be raised on luxury goods, 'voluntary' subscriptions from the

[21] D. Ebeling and F. Irzigler *Getreideumsatz, Getreide- und Brotpreise in Köln, 1368–1797,* Wien: Bohlau Verlag, 1977, p. xxxii.
[22] See D. Ebeling, 'Versorgungskrisen und Versorgungspolitik während der Zweiten Hälfte des 16.Jahrhunderts in Köln', *Zeitschrift für Agrargeschichte und Agrarsoziologie,* 27 (1), 1979, pp. 32–59.

rich were asked for, or the operation was financed by credits.[23] Some city authorities were alerted only by the advent of a crisis while others relied on a network of agents and merchants as well as on their own officials who travelled widely to buy grain and dampen price increases at home.[24] As long as this was a temporary measure the strains put on public finances were not insurmountable. Debt had to paid back, of course, presumably at a date when real income was not squeezed by high prices, and so in this way an intertemporal redistribution of consumption was accomplished. The latter half of the eighteenth century proved fatal to these schemes, however, because prices continued to increase for about half a century. The agencies responsible for grain supply accumulated huge debts as a consequence of their attempts to keep prices down through subsidies to the bakers and to consumers. This was most evident in eighteenth-century Rome, where the generous subsidies were made *permanent* in the latter half of the century. Consumers suffered less from grain price increases in Rome than elsewhere in the Mediterranean area, and Roman bakers paid less for their grain, which made them comply with the low-price policy. In the end the subsidies had to be abandoned because the accumulated public debt became too large, and because of the more liberal outlook of the early nineteenth-century pope, Pius VII.[25] However, Rome was not the only public granary that went astray in this period; the highly efficient *Kornkasse* of Cologne, for example, had to halt its operations for the same reason. In fact, very few public granaries survived the first decades of the nineteenth century.

Public granaries

Inadequate inventories for carry-over have been shown to be related to the excessive risks and zero expected earnings inherent in carry-over speculation, and to the externalities associated with carry-over-induced price stability. But why would public granaries and their carry-over be more profitable than private speculation? The answer is, of course, that they were not. With few exceptions public granaries were unable to

---

[23] See, for example, E. Scholliers, *De levensstandard in de XVe en XVI eeuw te Antwerpen*, Antwerp, 1960, p. 52, and C. Vandenbroeke, 'Agriculture et alimentation', *Centre Belge d'histoire rurale*, 49, 1975, pp. 139–234; D. Balani, *Il vicario tra città e stato. L'ordine publico e l'annona nella Torino del Settecento*, Turin: Deputazione subalpina de storia patria, 1987; H. Hillebrand, 'Die Getreidepolitik und Brotversorgung der Reichsstadt Aachen', *Zeitschrift des Aachener Geschichtsvereins*, 45, 1923, pp. 1–66.

[24] See the detailed account of the ambitious policies of sixteenth-century Cologne, in D. Ebeling, 'Versorgungskrisen'.

[25] See J. Revel, 'Le grain de Rome et la crise de l'annone dans la seconde moitié du XVIIIe siècle', *Mélanges de l'école française de Rome, Moyen Age-Temps Modernes*, 84, (1), 1972, pp. 201–82.

remain financially solvent over long periods. They relied on public funding raised from taxation and credit. The idea was to buy grain when and where it was cheap and sell when it was expensive, to increase the price when it was depressed, and to depress the price when it was too high.[26] Grain is a perishable product and the risks of fermentation, insects, rot, rats, etc. were always present, forcing managers to sell prematurely, sometimes without even covering the purchasing price. Time and again the public granaries had to apply for financial aid from city authorities or central governments. If the memory of a recent dearth was still alive, the resources usually came forward. But a series of good harvests made it difficult for the granary to renew its stocks. Bakers and consumers did not want to buy old grain, often of inferior quality, when there was plenty of new cheap grain around. As a consequence, the public granary made losses. The chances of getting the necessary funding for their deficits depended on how present was the memory of the preceding dearth. But sometimes that memory was too short: public granaries could then be found half empty and underfunded, or insufficiently stocked, at the outbreak of a dearth. Import subsidies to merchants, and other ad hoc means, were then tried in order to improve supply and dampen the rise in price. Experience from modern crisis management in developing nations suggests that confidence in public provisioning policies helps stabilise prices. The logic is obvious: if merchants know that prices will not be permitted to increase dramatically they will refrain from short-term speculative hoarding which would otherwise generate a self-fulfilling prophecy and stimulate a price bubble.[27] For this policy to be effective public authorities must be able to extend *credible* promises which, then as now, they sometimes could, but not always, keep.

Needless to say, bakers did not turn down the opportunity of buying grain below market price from the public granary. When the public granary had to cover costs accumulated when subsidising bakers and consumers and tried to charge bakers and consumers a price above the ruling market price, there was little understanding or enthusiasm.[28] The

---

[26] Frederick the Great of Prussia, in echoing his predecessor, expressed it this way:
   Die Bestimmung ist . . . das Gleichgewicht zu halten zwischen den Städten und dem Platten Lande, in den Städten zu verkaufen wenn das Getreide zu teuer, auf dem Lande zu kaufen wenn es zu wohlfeil ist.' (Quoted in W. Naudé and U. Stalwiet, *Die Getreidehandelspolitik und Kriegsma gazinverwaltung Preussens 1740–1756*, Berlin: Acta Borussia, 1910, p. 179)
[27] M. Ravallion, 'Famines and economics', *Journal of Economic Literature*, Vol. (3), (September 1997),pp. 1205–42, esp. section IV.5.
[28] The managers of the moderately successful public granary in Lyons experienced this, and time and again the city authorities had to subsidise its activities, which they did but with decreasing enthusiasm. See A. Rambaud, *La chambre d'abondance de la ville de Lyon 1643– 1777*, Lyons, 1911.

key to success for a local public granary, therefore, was its ability to establish a *monopoly in supplying the bakers*, or at least to force them to buy predetermined quantities of public grain when the granary had to renew its inventories. *La Chambre des Blés* in Geneva came close to operating such a monopoly over supply to bakers.[29] Ordinary consumers were free to buy grain in the public market, but since a large fraction of them lacked facilities to bake, they had to buy bread. The *Chambre* operated continuously from the end of the seventeenth century to the French Revolution, when Geneva was occupied. The basic principle was that bakers bought part of their grain from the *Chambre* below the market price in times of high prices and above the market price when prices were low. That the activities of the *Chambre* actually stabilised prices is evident, considering that frequent attempts were made to export bread from the city when it was relatively cheap and to import bread when prices were lower in the surrounding area. Maintaining control of the supply line to bakers was thus the most critical element for most public granaries. They all had to rely on some element of forced supply when prices were low, but in only a few cases was it possible to retain this authority over long periods of time. A similar experiment in nearby Lyons was only moderately successful.[30]

When public granaries also served a military purpose – that is, provisioning a standing army, and had the backing of a strong and determined state, as in Prussia in the eighteenth century – they became important participants in the market for grain. Although Prussia developed granaries for both civilian and military purposes, the military granaries were used occasionally in the Scandinavian countries to regulate supply. The sheer dimension of these operations – the public stocks in Prussia amounted to some 10 per cent of the normal harvest – and the prudent timing of purchases and sales makes it probable that they contributed to price stability.

There was a peculiar ambiguity towards private speculative stock-building, as has been pointed out above, but a more assertive attitude towards institutional carry-over. Religious institutions were encouraged to do this, and so also were corporations. In some cities corporations were ordered to keep stocks in exchange for the monopoly they had been granted. These were not public granaries in the strict sense of the word; however, the Livery companies in London were compelled to contribute

[29] H. Blanc, *La Chambre des blés de Genève*, Geneva, 1939. But see also A.M. Piuz and D. Zumkeller, 'Stocaggio dei grani e sistema annonario a Ginevra nel secolo XVIII', *Quaderni Storici*, 46, 1981, pp. 168–91.

[30] A. Rambaud, *La chambre d'abondance*. Although Rambaud is quite hostile to the idea of public granaries, he concedes that their activities had a price-stabilising effect: see pp. 80, 158–9.

to a granary managed by the Corporation of London, and it was in operation at least till the end of the seventeenth century. In Copenhagen, and in
many continental cities, a similar system operated for another century,
but with the Bakers' guild as the 'public' granary. In London the
Corporation set up a market to distribute its grain below the ruling
market price, but mainly to the poor sections of the city.[31] These peculiar
institutions, semi-private in nature but a substitute for public granaries,
raise the issue of whether it is reasonable to talk about public sector
crowding-out of private speculation. The Livery companies in London
cannot be seen as strangers to trade and commerce, and it is therefore
compelling to suggest that their efforts to establish a granary was a
response to, rather than a cause of, recurrent failures of the grain market
to deliver. Of course, it can be argued that the Corporation of London
was concerned about the political externalities generated by price volatility. Perhaps the lives and security of the grain dealers, and commerce in
general, were so threatened in times of dearth that 'business as usual' was
not an option. But this interpretation is not necessarily at odds with the
general thrust of the argument advanced here: externalities caused by
price stability called for concerted action, although in this particular case
a co-operative but binding obligation to the Corporation of London was
the device.

International disorder and autarchy

So far, it has been possible to offer an interpretation of the long-lasting
institutions governing grain markets as a rational response to the problems faced by local and national economies. When we turn to the regulation of external trade, it is not so easy. Most nations had a system of
quantitative trade restrictions affecting, at different points in time, either
exports, or imports, or both. Even grain-surplus regions, such as the
Baltic area, resorted to export prohibitions in times of severe harvest
failure.[32] It can be argued, of course, that this was a rational strategy from
the point of view of a single nation, in a 'prisoner's dilemma' type of
context, in which the outcome in the end was globally and individually
inefficient. Endemic international conflicts would make a reliable flow of
grain highly unlikely, and it certainly impeded the development of international trade. Given the possibility that other nations could resort to
trade restrictions without notice, the best response would be to try to

[31] R.B. Outhwaite, 'Dearth and government intervention in English grain markets,
1590–1700', *Economic History Review*, second series, 34, 1981, pp. 389–406.
[32] Danzig imposed – often short-lived – export bans as often as once every ten years in the
sixteenth century. See W. Naudé, *Die Getreidehandelspolitik*, p. 18.

attain self-sufficiency in food. More importantly, this lack of international order made the quest for autarchy almost universal. From the viewpoint of a single nation therefore, import restrictions, became the obvious way of attaining a sufficient internal supply of grain, thereby extending favours to the rural interests by causing an increase in level of prices. However, these restrictions were lifted when prices threatened consumers. Export prohibitions were used mainly in periods of insufficient supply and were always suspended when prices fell, alarming urban interests. Given the quest for self-sufficiency imposed by the uncertainty of the flow of merchandise, the ruling élites tried to balance conflicting interests by extending favours to both, but in different phases of the price cycle.[33] In the more centralised nations, such as Prussia, there were repeated negotiations between the concerned parties in the *Landtage* sessions. Rural interests pressed for export permits and got them when prices were low. The urban interest agitated for import permits when prices were high, and often enough these permits were granted. The urban lobby did not necessarily oppose free trade. In seventeenth-century Denmark, the wealthy merchants in Copenhagen and the landed interests represented by the aristocracy lobbied for the lifting of the temporary export restrictions sometimes introduced. In fact, the aristocracy had secured itself a say in all matters concerning trade policy.[34] In England, the outcome of the bargaining between conflicting interests clearly turned against urban interests when the bounty on export was introduced, because the bounty most probably increased the price of grain. From the late seventeenth century there were also constitutional barriers against frequent changes in trade policy. At the other extreme we have France, which not only regulated external trade but regional trade as well. In the rest of Europe, however, policies were usually designed to strike a balance between the two interest groups: to stop prices from falling too much by easing exports, and to restrain the increase during periods of scarcity by encouraging imports.

---

[33] There is a rival interpretation suggesting that grain regulations favoured urban interests against rural. See for example M.A. Romani, *Nella spirale di una crisi. Populazione, mercato e prezzi a Parma tra Cinque e Seicento*, Milan: A. Guiffrè, 1975. In Italy a straightforward distinction between urban and rural interests is very difficult to make since the urban élite were landowners. C. Vandenbroeke, on the other hand, suggests that governments were seeking compromises between landed interests and the demands expressed by the urban consumers. See his 'Agriculture et alimentation', pp. 154–5.

[34] See Olsen, 'Studier i Danmark's Kornavl og Kornhandelspolitik i Tiden 1610–60', *Historisk Tidsskrift*, 1942–4, pp. 462–3.

Public crowding-out of private virtues?

Did public granaries and market interventions deter private merchants from the grain trade and from storage for carry-over? In other words, can we talk of 'public crowding-out'? There are three separate issues which need to be looked into in answering these questions:

- First, how did public policy affect private carry-over?
- Second, to what extent did regulation hamper the development of stable trading networks?
- Third what were the short-term consequences for private trade?

The questions just raised will be answered in reverse order. In the short run and to the extent that public supply lowered prices, which it was meant to do, it could of course have affected private trade negatively. Merchants reacted on the basis of expected earnings and the larger they were, the larger the trade in grain would be. However, as was demonstrated in figure 4.1 (p. 69), the huge standard deviation attached to the expected returns implies that it would have been practically impossible to identify the effects of public policies from other types of 'noise' and it is therefore difficult to assess the *net* impact of regulation. It is also worth stressing that if the public provision was credible then price bubbles – that is, self-fulfilling expectations of price increases – could be evaded. But even if public provisioning policies merely replaced private supply, one should not rush to the conclusion that the policies were misguided if a constant supply could be obtained at a lower price level. They would not stand the test of being Pareto-efficient but 'efficiency' (in that rather narrow sense) was not at stake. The goal was an equitable distribution of scarce resources, generating social gains and lower crisis mortality for reasons discussed in some detail in chapter 2.[35] We here encounter the problem that the price which will give private traders sufficient incentives may not be a socially tolerable price, taking into consideration the consequences for those with low incomes, and more generally the negative externalities generated by inflated price levels. The issue of the public crowding-out of private initiative therefore misses the point both as regards the rationale of public intervention and its social determinants. In the first place the existence of positive externalities in price stability makes claims as to the superiority of market outcomes unsustainable *per se*. Equally important is the fact that efficiency was not a sufficient ambition for public policy. On moral grounds and more impor-

---

[35] Alan Everitt, by no means an uncritical historian of the early modern regulation system in England concludes: 'The scheme as a whole [i.e. regulation] was in fact a form of rationing on behalf of the poor'. In 'The marketing of agricultural produce', in Thirsk (general ed.), *Chapters*, vol. 4, p. 134.

tantly for understanding actual policies a 'fair' distribution – in the sense that the worst consequences of subsistence crises were to be avoided – helped to preserve social order and was therefore also in the interest of an élite eager to remain so. While it is easy to see motivation for these policies as a short-term remedy and in the midst of a subsistence crisis it is more doubtful whether regulation is tolerable if it leads to *permanent* negative effects on the volume of trade and stifles the development of trading networks. However, there is no firm evidence that this actually was the case.

It is worth stressing that the nature and extent of intervention in grain markets differed widely between normal years and periods of crisis. Only during the latter were corn factors actually supervised and policed in a systematic way. In normal years authorities practised 'benign neglect'[36] of the rules that were supposed to govern market dealings.[37] The important implication is that although merchants rightly complained about the close supervision and tight leash they experienced during a dearth, little or nothing stopped them from pursuing 'business as usual' once normality had been re-established. As a consequence there seems to be continuity in the evolution of trading networks and marketing procedures of agricultural produce amounting to increased specialisation and efficiency in transactions and to some extent in transport.[38] By the eighteenth century it seems as if those set to supervise the markets had gained a fairly sophisticated view of how markets operated, which stopped them from unnecessary policing. Most importantly they understood that the authoritarian methods of governing markets were at best inefficient except in the very short run.[39] Ultimately, a continuing development in trading practices and networks should show in an increased integration of markets. And so it did; markets became better integrated both regionally and nationally over long stretches of time, which will be explored further in chapter 5. Might market integration have proceeded at a faster rate in the absence of regulation? We do not have an answer to that question, but it should be emphasised that the most serious barrier to trade was the high cost of transport.

Finally, there is the effect of public policy on private carry-over. Did

---

[36] The expression is borrowed from Steven Kaplan. See his *Provisioning Paris*, Ithaca, Cornell University Press, 1984, pp. 30–2.

[37] A similar dichotomy of inactivity in normal years and (hyper)activity during dearths is found in most countries. See Everitt, 'The marketing of agricultural produce', in Thirsk (general ed.) *Chapters*, vol. 4, p. 130 for England.

[38] See for example Chartres, 'The marketing of agricultural produce', in Thirsk (general ed.), vol. 4, pp. 170– 1, 199, 217.

[39] S.Kaplan, *The Bakers of Paris and the Bread Question 1700–1775*, London: Duke University Press, 1996, p. 518.

public granaries deter private speculative carry-over because it affected expected prices negatively? This is not an easy subject because the answer depends on one's conviction regarding the nature of private carry-over. Was it a profit-maximising pursuit, as some believe it was, or did it follow some mechanical rule? We discussed that issue on pp. 55--62, and our tentative conclusion favoured the latter explanation, in the sense of some simple decision rule such as: always put aside some grain if possible. The *expected* earnings did not offer obvious incentives for carry-over and the uncertainty as regards the actual return implied that the costs in finding and making the correct decision actually deterred profit-maximising speculation. A rule-of-thumb could therefore be considered a rational reponse to the storage problem. If this hypothesis is correct, one should not fear considerable crowding-out from public granaries since storage decisions were not sensitive to the pecuniary aspects of storage.

Much of the case for public intervention rests on its effect on price stabilisation. It would be interesting to know whether price volatility actually decreased as a consequence of the policies introduced. In order to answer that question properly we would need a counter-factual, a record of prices in markets not affected by public policies. It is obvious that the de-regulated markets of the late nineteenth century will not do as counter-factuals since transport prices had declined considerably in the meantime, increasing integration and stabilising prices. Among pre-industrial markets it is not easy to find a counter-example because the price records we have derive from the subsistence bureaux of cities around Europe, and therefore almost all from markets in which there was political intervention. It is true that there are other sources, mainly from institutions (such as hospitals and monasteries), but they lack the regularity of the former and are also mainly from regulated markets. There is one possible counter-example, London, which had both a comparatively free grain trade and good data, although only for the eighteenth century (table 4.3). The data source refers to Navy victualling; it displays higher volatility than other contemporary regulated markets, with the partial exception of Toulouse.

It would be premature to conclude that the difference between (say) Pisa, Cologne or Vienna, on the one hand, and eighteenth-century London, on the other, is explained by the stabilising effect of public intervention. Nevertheless, the comparison fails to corroborate the alleged counter-productive effects of public intervention.

There is also another piece of evidence which lends some support to the interpretation that public intervention contributed to price stability. It is possible to generate a 'counter-factual' by looking at periods in a given

Table 4.3 *Price volatility in regulated and non-regulated markets, 1685–1801, standard deviation of the residual in a random-walk model of wheat prices*

Period		(per cent)
London	1685–1801	8.1
Toulouse	1635–1800	8.1
Ruremonde	1635–1796	6.3
Pisa	1635–1789	5.7
Cologne	1635–1796	6.1
Vienna	1692–1800	5.8

Sources: See Sources (pp. 156–9).

nation *with* and *without* ambitious regulation. That counter-factual assumes, however, that all other intervening factors – such as the underlying harvest shocks, monetary shocks and the degree of market integration – did not change sufficiently to serve as *the* cause. When we analysed the English early modern series in chapter 3 (cf. tables 3.3 and 3.4, pp. 57–8) we found a large drop in volatility – measured as the standard deviation of the residual in a trend stationary model – after the introduction of the *Book of Order* regulation by the end of the sixteenth century. The size of that decline is larger than might be expected from a gradual improvement in market integration, although admittedly this interpretation is tentative. It is possible that a much more stable monetary regime also contributed to the decline in volatility. However, it is less likely that there was a change in the nature and extent of the underlying harvest shocks between the periods.

As a final note it is worth discussing to what extent the existing policies crowded-out other more appropriate (political) means of accomplishing consumption stability. Since the consequence of an increase in prices on consumption is measurable only in relation to the level of income and its distribution, it cannot be taken for granted that the only (or best) way to protect consumption of food is through intervention in food markets. One might also want to ask why insurance did not develop as a private alternative. The answer to that is probably that a subsistence crisis constitutes what a private insurer would call a *force majeure* which would, by definition, exclude the normal workings of insurance. Indeed, the commitment of the state or the local council to help in a crisis might be interpreted as a substitute for a probable private insurance failure – that is, the state emerged as the insurer of last resort. It is worth noting the symmetry of this relationship. In years of harvest failures producers were enjoying the implicit import tariff of high transport costs for foreign grain which permitted prices to soar, but good government then came to the assistance of consumers by stimulating or subsidising import or selling grain from the granaries. In abundant years, consumers benefited from the implicit export duty of high transport costs which pushed down price. But then governments introduced export bounties or filled the public granaries, which lifted prices from the level they would otherwise had taken.

What were the policy choices? Entitlement protection through income support might in principle do the job without any need for direct intervention in the supply of grain or pricing of bread. What emerges here is a choice between a selective way of securing consumption at a desired level with *entitlement protection*, targeting specific vulnerable groups, and a more general policy of relying on market intervention. The historical record suggests an evolution away from intervention in markets and towards selective entitlement protection. The fact that the decline of comprehensive grain policies occurred comparatively early in England and with the development of the Poor Laws is striking and probably not accidental. There were also attempts outside England in the eighteenth century to introduce selective policies. There were, for example, efforts at diverting crowding-out effects of price-stabilising measures by establishing a two-tier price structure. Subsidised grain was primarily sold to the poor at below-market prices, while the rest of the population had to rely on the free market. The rationing system could be either informal – the better-off would feel ashamed of getting their supplies from this market – or be based on explicit controls over those making their purchases in that market.[40]

Yet what finally opened the way for selective means testing in the nineteenth century was a reduction in price volatility as markets became more integrated and as income improved. As a consequence, large groups previously affected by the poor performance of grain markets were no longer at risk and those still exposed to the whims of the market were better helped by entitlement protection. Policies could become more selective, and they did so.

---

[40] See, for example, P. Stolz, *Basler Wirtschaft in vor- und frühindustrialer Zeit*, Basle: Shulthess Verlag, 1977, pp. 112–15.

5 Market integration and the stabilisation of grain prices in Europe, 1500–1900

The measurement of market integration

It has been argued in previous chapters that given the high costs of transport, the slow flow of information and the risky nature of local harvest carry-over, harvest fluctuations necessarily had a large impact on supply and prices. But changes in transport and information technology increased opportunities for trade and arbitrage and stimulated integration of markets. In this chapter the *extent* of market integration through time and its impact on price stability will be documented and analysed. However, to assess the extent of market integration we need a *standard*. The basic idea applied here is that market integration is related to the homogeneity of information in different markets and the opportunities for arbitrage and trade – that is, for exploiting the gains from moving goods from where prices were low to where prices were high. If all participants shared the same information and transport costs were negligible or stable, price levels would be expected to converge to some equilibrium ratio, of which 'the law of one price' must be considered the ultimate one, indicating that price in different locations is equal. However, the law of one price seldom applies literally because transport costs are positive. Markets can be perfectly well integrated when price differentials reflect the transport cost between them. For example, markets A and B might have an equilibrium price ratio A/B = 90lire/100lire = 0.9 which then can be interpreted as market A supplying Market B at a transport cost of 10 lire.

It is a well known and an extensively documented fact that price levels between different markets of a homogeneous good, such as wheat, have converged in the very long run, although the most dramatic decline in intercontinental price differentials occurred during a comparatively short period in the nineteenth century, when there were dramatic changes in transport and information technologies.[1] Nonetheless, convergence is a

---

[1] L. Jörberg detects converging corn-prices in Northern Europe and declining regional price variance in Sweden during the eighteenth century, see L.Jörberg, *A History of Prices in Sweden*, vol. 2, Stockholm: Lund: C.W.K. Gleerup 1972. Price convergence between

transitory event and therefore not a sufficient standard of market integration. Some measure of the robustness of the equilibrium price ratio between identical goods in different markets is preferable. 'Robustness' here refers to two inter-related characteristics. First, we want to know whether there is an equilibrium price ratio between markets, such as the law of one price; second, how fast that equilibrium is re-established if there is an exogenous shock to the economy, such as new information about a local or distant harvest failure. The advantage of this view is that it combines the two essential elements in market integration: information and arbitrage or trade. If information flows rapidly and the opportunities for trade are good, the price movements triggered by the exogenous shock should be more or less identical in all markets. It would be unwise, however, to restrict the use of the concept of market integration to that of an absolute standard – that is, a standard with which we can judge whether there is market integration or not. The extent of market integration can be analysed in this framework if we look at the speed at which the equilibrium is restored.

It is worth noting that we are focusing both on adjustments – i.e. changes – *and* an equilibrium ratio of levels. Looking at changes alone might be misleading if the time series are non-stationary, which they usually are. A high correlation between price changes – i.e. rough synchronisation between the first-difference of prices in two markets – need not necessarily imply a long-run equilibrium relation, but *if* there is such an equilibrium relation then there must be adjustments to shocks, so that equilibrium is restored. In general, the more integrated markets are *the faster will adjustments back to equilibrium be*. Since market integration is helped by falling relative costs in transports of goods and information, we would expect *market integration to increase over time*. That expectation is corroborated by the empirical analysis presented below. The other aspect analysed in this chapter is the effect of market integration on price volatility. We will argue that prices of agricultural output in the period under review are primarily driven by supply shocks; demand cannot be expected to be very volatile owing to the fact it is income-inelastic. But supply shocks are independent and local and thus make for profitable interchange (arbitrage) between regions, reducing price volatility when the trade and information flows become cheaper. Hence we would expect

footnote 1 (*cont.*)

North America and Britain was more dramatic. The price differential between the higher Liverpool wheat prices compared to Chicago declined from 50–60 per cent in the 1870s to 5–10 per cent 30 years later. See C.Knick Harley, 'The world food economy and pre-World War I Argentina', in S.N. Broadberry and N.F.R. Crafts (eds.) *Britain in the International Economy*, Cambridge: Cambridge University Press, 1992, pp. 244–68.

price volatility to *decline with the extent of market integration and over time.* These expectations are confirmed on pp. 106–13.[2]

An equilibrium error-correction model

Of the possible equilibrium relations – relations for which there is a straightforward interpretation – between prices of identical goods in two markets, the law of one price, adjusted for transport costs if necessary, is the ideal one. The existence of an equilibrium relation indicates that markets are 'efficient' in the sense that agents use all available information. We will focus on an equilibrium relation which entails the law of one price in the literal sense of the word but also allows for other equilibria – more specifically, a constant-price ratio. There are two reasons for adopting the constant-price ratio rather than the law of one price as the equilibrium relation between markets. First, price might be permanently higher in grain-deficit regions than in surplus regions, with the price differential reflecting the transport cost from the surplus to the deficit region. A price differential might also reflect a quality difference between the goods.

A second reason for using the constant-price ratio as the equilibrium relation is that it greatly facilitates the analysis of international market integration, because it means that there is no need to convert prices quoted in national currencies to the same monetary unit. It is true we thereby cannot test the law of one price, strictly speaking, but that is not our primary concern. The empirical analysis must, however, be restricted to periods with stable metallic contents in the monies used.[3]

If there is an equilibrium relation we would be interested in knowing how fast prices return to that equilibrium after a disturbance – a so-called *innovation* – in the price series. The faster local prices return to the equilibrium the more integrated must markets be, an indication that the

---

[2] In French historiography, this link between market integration and price stabilisation has been disputed from the presumption that well functioning regional provisioning systems were disrupted by integration. As will be seen below, there is little substance in this view. See J. Meuvret, *Le problème des subsistances à l'époque Louis XV. Le commerce des grains et la conjoncture,* Paris: Editions de l'Ecole des Hautes Etudes en Sciences Sociales, 1988. There is a sympathetic survey of Meuvret's impressive work by G. Grantham in 'Jean Meuvret and the subsistence problem in Early Modern France', *Journal of Economic History,* 49 (1), 1989, pp. 43–72. See also L. Tilly, 'The food riot as a form of political conflict in France', *Journal of Interdisciplinary History 2,* 1971, pp. 184–200.

[3] This simplification is not without costs, however. It is plausible that when price differences between two markets exceed the transport costs there are true adjustment processes going on re-establishing the equilibrium. However, price differences may sometimes be smaller than transport costs, and there will not necessarily be any adjustment taking place. However in the analysis pursued we treat all out-of-equilibrium movements as adjustments. There might therefore be a downward bias in the estimates of the speed of adjustment.

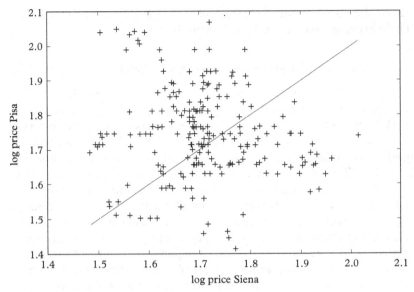

Figure 5.1 Monthly observations of wheat prices in Pisa and Siena, 1560–1580
Sources: See Sources (p. 158).

impact of local conditions is dwindling. This approach is a comparatively new way of analysing time series which are non-stationary, and in which their non-stationarity arises from a common factor.[4] Two examples will help illustrate the intuition behind these models. In figures 5.1 and 5.2 plots of monthly prices of wheat in two Tuscan cities in the sixteenth century (Siena and Pisa) and two French nineteenth century urban markets (Arras and Rouen) are displayed. Let us first examine the Italian case (figure 5.1).

The underlying series for these plots are both non-stationary, which means that none of them has a tendency to return to a particular value. The combinations of observations of monthly prices are vaguely clustered around a straight line, which is an 'equilibrium relation' in the sense given to that concept above, in this particular case, it expresses the law of one price. That is, along this line prices are identical in the two markets at a given point in time. Although few observations are actually found on that very line it is a sort of 'attractor' in that it prevents prices from wandering too far and permanently in two-dimensional space. An outlier in

---

[4] An introduction to this literature can be found in R.F. Engle, and C.W.J. Granger, (eds.), *Long-run Economic Relationships. Readings in Cointegration*, Oxford: Oxford University Press, 1991.

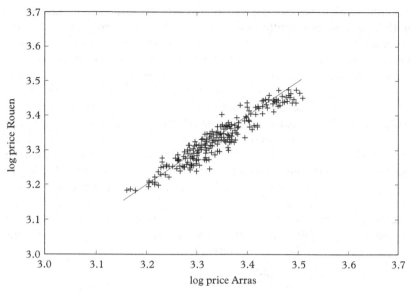

Figure 5.2 Monthly observations of wheat prices, Arras and Rouen, 1867–1886
Sources: See Sources (p. 157).

this space implies that the price differential between markets is high, a situation that would stimulate arbitrage and trade, reducing the price differential. It must be pointed out, however, that the power of the 'attractor' is fairly weak. It takes several years to 'correct' a disturbance. Tracing a sequence of plots – i.e. following the price from month to month – would not produce a permanent divergence from the straight line. Nor would the plot remain located at the same side of the line; instead, it would cross the line repeatedly.

Turning our attention to figure 5.2, the 'attractiveness' of the 'law of one price ' has increased, as revealed by the fact that the cluster of prices along the straight line has narrowed considerably. What makes for the difference between the two graphs (both figures 5.1. and 5.2 are on log scales, so they are strictly comparable) is not the distance between the cities in the two examples (it is roughly equal) but that figure 5.2 relates to the nineteenth century and figure 5.1 to the sixteenth century. Clearly the transport and transaction costs were higher relative to the price of grain in the sixteenth century and information flowed less rapidly, with the result that markets were less integrated.

The economic mechanism behind the existence of an equilibrium relation (the law of one price or a constant-price ratio) will work more smoothly with lower costs of transport and faster information flows. This is first because price differentials will be discovered more quickly, and secondly because the lower transport costs will invite traders to make profits from fairly small price differentials between the cities. As a way of understanding this mechanism intuitively, imagine a band within which prices in a single market can vary without making export or import trade profitable. The higher transaction and transport costs, the larger will the width of that band be: prices in the single market can move freely within the band as long as they do not touch. Arbitrage corrects the local price if it crosses the band limits – that is, price cannot diverge permanently from equilibrium. The class of models describing this process are called 'equilibrium error-correction models'. Such models can be applied to non-stationary data which are 'combined' through some linear equilibrium relation and therefore are said to be *cointegrated*. A simple version of such a model has the following characteristics (but see the appendix to this chapter, p. 114, for the precise mathematical formulation):

$$\Delta P^A_{\ t} = \alpha(P^A_{\ t-1} - P^R_{\ t-1}) + \epsilon_t$$

where P refers to *log* of price, superscripts A and R refers to two markets – for example, Arras and Rouen, respectively – α is the error-correction parameter and ϵ is a white noise, or a random variable with constant variance and zero mean. The story told by this equation is simple. The direction of change in price, ΔP, in Arras a particular month, t, will be determined by the price differential between Arras and Rouen the previous month, $t-1$, and the random variable ϵ which describes the unanticipated shocks – that is, new information at time t. If prices were higher in Arras than in Rouen that would exert a downward pressure on prices in Arras at time t given the innovation, the random shock ϵ_t. If, on the other hand, prices were higher in Rouen at time $t-1$ this would generate an upward pressure on prices in Arras. The expected sign on α is consequently negative and the larger its numerical value the faster will equilibrium be restored.

Models of this type – see the appendix for details – have been used in the estimation of the speed of adjustment back to equilibrium in markets that proved to be cointegrated. A large number of European markets for wheat from c.1500 up to the First World War have been analysed. These markets are spread over most of Europe and are plotted in figure 5.3.

The results from the analysis are reported in tables 5.1–5.4. The periods chosen for analysis were imposed by the following considerations. In international comparisons, it was necessary to control for monetary disturbances, so periods under scrutiny were largely periods with monetary stability. Furthermore a series must not have too many missing

Figure 5.3 Location of market towns analysed in this chapter

observations. The tables are organised as follows. Column (1) presents the cities and time periods for which the cointegration tests and the estimation of the error-correction parameter have been performed. Column (2) reports on whether markets were cointegrated or not. A plus sign means that the price series are cointegrated, while a minus sign means that they are not. The hypothesis that equilibrium is a constant-price ratio is then tested and the test probability is reported in column (3).Column (4) presents the α parameters if the hypothesis of a constant-price ratio is accepted and it measures the speed of adjustment – the monthly percentage adjustment – of the specified market to the constant-price ratio between cities in an error-correction model; throughout the tables the signs on the parameters have been omitted. Column (5) reveals whether there is weak exogeneity or not. The adjustment parameter for the exogenous market is put in brackets and it is insignificant. 'Weak exogeneity' in a market implies that its price has an 'impact' on the price in the other market without being itself affected by the price in that market. It is sometimes referred to as 'market leadership', but this can be misleading since it basically reflects asymmetries of information between markets. If one market systematically gets new information before the other it will turn up as a market leader without actually dominating the other market in the literal sense of the word. We would expect 'market leadership' to *disappear in a perfectly integrated market* because the informational asymmetries which it reflects are bound to disappear when new and efficient information technologies, such as the telegraph, emerge at the end of the nineteenth century.

Table 5.1 shows clear signs of regional integration. In Tuscany, for example, Siena and Pisa seem already to be integrated in the sixteenth century and are becoming increasingly integrated as time goes by, as illustrated by the increase in α. There are signs of a Mediterranean integration (Pisa and Toulouse), but the results for France are inconclusive, as reflected by the failure to accept the hypothesis of a constant-price ratio between Paris and Toulouse. Surprisingly Paris and Pisa behave better in this respect. It is worth stressing that the speed of adjustment is slow. The half-life of a shock to one market – that is, a deviation of price in that market from the equilibrium – is around 1½–3 years. It must also be pointed out that results are sensitive to the period chosen, which suggests a fragile nature of market networks in this period. The analysis has been restricted to periods where there are no documented monetary disturbances, the latter being quite frequent in these centuries with monetary financing of government spending by means of debasement of the currency. It is not always possible to give a plausible explanation for the recorded weak exogeneity or 'market leadership'. In some cases it seems

Table 5.1 *Results from equilibrium error-correction tests, European cities, sixteenth and seventeenth centuries*

(1)	Cointegration (2)	H_1 (3)	α (4)	Weak exogeneity (5)
Paris Toulouse } 1600–20	–			
Paris Cologne } 1660–80	–			
Toulouse Cologne } 1660–80	–			
Pisa Cologne } 1660–80	–			
Siena Pisa } 1560–80	+	0.29	(0.006) 0.053	Siena
Siena Pisa } 1680–98	+	1	(0.012) 0.081	Siena
Pisa Toulouse } 1655–90	+	0.31	0.051 (0.027)	Toulouse
Pisa Paris } 1655–90	+	0.14	0.03 (0.02)	Paris
Toulouse Paris } 1655–90	+	0.01		

Sources: See Sources (pp. 156–9).

counter-intuitive, such as Siena 'dominating' prices in Pisa, the latter being directly affected by international trade and new information closer to the important port of Leghorn (Livorno). However, in this particular case Siena's 'market leadership' might be more apparent than real, since the Siena prices used are monthly *averages* while Pisa's are the price on the first market day of every month. By and large, there is reason to be careful in analysing integration of markets, when price series are not strictly identical in design. That Paris is weakly exogenous relative to Pisa might reflect the lagged impact on Pisa of information from Northwestern Europe and the Baltic ports. The implication here would then be that the overall impact of these markets were more pervasive than the impact of the Mediterranean markets.

Table 5.2 *Results from equilibrium error-correction tests, European cities, eighteenth century*

(1)	Cointegration (2)	H₁ (3)	α (4)	Weak exogeneity (5)
Pisa } Siena } 1730–50	+	0.06	0.073 0.05	No
Pisa } Toulouse } 1730–50	+	0.1	0.055 (0.038)	Toulouse
Pisa } Vienna } 1730–50	+	0.17	0.02 (0.0)	Vienna
Pisa } Ruremonde } 1730–80	+	0.79	0.03 0.027	No
Toulouse } Ruremonde } 1730–80	+	0.13	0.026 0.029	No
Vienna } Ruremonde } 1730–80	+	0.8	(0.011) 0.028	Vienna

Sources: See Sources (pp. 156–9).

By the time the advocates of liberalisation of grain markets had entered the intellectual scene in the mid-eighteenth century, there were consistent signs of an emerging integrated European wheat market, with Ruremonde, presently in the Netherlands, representing Western Europe, Vienna representing Central Europe and Pisa and Toulouse representing Southern Europe. Yet adjustments to shocks still took a rather long time, as can be gathered from the low α values in table 5.2. However, 'market leadership' or informational asymmetries were beginning to disappear. Dramatic changes in transport costs probably accounted for little of the new phase in market integration; what counted was the slow emergence of a robust trading network and homogeneous information penetrating Europe at a faster rate. In order to estimate the simultaneous speed of adjustments, the combined effect of α values in the pairwise tests which indicate no 'weak exogeneity' must be calculated.

Not until the mid-nineteenth century when the modern information and transport systems have emerged do we find evidence of swifter adjustments to shocks. Around then, α values doubled or tripled. In the free-trade era of the mid-nineteenth century the half-life of a price deviation was down to three to four months from two years or more a century

Table 5.3 *Results from equilibrium error-correction tests, European cities, nineteenth century*

(1)		Cointegration (2)	H_1 (3)	α (4)	Weak exogeneity (5)
London Brussels	1845–72	+	0.38	0.094 0.082	No
London Toulouse	1845–72	+	0.17	(0.037) 0.06	London
London Bordeaux	1845–72	+	0.08	(0.052) 0.063	London
Brussels Toulouse	1855–72	+	0.71	(0.07) 0.22	Brussels
Brussels Bordeaux	1855–72	+	0.13	(0.029) 0.239	Brussels
Brussels Lyons	1855–72	+	0.12	(0.054) 0.22	Brussels
Brussels Rouen	1833–72	+	0.37	0.072 0.102	No
Brussels Vienna	1867–84	−			
Vienna Rouen	1867–84	+	0.48	(0.016) 0.106	Vienna

Sources: See Sources (pp. 156–9).

earlier in international markets, such as London, Brussels and Toulouse. Furthermore – as expected – information flows no longer seem to have discriminated between open markets such as London and Brussels. But why are these two markets weakly exogenous in relation to the French markets? One explanation would point out the central role of England in world grain trade *and* its openness. Note, however, that the French prices respond very fast to the price shocks from abroad so it is not an isolated market in any sense, which has to do with the fact that France was pursuing free-trade policies in the periods covered by the analysis reported in table 5.3. Vienna is apparently not well integrated in the European grain market; the cases of pairwise tests including Vienna for which

Table 5.4 *Results from equilibrium error-correction tests. French cities,*
nineteenth century

(1)	Cointegration (2)	H_1 (3)	α (4)	Weak exogeneity (5)
Toulouse Bordeaux 1855–72	+	0.24	0.315 (0.108)	Bordeaux
Toulouse Rouen 1860–80	+	0.29	0.135 (0.025)	Rouen
Toulouse Rouen 1867–1913	+	0.78	0.084 0.055	No
Toulouse Marseille 1885–1913	+	0.13	0.083 0.068	No
Toulouse Lyons 1885–1913	+	0.05	0.104 0.216	No
Rouen Bordeaux 1855–72	+	0.51	(0.09) 0.18	Rouen
Rouen Marseille 1885–1913	+	0.48	0.114 (0.058)	Marseille
Rouen Lyons 1885–1913	+	0.14	0.164 0.153	No
Lyons Marseille 1885–1913	+	0.41	0.128 0.068	No

Sources: See Sources (pp. 156–9).

cointegration has been detected are rare. (Only a few of the many tests
performed are reported in table 5.3.) However, its poorer integration with
other European markets may be more apparent than real. Austria's comparatively unstable monetary regime in the second half of the nineteenth
century may have been a contributing factor in the sense that independent shocks to the national price level in Vienna may have disguised the
integration.

In the late nineteenth century there was still a difference between the
nature of international and national integration. Table 5.4 reports on the
evolution of market integration in France in the nineteenth century and it
is worth comparing these results with the nineteenth-century results in

table 5.2. The speed of adjustment was much faster in national markets, with a half-life of a shock down to two or three months. Transport costs – as revealed by geographical distance – were not the only contributing factor behind integration. National boundaries independently slowed down the speed of adjustment, to the extent of adding a month or so to the half-life of a disturbance. National boundaries exerted this impact because they had an influence on the transmission of information, or because of informal or formal barriers to international trade other than tariffs.

It is worth noting that informational asymmetries remained in force at a national level for that part of the nineteenth century that preceded the telegraph. In some cases, such as the analysis of Toulouse and Bordeaux, it is easy to explain the weak exogeneity of the port of Bordeaux on the Atlantic coast, or another important grain port, Marseille in relation to Northwestern Rouen. These two ports, on the other hand, are both directly tied to the international trading network and are therefore, from an informational point of view, equals. Most cases of weak exogeneity vanish in the last decades before the First World War, however. Marseille also stands out (not all results are reported in the tables) as somewhat untypical and poorly integrated with the rest of France. Not until the end of the nineteenth century did Marseille consistently form part of the national French market.

It may be useful to display the meaning of the α parameter by relating it to the time it takes for a disturbance to be 'absorbed'. That process is displayed in figures 5.4 and 5.5. In figure 5.4 the story goes as follows. Imagine a 10 per cent price increase in a market which exhibits weak exogeneity – i.e. one unaffected by price in the other market. The curve illustrating this process first jumps from 100 to the value 110 and remains at that level along the time axis. The other market adjusts to the higher price in the 'market leader' at a rate given by the adjustment parameter, $\alpha = 0.04$. That particular value is an average of the speed of adjustments found in the seventeenth and eighteenth centuries for markets that adjusted to some leading or dominating market. The lower of the two curves approaching the 'market leader' has been generated by this typical pre-industrial speed of adjustment. The other curve is generated by $\alpha = 0.31$ (Toulouse–Bordeaux 1855–72, with Bordeaux as the market leader) which was the highest parameter detected in the analysis where we also had weak exogeneity. The long historical process of market integration over three centuries described in this chapter can be seen as a shift from the lower to the higher of the two curves.

The other important aspect of market integration was the disappearance of market leadership or informational asymmetries. A series of cases

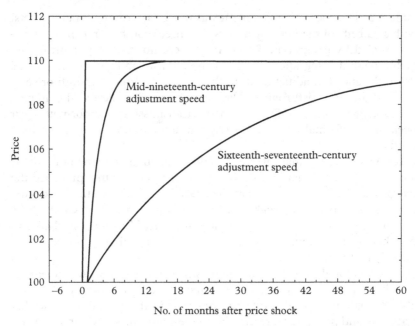

Figure 5.4 Adjustment of a 'follower' market to a price shock in a dominating (weakly exogenous) market, with adjustments speed at 0.04 and 0.31, respectively
Source: Calculations based on tables 5.1–5.4.

from the eighteenth and nineteenth centuries are illustrated in figure 5.5. In this case, the shock first hits one of the markets but both economies adjust. The slowest adjustment is found between Pisa and Ruremonde in the 1730–80 period, which is approximately equal to that found between Toulouse and Ruremonde in the same period. It is clear that Southern and (North)western Europe was integrated at that time. The two other pairs of adjustment curves refer to London and Brussels in the mid-nineteenth century and Rouen and Lyons a little later. Although London and Brussels are much closer to each other than French cities Rouen and Lyons, it seems as if territorial boundaries have an independent retarding effect on adjustment. Note that the half-life of a shock among two markets in different nations is one–two months longer than that of a shock in the French market (not displayed in the figure but documented in tables 5.3 and 5.4) at about the same time.

The analysis performed in this chapter is quite demanding when it comes to the *frequency* of observations in the data. For that reason, we have not been able to extend a comparable analysis to England and

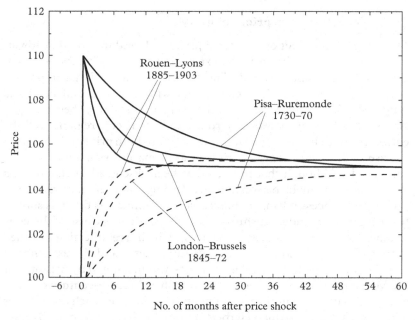

Figure 5.5 Mutual adjustment in pairs of European markets, eighteenth and nineteenth centuries
Source: Calculations based on tables 5.1–5.4.

Scotland. However, there are strong reasons to believe that what we have witnessed in continental Europe was typical also of Scotland and Wales. The early view that England remained separated in local or regional markets has been replaced by the view that England constituted a national market by the early eighteenth century.[5] Given the easy access to waterways and the coastal transports, this seems plausible. Research on Scotland also indicates a high degree of integration. If the extent of price volatility is seen as negatively correlated with integration – a view which will be discussed further below – then Scotland was becoming more integrated over the seventeenth and eighteenth centuries. There is a sizeable drop in price volatility in the long run.[6]

[5] C.W.J. Granger and C.M. Elliot, 'A fresh look at wheat prices and markets in the eighteenth century', *Economic History Review*, 20 (2), 1967, pp. 257–65.
[6] A.J.S. Gibson and T.C. Smout, 'Regional prices and market regions: the evolution of the early modern Scottish grain market', *Economic History Review*, 48 (2), 1995, pp. 258–82.

The decline in price volatility

Market integration not only affected price levels and the speed of adjustment to equilibrium but also the extent of price volatility. As discussed extensively in chapter 2, a decline in price volatility is an important welfare improvement.[7] Market integration will decrease the effect of local supply shocks on local prices, and foster price stability, because geographical arbitrage between surplus and deficient regions will be enhanced. With inelastic demand with regard to both price and income, it is reasonable to look at price variations as primarily originating from the supply side. Although that problem has been discussed in chapter 1, a short reminder might be worthwhile. An important characteristic of a production process relying on nature, soil and climate is that it is subject to local but independent disturbances (independent because of the large number of intervening causal factors) which are affecting planned output. The independence of local disturbances – and the existence of global stability, relatively speaking at least – was first noted by Aristotle for the Mediterranean world, and was revived in eighteenth-century political economy with an impressive number of adherents such as Charles Davenant, Claude-Jacques Herbert and Anne Robert Jacques Turgot, who turned it into a forceful argument for free trade. Herbert's and Turgot's argument can be summed up as follows: planned output was based on some notion of an expected (equilibrium or normal) price, but actual output differed widely from that desired output. In segmented markets, such output variations shared by all local producers were bound to have large effects on local price, since local producers (say, in a village or a region) in a segmented market were large relative to the market demand. However, if disturbances were local, independent and with a zero mean, there was an equivalence between global or aggregate planned output and realised output in a sufficiently large integrated economy. Consequently there was a rationale for inter-local or inter-regional trade, and such trade would stabilise local prices, because the high-price regions would attract grain from low-price regions. The intuitive way of seeing the price-stabilising effect of market integration is to interpret market integration as an increase in the number of substitutes – such as wheat or other types of grain from other regions – for the locally produced wheat. The implication would be that the local producer which previously faced a downward-sloping demand curve now faced an increasingly elastic, and in the end a perfectly elastic, curve. As market integration proceeds local supply shocks become small relative to the wider market, and shocks will

---

[7] The argument can not be repeated here. See M. Ravallion, *Markets and Famines*, Oxford: Clarendon Press, 1988.

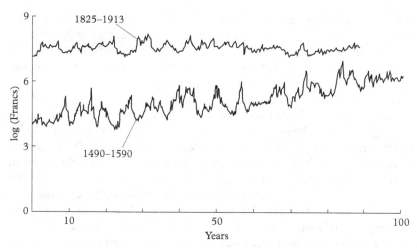

Figure 5.6 Price (in logs) of wheat, Toulouse, 1490–1590 and
1825–1913
Source: See Sources (p. 158).

affect neither local supply nor local prices. It is sufficient for integration to
be price-stabilising if aggregate harvest varies less than local harvests.

It is important to stress that price volatility in a single market will necessarily be high as long as transport and storage costs are high, and information flows erratically. Price volatility is therefore to a great extent
technologically determined. We observed in chapter 4 that price volatility
was lower for expensive grain than for cheaper varieties. The obvious
interpretation is that, transport costs being additive, transport's share of
the total cost of wheat is smaller than for (say) rye. The conjecture then is
that wheat markets are better integrated because the barriers to trade are
smaller. As costs of information and the transmission and transport of
goods fall, we would expect price volatility to fall over time. Figure 5.6
traces the evolution of price of wheat in Toulouse for two periods,
1490–1590 and 1825–1913, and it is obvious that volatility was smaller in
the nineteenth century. In fact, volatility seems to have declined throughout the entire period, even if this is not shown in the figure.

Before further documenting the evolution of price volatility, a meaningful definition of 'volatility' is in order. Let us start with an ad hoc definition such as the average monthly percentage change in price, which is
simply the sum of monthly changes (ignoring the sign of the change)
divided by the number of observations. Measured in this way, volatility
declined steadily from some 7 per cent in the sixteenth century to 3 per
cent during the last four decades before the First World War. Measuring

volatility instead by deviations from a trend or from some smoothing process (for example, a moving average) would produce a much larger fall in volatility. Depending on the smoothing method adopted, volatility would have been between four to five times higher in the sixteenth century than in the last half of the nineteenth century.

None of these measures has an explicit foundation or rationale, however. It is unlikely that contemporaries could discern a trend or some moving average in the price movements they faced. Is it possible to derive a volatility measure from the general argument pursued in this book that volatility is inversely related to welfare? One way of looking at the problem starts from the premise that adjustments to changes take time – for example, nominal wages may catch up but they do so with a time lag. The reason for this is, of course, that wage claims are related to expected costs of living. The relevant volatility concept should therefore entail the idea of *unexpected* changes. To determine what the 'unexpected change' is can be quite problematic, however. It presupposes an econometric model, but sophisticated models were not available. We have, instead, chosen a simple model, a random walk, which often performs reasonably well although not strictly the best at all times. A random walk suggests that expected price equals price today, so the unexpected element – the error – is the innovation in the series which is supposed to be random, reflecting the fact that price changes are driven by new information which is in itself a random event. By implication, the hypothesis states that all available information is used in a rational way by participants in the market and, as a consequence, that all relevant information is expressed in the current price. Current price will not change unless in some future period new information is brought in. The logic here is that if you know today of some future event it will be captured in current information *and* price. For example, assume that it is known that price will decrease by 10 per cent tomorrow. The immediate outcome will be that consumers will postpone purchases, so that prices fall today. The nature of *new* information is that it is not known currently, and therefore it is plausible that it is random. The expectation of price tomorrow will therefore be today's price.

The essential test criterion for a random walk is that you can exclude any significant and systematic impact of past price on innovations in the series. As pointed out in previous chapters we cannot do that. If there is such an impact there is some information around which participants are not using rationally. As is shown in the appendix (p. 114), the inclusion or exclusion of a deterministic seasonal component affects the lag structure although the deterministic seasonal component is seldom significant. However, in terms of the size of the residual – that is, the unexpected or unexplained change – the difference between a pure random walk and

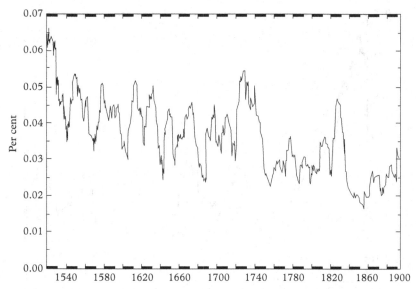

Figure 5.7 Standard deviation of the residual in a random-walk model of monthly wheat prices, Toulouse, 1500–1900, recursive estimation, per cent
Source: See Sources (p. 158).

one including lags is trivial, so it is good enough to measure volatility as compared to the 'best' model. It is likely that if contemporaries held any views about price behaviour, the random walk wins on its simplicity compared to models with complicated autoregressive properties.

Before we proceed to a discussion of the results in figures 5.7 and 5.8 and table 5.5, which clearly indicates a decline over time in the residual-cum-volatility measure, we must counter the econometrician's suspicion that the decline in the residual shows that the model is poorly specified. Might some other model not do better in terms of residual variation for the early periods in our study? Perhaps, but it is difficult to imagine what that model would be like. As pointed out previously, adding lags has only trivial effects and – most importantly – does not change the pattern of declining residual variance over time. The interpretation of the results discussed on pp. 100–1 on faster adjustment to shocks was that the larger community had faster access to the same information. That means that the nature of information changed over time. In the early periods information on the local supply conditions dominated the information flow while, as we enter the eighteenth and nineteenth centuries, the weight of local information (and the local supply shock) was diminishing. So what

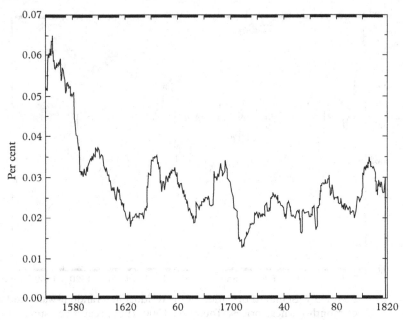

Figure 5.8 Standard deviation of the residual in a random-walk model of monthly wheat prices, Pisa, 1560–1820, recursive estimation, per cent

Source: See Sources (p. 156).

is at stake here is not the random nature of new information but that information in well integrated markets reflected the different fortunes of many markets, some with bumper harvests and others with poor harvests. This information displayed smaller aggregate shocks because local outliers were smoothed away. This might not be the whole story, however. If the demand for wheat becomes less price-inelastic, which it probably did in the nineteenth century with the increasing availability of substitutes, then a given supply shock will have a smaller effect on prices.

In figures 5.7 and 5.8 the standard deviation of the residual – the measure of our ignorance – is estimated in a recursive random-walk model. That procedure can be described as a 'window' moving over time. A constant number of observations is used, but as you move forward in time new observations are replacing the oldest ones and the parameters are therefore re-estimated. That way, the residual usually comes out smaller than if you make the estimate on the entire period. Figure 5.7 displays the residual for Toulouse over a period of four centuries, and although the residual varies a lot there is a visible and steady downward trend. The residual for Pisa in figure 5.8 also starts from a high level in the sixteenth century, but declines rapidly. You might detect a slightly lower residual in the eighteenth century than in the seventeenth century. For both Pisa and Toulouse, you have an expected increase of the residual as the post-revolutionary wars in Europe around 1800 troubled trading networks.[8]

Let us now turn to table 5.5, which reports estimates of the standard deviation of the residual in a seasonally adjusted random-walk model for a large number of markets of wheat, rye and barley during four centuries. The parameters have been estimated for the stated period – i.e. non-recursively – and the level of the residual is therefore higher. The main results confirm those found in the graphs and can be summarised as follows. There was a substantial decline in volatility over time, although it was not necessarily continuous. There was a sixteenth and seventeenth century maximum around 6 and 10 per cent. There was an *ancien régime* low at 5 per cent which some markets had already attained in the seventeenth century, and by the end of the nineteenth century the residual standard deviation had declined to between 3 and 4 per cent. As has already been pointed out, cheaper grains with relatively higher transport and storage costs display higher volatility.

The Cologne series stands out as exceptional both for its low level and lack of downward trend. One reason for the low volatility is Cologne's privileged geographical location. The city had access both to Baltic grain via the Low Countries, and to a large part of West and Central Europe through the Rhine and its tributaries. However, it is also worth speculating whether or not the ambitious price-stabilising policy followed by the Cologne city council contributed to the observed stability. Pisa was also a well located market with an active grain policy and a diverse hinterland, with supplies from the entire Mediterranean world, including ports on the Black Sea. It is worth noting that the residual standard error for Cologne and Pisa in the seventeenth century was at a level which seems to be a sort of *ancien régime* minimum, and that only in the era of the nineteenth-century transport revolution are lower residuals attained elsewhere. In light of the discussion in chapter 4 it is worth noting that in most markets price volatility comes down after the highly volatile late sixteenth century had activated interventionist provisioning policies. Somewhat surprisingly, the London series exhibits relatively high residual standard deviation. On the face of it, as a Navy victualling series, one would suspect instability to be smaller than in the '*mercuriale*'

---

[8] The recursive method implies that you cannot single out a particular year for a given residual, since it is estimated on the basis of a 'window' of 10 years. The time axis therefore is approximate.

Table 5.5 *Standard deviation of the residual in a random-walk model of monthly prices, European markets, c. 1500–c. 1913, per cent*

Brussels	1569–1635	1635–96	1801–87	1820–87	1870–87
Wheat	8.0	5.7	6.3	5.9	5.1
Rye	9.1	7.6			

Cologne (Köln)	1532–1635	1635–1796
Wheat	5.4	6.1
Rye	6.5	6.9

Ruremonde	1599–1635	1635–1796
Wheat	6.1	6.3
Rye	7.3	7.8

Siena	1546–1635	1635–1765
Wheat	7.5	6.6

Utrecht	1535–1635	1635–1690
Wheat	6.4	—
Rye	7.4	5.3

London		1685–1735	1725–75	1745–95	1765–1801
Wheat		9.0	6.7	6.5	8.6

Vienna (Wien)		1692–1800	1790–1820	1825–1913	1875–1913
Wheat		5.8	9.2	6.1	4.5
Rye		8.0	10.6	6.8	4.5
Barley		9.5		7.2[a]	

Toulouse	1486–1635	1635–1800	1790–1820	1825–1913	1875–1913	1890–1913
Wheat	10.3	8.1	8.3	4.8	4.5	3.4

Lyons						
Wheat				4.7	3.6	3.3

Rouen						
Wheat				5.3	4.4	4.4

Pisa	1550–1634	1635–1789
Wheat	8.8	5.7
Rye	10.4	9.7
Barley	13.1	9.1

Notes:
[a] 1825–1882.
— The analysis has not been possible to perform.
Sources: See Sources (pp. 156–9).

series, because a government agency ought to have some market power as a buyer. It is also interesting because contemporary liberal writers on the Continent constantly referred to the apparent stability of the English market which, it was argued, had to do with the lack of tight regulation.

The French Revolution and the disruption of international trade before and during the Napoleonic wars predictably increased instability, as mentioned above (cf. Vienna in table 5.5). Over the four centuries covered by these series, residuals were reduced to between a third and a half of their sixteenth-century levels. Although all series exhibit very low residual levels in the early or mid-eighteenth century (between 5 and 6 per cent), the residual by the end of the nineteenth century had dropped to 4 per cent or less. For all series that can be followed over very long stretches of time – i.e. Toulouse, Brussels and even Vienna – the 'all-time-low' came towards the end of the nineteenth century. There is therefore little support for the idea that market integration actually increased price volatility when it disrupted local trading networks. Although figures 5.7 and 5.8 indicate that there was repeated spells of high residual standard deviation, the extent of this volatility diminished over time.

Did changes in the pattern of harvest disturbances play a role for this long-term decline in price volatility? The little we know about changes in yields does not support such an interpretation. Technological progress in farming was slow, and while yields increased there is to my knowledge no evidence that yield variance changed much. My expectation was that the nineteenth century would be the only period covered in this study in which a decline in fluctuations might occur because of the introduction of new techniques. But that expectation cannot be corroborated, at least not for the pre-chemical fertiliser age. For the nineteenth century we have wheat 'yields per unit of land' data for France, 1825–70, and the conclusion that emerges is that there was no decline in yield fluctuations.[9] The fact that market integration increased, and in the absence of any other obvious cause, makes it probable that the decline in price volatility was the product of market integration, and not a gift of Nature.

---

[9] The data on which this generalisation is based were published by the French Ministry of Agriculture as *Récoltes des céréales et des pommes de terre de 1815 à 1876*, Paris, 1878.

APPENDIX

Mette Ejrnæs

This appendix deals with three topics. It starts by explaining how incomplete time series can be completed. It then discusses different autoregressive representations of the time series by analysing a particular but fairly typical series of wheat prices. Finally the methods used in the co-integration analyses are presented.

Missing observations

Most price series are incomplete – that is, we lack observations for some months. If missing observations are not too frequent we can generate the missing observations by interpolation. However, if there are many missing observations an adequate interpolation is not possible. In such cases, we have to restrict the use of time series to periods with few or no missing observations, which sometimes means that the periods covered in the analysis will be fairly short.

The idea underlying the interpolation is to predict the missing observation on the basis of available information. The interpolation for this analysis is made by using the Kalman filter.[1] The Kalman filter uses the known values of the time series to predict the unobservable. This means that the interpolation is not based on any *a priori* knowledge.

The interpolation is performed by estimating a general time-series model called ARIMA.[2] Based on the estimated parameters in the model the missing values are calculated. For this analysis the interpolation is performed by using the TRAMO (*T*ime Series *R*egression with *A*RIMA Noise, *M*issing Observations and *O*utliers) program by Victor Gomez and Agustin Maravall.[3] The program computes the interpolators of missing observations, and it is possible to include different deterministic components. For the interpolation of monthly wheat prices a seasonal deterministic component is included.

The advantage of interpolation is that we do not lose observations. All the information in the time series is used. Unfortunately, this method

[1] L. Fahrmeir and G. Tutz, *Multivariate Statistical Modelling Based on Generalized Linear Models*, New York, Springer Verlag, 1994, pp. 263–7.

[2] W.H. Green, *Econometric Analysis*, 2nd edn., Englewood Cliffs: Prentice-Hall International Editions, 1993, pp. 539–49.

[3] V. Gomez and A. Maravall, *Program TRAMO, Time Series Regression with ARIMA Noise, Missing Observations and Outliers*, Manual European University Institute Florence, 1994, mimeo.

cannot be used if there are too many missing observations. In these cases, it has been necessary to shorten the time series to periods with complete data. For that reason, the starting point and/or the final point of the time series are occasionally determined by the quality of the data.

The autoregressive process

One of the most simple models for stationary time series and probably the most widely used is the autoregressive process. This model is actually a stochastic difference equation, which means that the explanatory variables in the model are the lagged dependent variables. The model is given by

$$y_t = \sum_{j=1}^{k} \varphi_j y_{t-j} + \epsilon_t \qquad t = k, \ldots, T$$

such that $\epsilon_1, \epsilon_2, \ldots, \epsilon_T$ are independently normally distributed terms with mean 0 and variance σ^2.[4]

In this type of model the value of y_t is explained by the history of the time series and the model is called a dynamic or an autoregressive model.

One of the reasons why this model is very frequently used is its potential good fit when only one class of data is available, such as a price series of a particular good, even though the economic interpretation of the model is not always straightforward. However the lagged dependent variables can be expected to contain information on other relevant but unidentified variables. In the light of the efficient-market hypothesis we expect only the coefficient of the first lagged dependent variable to be significant and $\varphi_1 = 1$. The model is then called a random-walk model

$$y_t = y_{t-1} + \epsilon_t \qquad t = 1, \ldots, T$$

We will now assess the merits of different autoregressive representations of the price data.

The autoregressive model for wheat prices

In this section an empirical analysis of the wheat prices is presented.[5] We are using an autoregressive model to estimate the price series. The estimation and all the graphs are made by using GAUSS.

---

[4] T.W. Anderson, *The Statistical Analysis of Time Series*, New York: Wiley Classical Library, 1994, p. 164.
[5] The source used here is the Pisa series referred to in the Sources (p. 156).

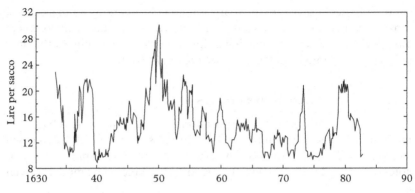

Figure 5A.1 The level of the wheat price, Pisa, 1633–1682

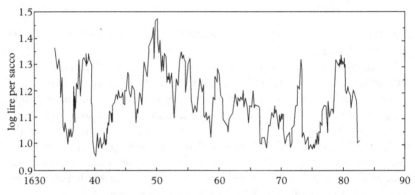

Figure 5A.2 The log of the wheat price, Pisa, 1633–1682

The data set is wheat prices in Pisa from January 1633 to December 1682. The prices are monthly observations, quoted the first market day in every month. Hence, the time series consists of 600 observations. Figure 5A.1 shows the time series.

It is obvious that the time series is non-stationary. The graph indicates that the variance increases when the price increases. The usual way to handle this problem is through logarithmic transformation of the time series. The transformed time series is shown in figure 5A.2.

Very often the price series turn out to be integrated of order 1.[6] This means that the level of the prices is a non-stationary process while the first difference is a stationary process.[7] To examine this property, the first differences are shown in figure 5A.3.

[6] P.G. Ardeni, 'Does the law of one price really hold for commodity prices?', *American Journal of Agricultural Economics*, 71(3), 1989, pp. 661–9.

[7] M. Hatanaka, *Time-series based econometrics*, Advanced Text in Econometrics, Oxford: Oxford University Press, 1994, p. 17.

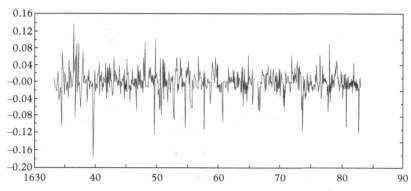

Figure 5A.3 The differences of the wheat price, Pisa, 1633–1682

The graph of the first differences (figure 5A.3) indicates that the price series is integrated of order 1. The Durbin–Watson test statistic is 0.08, which also indicates that the time series is integrated of order 1.[8] We will from now on assume that

$$y_t = \log(p_t) - \log(p_{t-1}) \qquad t = 2, \ldots, 600$$

is a stationary process.

When the price series consists of monthly observations we expect a seasonal variation during the year. To get a general overview of the seasonal fluctuation the mean and the standard deviation of every month is computed and displayed in figure 5A.4 and figure 5A.5.

The figures illustrate that there exist seasonal variation in both mean and variance. By including a deterministic seasonal component we remove only the seasonal pattern in the mean and the seasonal pattern in the variance will remain in the data. For that reason, we do not include a deterministic seasonal component.

In determining the model, we have to decide which lags we want to include. In order to find the model, we use autocorrelations. A high numerical value of autocorrelation indicates that the corresponding lagged variable should be included in the autoregressive model.

The autocorrelations and the 95 per cent significant bands are shown in figure 5A.6. The figure indicates that lag 1, lag 12, lag 24 and lag 36 are significant, which means that the model has a seasonal cycle of one year's duration. For that reason, we estimate an AR model with lag 1, 12, 24 and 36 of the dependent variable:

$$y_t = \alpha_0 + \alpha_1 y_{t-1} + \alpha_2 y_{t-12} + \alpha_3 y_{t-24} + \alpha_4 y_{t-36} + \epsilon_t$$

[8] W.H. Green, *Econometric Analysis*, pp. 423–5.

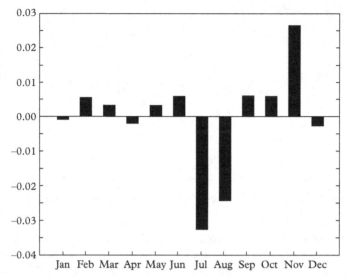

Figure 5A.4 The monthly average of the differences of the wheat price, Pisa, 1633–1682

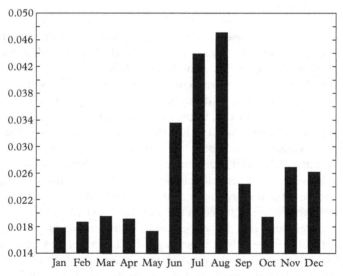

Figure 5A.5 The monthly variance of the differences of the wheat price, Pisa, 1633–1682

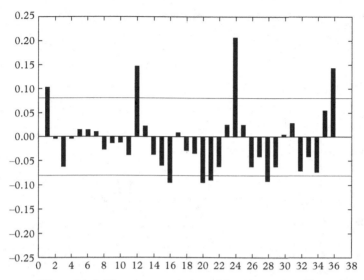

Figure 5A.6 The autocorrelation of the wheat price, Pisa, 1633–1682

where $\epsilon_t \sim Nid(0, \sigma^2)$. The estimation of the model shows that the estimated coefficients of the constant term and of lag 36 are insignificant, and they are therefore excluded. The final model is

$$y_t = \alpha_1 y_{t-1} + \alpha_2 y_{t-12} + \alpha_3 y_{t-24} + \epsilon_t.$$

The parameters in the model are estimated by Ordinary Least Square (OLS) and the result of the estimation (standard deviation in parenthesis) is:

$$\hat{\alpha}_1 = 0.103 \quad \hat{\alpha}_2 = 0.125 \quad \hat{\alpha}_3 = 0.196 \quad \hat{\sigma}^2 = 0.00476.$$
$$\text{(0.00394)} \quad \text{(0.00404)} \quad \text{(0.00406)}$$

In the subsequent analysis of the residuals we find that the residuals are almost normally distributed with mean zero. The residuals do not reveal any signs of autocorrelation, so we conclude that they are normally and independently distributed. Another kind of misspecification is model instability. In order to examine the stability of the model, we exploit recursive estimation.

Recursive estimation

In time-series models it is very often the case that the model data fits only for very short periods. Therefore we will examine if the model fits the data for the entire period and if the parameters are constant throughout. When

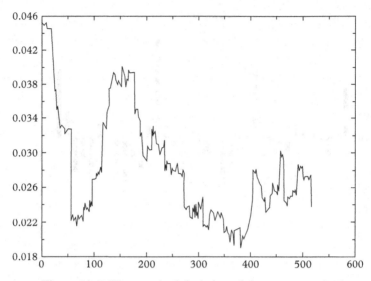

Figure 5A.7 The standard deviation of the error term in the recursive analysis of the autoregressive model

we have 600 observations it is possible to split the periods into sub-periods. The underlying idea of recursive estimation is to divide the period into sub-periods and then estimate the parameters on the sub-series. In contrast to the common recursive estimation, we do not extend the data set.[9] Every estimation is based on a five-year sub-period, which consists of 60 observations. The starting point of the sub-period is moved one observation at a time, so the sub-periods are overlapping. The estimation is performed 516 times using OLS.

The estimation of σ^2 from the recursive estimation is shown in figure 5A.7. The first point on the graph is the estimate of σ^2 based on the period from January 1635 to December 1639, the next point is based on the period February 1635 to January 1640, and so on.

The graph of the standard deviation of the error term can be used in an economic context. The error terms can be interpreted as the unexpected shock on the prices. The variance of the error terms measures the impact of the shock on the prices. Figure 5A.7 shows that the standard deviation is in general decreasing through the period. The peaks in the graph are caused by outliers.

The result of the recursive analysis shows that the parameters in the model are non-constant. This indicates that it is difficult to use one auto-

[9] G.E. Mizon, 'Modelling relative price variability and aggregated inflation in the United Kingdom', *Scandinavian Journal of Economics*, 93(2), 1991, pp. 189–211.

regressive model for a long period, and that the model changes through the period.

Random-walk model

Given the lack of robustness of the parameters in the model analysed above it would be worthwhile to look more closely at the random-walk model or the efficient-market hypothesis, which has a straightforward economic interpretation. A 'random walk' is a special case of an autoregressive model for which it is assumed that the increments or first differences are white noise. The model is given by

$$y_t - y_{t-1} = \epsilon_t \qquad \text{for } t = 1, \ldots, T$$

where ϵ_t is independent and identically distributed with zero mean and variance σ^2. The conditional mean is given by

$$E(y_{t+1} | I_t) = y_t$$

where I_t is the information set at time t.

In the context of monthly wheat prices, we will allow for seasonal variation throughout the year. In contrast to the general autoregressive process we do not have the opportunity to include a lag of order $12, 24, \ldots$, which allows seasonal variation. We therefore assume that every month has a different price level, which means we have a January level, a February level, ... and a December level. This seasonal adjustment is described in Johnston.[10] The random-walk model with seasonal variation can be written as

$$y_t - y_{t-1} = \psi' S(t) + \epsilon_t \qquad \text{for } t = 1, \ldots, T$$

where S is a 12×1 vector given by

$$S' = (1_{\{t=jan\}}, 1_{\{t=feb\}}, \ldots, 1_{\{t=dec\}})$$

and ψ is a 12×1 vector containing the associated coefficients. The only parameter in the model besides ψ is the variance of the error term σ^2. The parameters in the model are estimated by OLS.

The recursive estimation can be performed as described in the case of the general autoregressive process. In this case, one can give the recursive estimate of the variance an economic interpretation. In this model, the error term can be interpreted as a shock. The shock contains new information and therefore influences the price. The variance of the error term measures how great an impact the shock has on prices. We therefore con-

---

[10] J. Johnston, *Econometric Methods*, 1994, pp. 234–5.

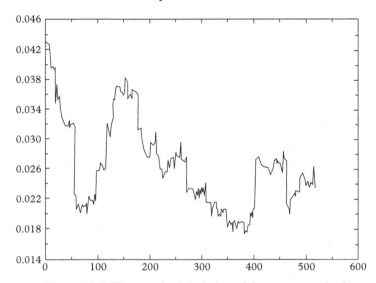

Figure 5A.8 The standard deviation of the error term in the recursive analysis of the random-walk model

jecture that the variance will decrease over time, concurrently with more integrated markets, which will smooth the shocks. Figure 5A.8 shows the variance of the error term in a random-walk model. In terms of the standard deviation of the error term the difference between the autoregressive model described above and a random-walk model is trivial, as can be seen from a comparison of figure 5A.7 and figure 5A.8.

The cointegration analysis

In this section, the statistical model for the cointegration analysis is presented and a few comments on the test procedure given. A discussion of the statistical aspects of cointegration analysis is not given, but can be found in Johansen.[11] This appendix describes the particular model used in the analysis in this book. The results of the estimation technique are assumed to be known. This section describes how the cointegration analysis is performed, and how to interpret the results.

The error-correction model

The idea behind cointegration is that there exists an equilibrium relationship between certain variables. If the variables in a certain period are out

[11] S. Johansen, *Likelihood-based Inference in Cointegrated Vector Autoregressive Models*, Oxford: Oxford University Press, 1995.

of equilibrium, they will try to adjust to the equilibrium in the next period. This model is called an 'equilibrium error-correction model' because the variables adjust if there is an error in relation to the equilibrium. The error-correction model of two variables can be formulated mathematically. Let the equilibrium be given by

$$B_1 y_{1t} + B_2 y_{2t} + \beta_3 = 0 \qquad \text{for all } t = 1, \dots, T \tag{5A.1}$$

where y_{1t} is variable number 1 and y_{2t} is variable number 2, both observed at time t. β_1, β_2 and β_3 are the equilibrium coefficients, which are called the coefficients of the cointegration vector. The variables y_{1t} and y_{2t} are in equilibrium if they fulfill (5A.1). The error-correction model is given by

$$y_{1t} = \alpha_1 (\beta_1 y_{1t-1} + \beta_2 y_{2t-1} + \beta_3) + y_{1t-1} \qquad t = 2, \dots, T$$

$$y_2 = \alpha_2 (\beta_1 y_{1t-1} + \beta_2 y_{2t-1} + \beta_3) + y_{2t-1} \qquad t = 2, \dots, T$$

where α_1 and α_2 are called the adjustment coefficients. Assume the variables are out of equilibrium at time t, for example,

$$\beta_1 y_{1t} + \beta_2 y_{2t} + \beta_3 > 0 \text{ and } \beta_1 > 0$$

and the adjustment coefficient, α_1, is negative. Then the value of y_{1t+1} becomes smaller than y_{1t}, and in the next period the variables are closer to the equilibrium. If α_1 is positive the variables will move away from the equilibrium and if α_1 is zero y_{1t} will not adjust at all. The numerical value of α_1 indicates the speed of the adjustment.

We now assume that the variables y_{1t} and y_{2t} are stochastic variables. The stochastic version of the error-correction model is formulated by

$$\Delta y_{1t} = y_{1t} - y_{1t-1} = \alpha_1 (\beta_1 y_{1t-1} + \beta_2 y_{2t-1} + \beta_3) + \epsilon_{1t} \qquad t = 2, \dots, T \tag{5A.2}$$

$$\Delta y_{2t} = y_{2t} - y_{2t-1} = \alpha_2 (\beta_1 y_{1t-1} + \beta_2 y_{2t-1} + \beta_3) + \epsilon_{2t} \qquad t = 2, \dots, T \tag{5A.2}$$

where ϵ_{1t} and ϵ_{2t} are normally distributed error terms. By means of co-integration analysis one can determine whether or not the variables adjust to equilibrium and to find the estimated equilibrium, if it exists.

The model in our analysis is a little more general than (5A.2), and is given by

$$\Delta y_{1t} = \alpha_1 (\beta_1 y_{1t-1} + \beta_2 y_{2t-1} + \beta_3) + \sum_{i=1}^{k} (\gamma_{i(11)} \Delta y_{1t-i} + \gamma_{i(12)} \Delta y_{2t-i})$$

$$\tag{5A.3}$$

$$+ \sum_{j=1}^{11} \varphi_j s_t + d_t + \epsilon_{1t}$$

$$\Delta y_{2t} = \alpha_2 (\beta_1 y_{1t-1} + \beta_2 y_{2t-1} + \beta_3) + \sum_{i=1}^{k} (\gamma_{i(21)} \Delta y_{1t-i} + \gamma_{i(22)} \Delta y_{2t-i})$$

$$+ \sum_{j=1}^{11} \varphi_j s_t + d_t + \epsilon_{2t}$$

where k is the number of lags included in the model, γ the coefficient of the lags, s_t a deterministic seasonal component (as described in the section on the random-walk process, pp. 121–2) and d_t a dummy variable. The reason why we include these extra terms is to obtain a better description of the data. By including a deterministic seasonal component we allow for different levels during a year. The dummy variable is included to get rid of outliers. These dummy variables are used in only a few cases if the outliers are very large.

The error-correction model can be written as

$$\Delta y_t = \begin{pmatrix} \Delta y_{1t} \\ \Delta y_{2t} \end{pmatrix} = \begin{pmatrix} \alpha_1 \\ \alpha_2 \end{pmatrix} (\beta_1 \beta_2) \begin{pmatrix} y_{1t-1} \\ y_{2t-1} \end{pmatrix} + \begin{pmatrix} \alpha_1 \\ \alpha_2 \end{pmatrix} \beta_3 \qquad (5A.4)$$

$$+ \sum_{i=1}^{k} \begin{pmatrix} \gamma_{i(11)} & \gamma_{i(12)} \\ \gamma_{i(21)} & \gamma_{i(22)} \end{pmatrix} \begin{pmatrix} \Delta y_{1t-i} \\ \Delta y_{2t-i} \end{pmatrix}$$

$$+ \Phi D_t + \begin{pmatrix} \epsilon_{1t} \\ \epsilon_{2t} \end{pmatrix}$$

$$= \alpha \beta' y_{t-1} + \alpha \beta_3 + \sum_{i=1}^{k} \Gamma_i \Delta y_{t-i} + \Phi D_t + \epsilon_t. \qquad (5A.4)$$

What we want to do is to examine whether the variables adjust to equilibrium, which means that the variables are given by (5A.4).

The cointegration model

In the context of cointegration an 'equilibrium' is a stationary relation between the variables. In a cointegration analysis we assume that at least two variables are non-stationary, but by differencing, the increments become stationary. The variables are then following an I(1) process, they are said to be 'integrated of order one'.

In a cointegration setup the error-correction model is given by a Vector Autoregressive (VAR) model:

$$\Delta y_t = \Pi y_{t-1} + \sum_{i=1}^{k} \Gamma_i \Delta y_{t-i} + \Phi D_t + \epsilon_t \qquad (5A.5)$$

where Π and Γ_i are 2×2 matrices. Φ is a $2 \times l$ matrix, where l is the number of dummies: 11 (seasonal dummies) *plus* the number of outlier dummies. The hypothesis concerning the number of stationary relations is formulated as a hypothesis on Π. The rank of the matrix Π is determining for the number of stationary relations:

- if Π has full rank, in our case two, it means both variables are stationary
- if Π has rank one, it means that there exists a stationary relation among the variables – the Π matrix is then given by $\Pi = \alpha\beta'$, where α and β are vectors, the model (5A.5) is then identical to (5A.4)
- if Π has rank equal 0, it means that there does not exist a stationary relation.

In the examination of the rank of the Π matrix the eigenvalues of Π are calculated. The eigenvalues measure the power of the adjustment. If there is a significant adjustment to a certain relation between the variables, we will accept the stationary hypothesis. In the analysis of wheat prices the value of the largest eigenvalue is reported. In the cases where a stationary relation exists, it is possible first to estimate and secondly to test different hypotheses on the cointegration vector, β, and the adjustment coefficients, α. The estimation is based on maximum likelihood and performed by the Johansen procedure.[12]

The advantages of using the Johansen method are stressed in Goodwin.[13] In Goodwin's article, multivariate cointegration is used to evaluate the law of one price for five international wheat markets. The analysis is based on monthly wheat prices from January 1978 to December 1989. The main conclusion is that the law of one price is violated when transportation costs are ignored. In contrast to this analysis, we limit ourself to a bivariate system, which makes it much more easy to interpret the cointegration vector.

The analysis of wheat prices

In our model, the variables are wheat prices in two different cities. The prices are logarithmically transformed, so

$$y_{1t} = \log(p_{1t}). \qquad (5A.6)$$

[12] S. Johansen, *Likelihood-based Inference*, 1995.

[13] B.K. Goodwin, 'Multivariate cointegration test and the law of one price in international wheat markets', *Review of Agricultural Economics*, 14(1), 1992, pp. 117–24.

Our main interest is in examining whether there exists a stationary relation between the prices in two different cities. If so, we would like to test hypotheses on the relation. The hypothesis is: the ratio of prices in two cities is constant:

$$\frac{p_{1t}}{p_{2t}} = c \text{ for all } t$$

$$\log p_{1t} - \log p_{2t} - k = 0 \text{ for all } t.$$

This hypothesis can be formulated as

$$H_1: \quad \beta_1 = 1 \quad \beta_2 = -1. \tag{5A.7}$$

The test is performed as a Likelihood Ratio-test, and the test statistics are asymptotically χ^2 distributed.

An alternative test of the hypothesis is proposed by Froot, Kim and Rogoff.[14] They examine the law of one price over 700 years for Holland and England. Instead of using cointegration, they construct a time series of the relative prices

$$x_t = \log(p_{1t}) - \log(p_{2t})$$

and test if it is stationary. The test is performed as an augmented Dickey–Fuller-test.[15] They find that the deviations from the law of one price are stationary at the 1 per cent level for barley, wheat and butter.

If the hypothesis H_1 is accepted, the adjustment coefficients are then estimated under the hypothesis H_1. These coefficients are normally distributed, and it is possible to calculate the standard deviation and the t value.

If one of the adjustment coefficients (let us say $\hat{\alpha}_2$) happens to be insignificant, the prices in city 2 are called weakly exogenous. The price in city 2 is then given by

$$\Delta y_{2t} = \sum_{i=1}^{k} (\gamma_{i(21)}\Delta y_{1t} + \gamma_{i(22)}\Delta y_{2t}) + \sum_{j=1}^{11} \varphi_j s_t + d_t + \epsilon_{2t+1}.$$

The prices do not adjust to equilibrium. The adjustment to the equilibrium takes place only in city 1. The price in city 1 is still given by (5A.3).

The cointegration analyses are performed by CATS in RATS (Cointegration Analysis of Time Series).[16] The estimation and the test procedures are illustrated by an example.

[14] K.A. Froot, M. Kim and K. Rogoff, 'The law of one price over 700 years', NBER Working Paper, 5132, 1995.
[15] W.H. Green, Econometric Analysis, 1993, pp. 48–9.
[16] H. Hansen and K. Juselius, 'CATS in RATS, Cointegration analysis of time series', Institute of Economics, University of Copenhagen, 1995, mimeo.

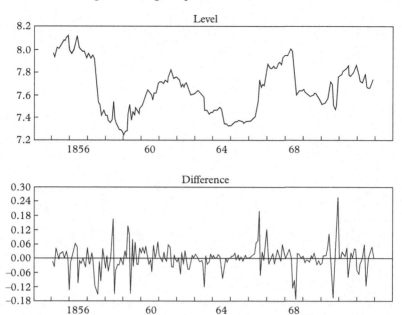

Figure 5A.9 The log price of wheat, Lyons, 1855–1872

An example

In this section, one of the analyses is presented in detail, the idea being to show how it is performed. For the remaining analyses only the results are reported.

The data

This is a cointegration analysis of the wheat prices in Bordeaux and Lyon over the period 1855–72.[17] The prices are transfored by the logarithm. Figure 5A.9 is a graph of the time series. The graph of the price in Lyons shows that the level of the price of wheat is non-stationary, but the differences seem stationary. For the price series of Bordeaux (Figure 5A.10) the level again is non-stationary while the differences seem stationary. The time series contains 214 observations.

The misspecification analysis

In order to obtain valid results of the analysis it is important that the error-correction model be well specified. This means that the residuals of

[17] The source used here is the Lyons and Bordeaux series referred to in the Sources (p. 157).

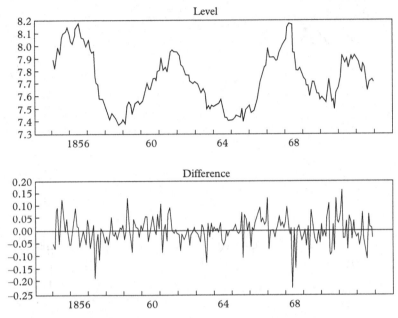

Figure 5A.10 The log price of wheat, Bordeaux, 1855–1872

the VAR model have to be almost normally distributed. After preliminary testing[18] we found that the best description of the VAR model was by including 1 lag, 11 centred seasonal dummies and a constant in the equilibrium. The model is then given by (5A.5), with $k = 1$. The misspecification tests show that the residuals have a higher kurtosis than expected. This means the distribution has heavier tails than the normal distribution; the excess kurtosis is due to some outliers. In this analysis, we have chosen not to include dummies to avoid the excess kurtosis. This choice is based on two considerations. First if we want to get rid of all the outliers we have to include a lot of dummies. It has not been possible to give all these dummies a economic/historical explanation, which means that it is difficult to interpret the results. Second, simulation studies show that the results of the cointegration analysis are almost unaffected by the presence of excess kurtosis. The excess kurtosis is found throughout the analyses.

[18] The preliminary testing includes different misspecification tests: a test for autocorrelation, tests for normality and a test for ARCH effects. These tests are a part of the standard procedure in CATS.

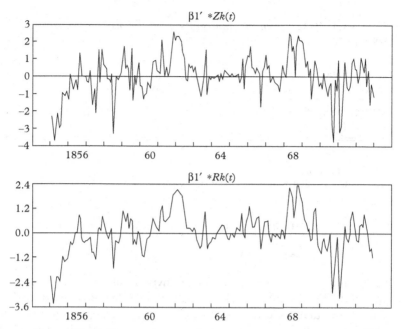

Figure 5A.11 The stationary relation between Lyons and Bordeaux, 1855–1872

The number of stationary relations

The number of stationary relation is determined by the value of the eigenvalues. The estimated values of the eigenvalues are 0.11 and 0.03. Based on the test statistic, the presence of one stationary relation corresponding to the eigenvalue 0.11 is accepted at a 10 per cent level. The stationary relation is estimated to

$$y_{Lyons} - 0.99y_{Bord} + 0.013 \qquad (5A.8)$$

and is shown in figure 5A.11.

The upper graph in figure 5A.11 shows (5A.8) while the lower graph shows (5A.8) corrected for seasonal dummies and lags.

The estimates of β indicate the hypothesis H_1. The Likelihood Ratiotest accepts the hypothesis with a p value of 0.87. The equilibrium under H_1 is then estimated to

$$y_{Lyon} - y_{Bord} + 0.081.$$

The estimates of the adjustment parameters are

Table 5A.1 *Results from the cointegration test, Lyons and Bordeaux,*
1855–1872

Period (1)	Cities (2)	λ (3)	Cointegration (4)	H_1^a (5)	α^b (6)	Weak exogeneity (7)
1855–72	Lyons	0.11	+	0.87	(0.081)	Lyons
	Bordeaux				0.214	

Notes:
[a] The test probability.
[b] The numerical value of the adjustment coefficient.

$$\hat{\alpha}_{Lyons} = -0.081 \quad t \text{ value for } \alpha_1 = -1.337$$

$$\hat{\alpha}_{Bord} = 0.214 \quad t \text{ value for } \alpha_2 = 3.459.$$

The t value is the test statistic for the hypothesis that the parameter is
equal to 0. The t value is t distributed with one degree of freedom. The t
value shows that the estimate of α_{Lyons} is insignificant, which means that
the price in Lyons is weakly exogenous, and does not adjust to equilibrium.

The results of the cointegration analysis

Table 5A.1 shows the contents of the cointegration analysis of Lyons and
Bordeaux. In column (3), the maximal eigenvalue is listed. Column (4)
indicates if there exists a stationary relation between the two price series.
To determine whether or not there exists cointegration we use a 10 per
cent significance level.[19] Column (5) contains the test probabilities of the
hypothesis given by (5A.7). In column (6), the estimate of adjustment
coefficients are listed and parentheses indicate that the estimate of adjustment coefficient is insignificant. Column (7) indicates if one of the cities
is weakly exogenous.

[19] As usual the 5 per cent significant level is used, but in determination of the number of stationary relations the 10 per cent level is normally used.

6 Authoritarian liberalism and the decline of grain market regulation in Europe, 1760–1860

Institutional change, welfare and efficiency

The last third of the eighteenth century witnessed a serious and systematic theoretical consideration of the adequacy of price-stabilising public intervention in grain markets, which marked the beginning of the end for traditional grain policies. This intellectual re-orientation inspired reforms which could hardly have been implemented, however, had it not been for the political authoritarianism which dominated political life during the Enlightenment. The reforms attacked the two major areas of *ancien régime* management of grain markets, as discussed at considerable length in chapter 4. Traditional grain policies had closely monitored the timing, location and admission to markets in order to combat the alleged exploitation of exclusive (insider) information. At times, there was an almost obsessive pursuit of transparency in commercial transactions in order to prevent agents from cornering the market, whether through sales and purchase contracts or inventory adjustments. That pursuit circumscribed the freedom of merchants and producers. Henceforth, much more faith was invested in the self-regulatory capacity of markets, and for that reason open access to markets was stressed. The second concern of traditional market management was the attempt to stabilise prices, either through stimulating external supply when it dried up or through open market operations through public granaries, which would buy when prices were low and sell when they were high. Increasingly, it was argued that these activities were better managed by markets.

France, where markets were most tightly regulated, was also the intellectual centre of the anti-regulation debate and a major arena of reform. But France is also the best illustration of how vulnerable reforms were to popular discontent triggered by unexpected price increases. The Habsburg monarchy, Scandinavia, Spain and Tuscany also entered a phase of reform at about the same time, while the deregulation of grain markets was delayed in Prussia until the early nineteenth century. The process of liberalisation had its setbacks in those parts of Europe as well, although a *cohabitation* of economic liberalism and political authoritarianism prevailed. The reforms were first imposed on an unimpressed and reluctant population which made the governing élites react nervously to shifts in public opinion. As a result, reforms and short but repeated spells of the traditional variety of intervention in grain markets alternated well into the nineteenth century. By the middle of the century the traditional manifestation of discontent with poor market performance, the food riot, had practically disappeared, signalling that active popular resistance to the principles of market pricing belonged to the past.

This chapter reviews the chronology and geography of reform and seeks to explain its success, its dependence on political authoritarianism and its slow pace. The intuition behind the explanation is simple, perhaps even simplistic. A key element is that grain markets in the nineteenth century performed better because increased integration reduced the impact of local disturbances in harvest outcomes on the local price of grain. That integration was stimulated by advances in the flow and reliability of information and by cheaper transport. Violent price fluctuations disappeared or became smoother, and the remaining milder fluctuations had less severe consequences on living standards because in an era of rising real wages, food constituted a diminishing fraction of total consumption for the typical household. Markets were consequently endorsed or tolerated by a wider coalition of social forces, while the social basis for the traditional interventionist policies narrowed. The elaboration of this intuition to a consistent explanation of institutional change is very problematic, however. The interpretation suggested here is based on a functional framework in which the existence of an institution is explained by its efficiency-enhancing characteristics. But it must be pointed out that the actual historical process in which the new institutions developed demonstrated that improvements were slow to emerge. They were also slow to be acknowledged and accepted. An understanding of the forces that bring about the introduction of deregulation must therefore be separated from explaining the ensuing stability of the new institutions. Only the latter issue is the proper subject of a functional explanation.

In a functional explanation a specific institution is shown to be instrumental – indeed, necessary – in obtaining an efficient outcome (or, more vaguely, a welfare improvement). To demonstrate, as was attempted in chapter 4, that the regulatory institutions of the *ancien régime* were 'efficient' in the sense that they corrected for market failures does not in itself constitute a functional explanation of these institutions. Neither will the argument that markets later performed much better lead to the functional explanation that unregulated markets ultimately prevailed *because* of this improvement in performance. A functional explanation states that (1) the institution to be explained has an efficiency-enhancing property, *and* (2) that it is necessary – i.e. that there are no functional alternatives in obtaining the efficient state – *and* (3) that it exists because of its efficiency-enhancing property. Economists and historians too often jump from (1) to (3) but there is no necessary relationship between them, in the sense that (1) implies (3), not even in conjunction with (2). A functional explanation requires a specification of a mechanism which ensures that institutions necessary to obtain efficient (or, more modestly, welfare-improving) outcomes actually prevail. One approach would be to argue that good institutions bring more satisfaction or gratification to members than bad institutions, and that the former will therefore be preferred to the latter. This comes close to saying that societies tend to obtain efficient outcomes or that there is a welfare-improving drift in society. This is not to say that we invoke some abstract or unidentified societal force: there ought to be a human agency involved in endorsing or selecting the good institution.

Before discussing under what conditions a welfare-improving drift actually is plausible, it is worth stressing that the formal requirements for a rigorous functional explanation have been fulfilled *if* it can be shown to exist. And in conjunction with (1) and (2) then (3) will follow.[1] The problem is, of course, that in general the idea that societies tend to attain efficient states is not self-evident. Pessimists would be inclined to see it as implausible. Path-dependence, which occurs when a particular past event constrains present alternatives, is an obvious case of persistence of non-efficient states. Conflicting interests might end up in sub-optimal outcomes, and the distribution of property and power can be such that improvements might be blocked. We cannot, in other words, rule out the persistence of inefficient institutions.[2] This insight will lead us to a type of

---

[1] The ideal functional explanation is, of course, evolutionary Darwinian biology in which an efficient attribute in a species exists because it enhances reproductive chances of that species. Only rarely will you find biological analogies in the social sciences, however. For illustrative purposes this might serve as an exception to the rule: in some industries firms are large because there are economies of scale. The competitive process, which is roughly analogous to natural selection in evolutionary biology, favours largeness and consequently the survival propensity of large firms will be greater than that of small firms, which will make for the extinction of the latter. In principle, the functional and efficiency-enhancing property of largeness might be latent – i.e. not intentionally desired or even acknowledged – as opposed to manifest. In practical life, it would be hard for managers not to observe the favourable consequences of size. When socio-economic *institutions* are discussed analogies to biological selection processes seem unconvincing, however, and manifest functions involving intentional design and a process of explicit, formal or informal, consent are probably the rule rather than the exception.

[2] See my 'Was feudalism inevitable?' *Scandinavian Economic History Review*, 39 (1), 1991, pp. 68–76 and the subsequent exchange with F. Galassi in vol.40 (2), 1992, pp. 34–43, on the efficiency of the manorial institution, in which I argued that there were functional alternatives, the peasant household. The prevalence of manorial organisation over the alternative in some parts of Europe had to do with the distribution of power which permitted an élite to limit the mobility of labour by brute force in an epoch with labour scarcity and free frontier land.

'political-economy' explanation in which policies and institutions are created to serve particular interest groups. However, in the particular case of grain market institutions one may want to point out the uniformity in the European experience.[3] Wherever the particular problem of grain-market instability was acknowledged, a similar set of institutions developed in the attempt to curb volatility. In anticipation of improved market performance caused by increased market integration, traditional institutions were gradually abolished. Then, finally, when anticipations turned out to be fulfilled unregulated markets were approved. To establish the fact of uniformity in the European experience is not a substitute for the elaboration of the welfare-improving mechanism, as specified above, but together with such a specification it would strengthen the functional argument. Until that is done it would be perfectly legitimate to conjecture that the observed uniformity merely reflected a similarity in some other underlying causal factor. The obvious candidate would be the argument that these societies shared a similar power structure, a pattern of vested interests, and that policies were shaped to suit these interests. What makes this type of explanation less attractive in the case of grain market regulation *and* deregulation is the fact, discussed at considerable length in chapter 2, that there were no major conflicting interests among producers and consumers as to the desirability of price stability. If more price stability was preferred to less by (almost) all it is likely that institutions promoting price stability would be preferred and endorsed. That is, the essential auxiliary requirement for a functional explanation, assuming that (1) and (2) were fulfilled – that there was a welfare-improving tendency at work in society in this particular domain – was present.[4]

What I have argued so far is that there existed a broad, although not perfect, consensus around the desirability of price stability. But the problem remains that it is very likely that the efficiency-enhancing properties of the reforms did not materialise immediately or become transparent and acknowledged. There was a popular and long-standing suspicion against grain merchants which biased the interpretation of daily events. An increase in prices, whatever its real cause, was most easily blamed on merchants and speculators, a fact which sustained traditional policies. The introduction of reforms is therefore likely to have had a chronology which differed from, and preceded, the wider acceptance and popular

---

[3] And outside Europe as well: similar institutions as those of *ancien régime* Europe emerged in China, for example. See P.-E. Will and R.B. Wong, *Nourish the People: The State Civilian Granary System in China, 1650–1850*, Ann Arbor: Center for Chinese Studies, The University of Michigan, 1991.

[4] On functional explanations see P.Halfpenny, 'Two-variable and three-variable functional explanations', *Philosophy of Social Science*, 11, 1981, pp. 27–32.

endorsement of markets. One should view the reforms as institutional innovations which were either accepted or rejected, depending on their perceived and real consequences. In other words, not only should the consequences matter but also how they were interpreted. Moreover, there were conflicting beliefs among the parties concerned in the early phase of reform as to whether deregulated markets could deliver price stability.

The first phase of reform did not primarily depend on the lack of transparency and conflicting perceptions because the promised and expected price stability simply did not obtain. One reason was that the transition from a system of a few authorised dealers in grain to a large number and a competitive state of affairs took time. And in the meantime the abuse of local monopolies might increase, which certainly would not pass unnoticed by an easily aroused populace. More importantly, grain markets were still not sufficiently integrated to obtain a reasonable degree of price stability. Besides, harvest failures were so frequent that the risk that they would coincide with a surge in reform activity was almost inevitable; reforms were therefore an easy target for the forces of traditionalism.

We should not therefore be surprised to find that institutional change faced formidable forces of inertia. I shall argue that the reformation in grain markets addressed all these forces of inertia in a variety of ways. The political authoritarianism of enlightened despotism seems to have been indispensable in the early phase of reform. It permitted a period of institutional innovation when the lack of transparency and the problems associated with transition from one market régime to another were creating an unfavourable climate for institutional change. As might be expected, the process from reform to consolidation was a lengthy process, with repeated setbacks. Even if reform policies did not explicitly rely on popular consent because political assemblies did not admit the common people, the masses were not entirely lacking in political resources. The food riot had long been an efficient political means of influence, in particular as long as the new pro-market ideology relied on a very narrow social base. The chronology of reform clearly indicates that, initially, the liberal credo was a minority view shared sometimes only by the entourage of the enlightened despot, and its early success was based on power rather than consent. Liberal reforms continued to be contested throughout the first half of the nineteenth century, although with diminishing vigour and dedication. Only as we approach the second half of the century did popular agitation change its focus from grain market regulation to *entitlement protection* – that is, from generalised market intervention to selective income support through social policies, public works and insurance schemes. It is consequently important to bear in mind that when markets were liberalised compensatory policies developed and consumption stabilisation increasingly relied on finely targeted measures. The beginning of this transformation to a modern market economy relied on a liberalism from above and was at times dependent on the active involvement of the courts and the police. But the stability of the market and a spontaneous order required more than this: it required visible proofs that markets were capable of delivering improvements relative to traditional grain policies. In other words, liberal reforms did not emerge because of popular support but they *survived*, once enforced, owing to popular consent.

Royals, élites and liberals

The first phase of reforms was intimately tied to the existence of reform-minded autocratic royals supported, encouraged and sometimes manipulated by their intellectual advisors – or, as was the case in Prussia under Frederick William III in the early nineteenth century – an enlightened and homogeneous bureaucracy which acted in the absence of a strong king. Market reforms were part of a desire to modernise agriculture, to strengthen the nation-state and to widen the tax base. The reformers also shared an intellectual heritage. At this early stage the reform-minded intelligentsia was a smallish group, a cosmopolitan clique, and although isolated, it had access to the ruling élite, which some of its members had been born into or adopted. The main intellectual inspiration was the teachings of the Physiocratic school, as discussed in chapter 1, although there were also indigenous liberal thinkers and reformers in, for example, such diverse environments as Sweden and Italy. In the main theatres of reform – France, the Habsburg monarchy, Tuscany, Spain and Sweden – the royals had a personal knowledge of and sympathy for Physiocratic ideas, although most of them were quite ecclectic in their use of them. What appealed was not necessarily the esoteric theoretical abstractions for which that school is remembered but the concern for agriculture at a time when financial stress cast a shadow over mercantilist subsidies to urban pursuits. While the impact of *les économistes* was inevitable in France, the fact that Gustavus III of Sweden, Joseph II of Habsburg Austria, Pietro Leopoldo of Tuscany and Carlos III of Spain were also inspired by Physiocratic thought indicates that this body of ideas had a general appeal. There were several strands of Physiocratic thought that proved congenial to the royals of the time. Most important, of course, were its endorsement of autocratic rule and the solutions it offered to the perennial problems of a lethargic agricultural sector victimised by huge variations in prices and earnings. Physiocratic political theory opposed new thinking on a division of power between legislative and executive functions and made taxation of the rent on land the unique source of revenue for the king. This 'single tax' was supposed to guarantee that the king, in his own interest, served the interests of the productive sector – i.e. the agrarian sector – by increasing its output.[5] The close relationship between the liberal thinkers and the enlightened despots was as much a pragmatic solution as based on political theory. To rally support from an autocratic ruler could turn out to be the quickest way of implementing enlightened new ideas since it entailed by-passing the resistance of the public and of vested interests in the grain-policy bureaucracy. Some liberals endorsed autocratic rule naively and unconditionally, while others developed a critique of political authoritarianism as they experienced the opportunism and frequent policy shifts of the royals.[6]

The first phase of reform in the 1760s–80s was primarily concerned with the deregulation of wholesale trade, traditionally limited to authorised dealers; barriers to entry were removed. This was a response to the belief that free entry increased the number of traders, making collusion more difficult. At about the same time, the guilds were deprived of some, though not all, of their privileges. There were three major areas of reform in the European move to grain market liberalisation:

• First, as already mentioned, came the liberalisation of internal trade – i.e. the establishment of free entry into the grain trade and acknowledgement of legitimacy of unrestricted contracting and the principles of market pricing.

• Second, external trade barriers became more transparent and predictable when the ad hoc quantitative restrictions vanished and were replaced by tariffs on a sliding–scale, that is, the tariff declined with the rising internal price.

• Finally by the middle of the eighteenth century tariffs became less protectionist or disappeared entirely, and the public 'production' of price stability through sales and purchases by public granaries was abandoned.

In order to understand the demise of public granaries in Europe it is essential, however, to note that in many cases old policies were not abandoned explicitly. For one thing, recurrent financial unaccountability

---

[5] The political theory was codified rather late in the evolution of Physiocratic thought by J.H. Le Mercier de la Rivière in *L'ordre naturel et essentiel des sociétés politiques*, Paris, 1767. Gustavus III, the Swedish king and reformer, who was impressed by Le Mercier, staged a *coup d'état* in 1772 to reintroduce autocratic rule. In the end, this proved to be a fatal step, although his was a reign of liberal reform. The tragic end of the story is told in Giuseppe Verdi's *Un ballo in maschera*.

[6] Anders Chydenius, the remarkable and original Finno-Swedish liberal praised Gustavus III of Sweden when he staged his *coup* in 1772. See his *Tal hållet vid vår allernådigste konungs, konung Gustav III's höga kröning*, Stockholm, 1772. Pietro Verri, the Lombard reformer, on the other hand became increasingly estranged from the very idea of enlightened despotism when he witnessed Joseph II's political opportunism.

meant that the activities of public granaries were interrupted for long periods during the *ancien régime*. The main reason for this was the excessive risks and frequent losses accruing when stored grain could not be sold off at the expected price; the result was the accumulation of huge debts. Not only did rats and rot reduce the inventories, but the limited life of grain forced the untimely renewal of stocks, bringing granaries repeatedly to *bancarotta*. During the old order it was often possible to generate support for a revitalisation of the granary in the aftermath of dearth but as liberalisation proceeded it became increasingly difficult to convince local councils or national parliaments to come up with the necessary subsidies. The last major attempt, though typically a local rather than a national experiment, concerned the Parisian *Caisse de la Boulangerie*. Its price-stabilising activity developed as a response to the crisis of the late 1840s; it is worth noting, however, that the premium over the market price of grain charged by the *Caisse* in periods of plenty was supposed to finance the losses incurred by the artificially low prices charged when grain was scarce. Although it actually succeeded in this delicate balancing act, its activities were comparatively short-lived and therefore merits being called *le dernier souffle* of traditional grain market regulation.[7]

Swedish ambiguity and Tuscan robustness

The chronology of reform did not differ much across the nations on the European Continent. It is convenient therefore to describe the Swedish case as a sort of *Idealtyp* reform, constituting in many ways an 'average' European experience. Sweden was an early starter in some respects, a slow starter in others, but never seriously out of step with other nations on the Continent.[8]

Internal trade was liberalised in 1775 by a decree based on the French reform of the 1760s. A translation was promptly and proudly dispatched to Turgot, then *Controlleur Général* in Paris, busy re-introducing the aborted reforms of the 1760s. The impact of Physiocratic thought on economic policy in Sweden has been downplayed in mainstream historiography, with Eli Hecksher setting the tone.[9] However, Hecksher had the grand design of Physiocratic ideology in mind. When the focus is limited

[7] See T. Hori, 'La crise alimentaire de 1853 à 1856 et la Caisse de la Boulangerie de Paris', *Revue Historique*, 552, 1984, pp. 375–401.
[8] The classical study of Swedish grain policies was written by K. Åmark, a pupil of Gustav Cassel and Eli Hecksher. See his *Spannmålshandel och spannmålspolitik i Sverige 1719–1830*, Stockholm: I.Marcus Boktryckeri, 1915. The subsequent devolution of traditional grain policies is analysed in J. Olofsson, *Arbetslöshetsfrågan i historisk belysning. En diskussion om arbetslöshet och social politik i Sverige 1830–1920*, Lund: Lund University Press, 1996.
[9] See E. Hecksher, 'Fysiokratismens ekonomiska inflytande i Sverige', *Lychnos* 1943, pp. 1–20.

to the liberalisation of the grain trade, the French intellectual inspiration is obvious. The French debate was quite familiar to the Swedish élite at the time through the writings by J.F. Kryger and C.F. Scheffer, both well placed and influential men. The former started off as a mercantilist writer and a civil servant in charge of manufacturing subsidies but later came under the influence of the liberalism of Herbert and Quesnay. He revealed no enthusiasm for other aspects of Physiocratic thinking, however.[10] Scheffer was closer to the Physiocrats (and to the future king, Gustavus III, since he was responsible for his education) adapting and translating their work into Swedish.[11]

The main elements of the Swedish reform were undoubtedly inspired by French precedent, although there were indigenous liberal voices. A sort of 'underdog liberalism' can be detected in the writing of the clergyman Chydenius, who represented the remote Northwestern part of Finland in the Swedish Parliament during the years of reform. In a series of pamphlets in the 1760s he attacked monopolies, mercantilist subsidies and discrimination against his region, which was prohibited from trading directly with foreign ports. He seems to have been unaware of the Physiocratic school, although he also saw the potential price-stabilising effect of free trade, which was a major ingredient in the French debate. Grain was not his primary concern but tar, the latter being a major export staple of his area. With price being determined in the world market the obligation to export tar through Stockholm increased storage, handling and transport costs, implying less income for his region.[12] The introduction of free internal trade in 1775–80 and the opening up of non-metropolitan ports to foreign trade had long been advocated by cities and regions outside the metropolitan areas which monopolised foreign trade, and it later became part of the political programme of Gustavus III and his counsellor Johan Liljecrantz who, without being a Physiocrat, had also borrowed some of their ideas.

[10] For an essay in the mercantilist tradition see J.F. Kryger, *Tankar om Swenske fabriquerne*, Stockholm, 1755. Kryger's liberalism is fully developed in his *Landtbrukets hjelp genom en fri spannemålshandel*, Stockholm, 1769.

[11] Scheffer translated and vulgarised the Physiocrats but he did it with a deliberate concern for local political conditions and constraints. On Scheffer's homespun 'Physiocratism' see L. Herlitz, *Fysiokratismen i svensk tappning*, Gothenburg: Meddelanden från Ekonomisk historiska institutionen vid Göteborgs universitet, 1974. A general discussion of economic thought in late eighteenth century Sweden is available in G. Ahlström, 'Swedish economic thought in the eighteenth century', in L. Jonung (ed.), *Swedish Economic Thought. Explorations and Advances*, London: Routledge, 1993, pp. 1–15.

[12] Chydenius opposes the exclusive shipping and trading rights of the major cities in *Wederläggning af de skäl hvarmed man söker bestrida Öster- och Wästerbotniska samt Wästernorrländiske städerne fri seglation*, Stockholm, 1765; the mercantilist subsidies are criticised in *Den nationale vinsten*, Stockholm, 1765 and the dangers of monopoly are exposed in *Källan till rikets wanmagt*, Stockholm, 1765.

The first wave of reform opened entry into wholesale trade and no longer restricted the location of transactions to open markets at particular hours. In a first step only the grain-surplus regions were permitted the new freedom; the remaining part of Sweden enjoyed the same rights from 1780. The exclusive rights given to cities to control trade diminished, but they survived in retail trade in grain and bread, at least in the larger cities. Not until 1846 were all remnants of the old legislation abolished, however. External trade was as a rule subject to frequent temporary quantitative restrictions, in Sweden as elsewhere. The important innovation was that unpredictable import and export bans were replaced by tariffs on a sliding scale, which made trade relations more transparent and regulated by predictable rather than ad hoc rulings. As has been argued previously, orders based on unilateral trade bans encouraged autarchy because they undermined confidence in the accessibility of foreign markets for sales and purchases.[13] In a transition period, tariffs on a sliding scale coexisted with temporary quantitative restrictions, but the latter became increasingly rare: by 1830 ad hoc trade restrictions had disappeared, although the abolition of protective tariffs had to wait until 1855. In this respect, Sweden conformed to the European pattern and timing.

Yet Swedish liberalism was ambiguous. While restrictions on internal and external trade were removed a system of public granaries was actually activated. During the late eighteenth century the granaries co-ordinated supply to the state-run distilleries and made ad hoc interventions to stop prices from reaching unacceptably low or high levels. During the last quarter of the eighteenth century an attempt was made to introduce in an orderly way policies which had earlier been pursued erratically. However, this activism did not pass unnoticed by critics and Parliament.[14] When the state-run distilleries were dismantled by the end of the eighteenth century the relative importance of public purchases declined considerably. At the same time, public granaries were reorganised and it was stressed that their open-market operations should respect the workings of normal trade and not deprive the grain merchants of their profit. Public granaries were also instructed to cover their own costs.[15] The new element is the policies pursued after 1830 aimed at identifying the groups

---

[13] Although all nations would be better off if all made their markets accessible, a single nation would gain by exploiting the openness of others while permitting itself the freedom to impose quantitative restrictions from time to time. This would be the dominant strategy and would lead to a sub-optimal state of generalised trade restrictions. See chapter 4 for an elaboration of this point.

[14] The advantages of private 'speculation' over public hoarding were argued by E. Schröder in a speech to the Royal Academy of Science. See his *Tal om nyttan av en utvidgad handel med inrikes spannmål*, Stockholm, 1792.

[15] See Åmark, *Spannmålshandel och spannmålspolitik*, 1915, pp. 254–6.

or individuals most at risk and to focus policy to assist them selectively. An element of entitlement protection was introduced and day-labourers were singled out as particularly vulnerable. The basic idea in the new policy was to finance public works – for example, road construction – and to employ those out of work because of harvest failure.[16]

In the first quarter of the nineteenth century Swedish agriculture was transformed from being a more or less permanent net importer of grain to a net exporter. The focus now shifted towards purchases of home-produced grain to stop prices from falling, either on a national or a regional basis. However the public granaries were not very successful at disposing of their surplus grain, and with the new ethos of sound financial accountability opposition mounted and the Parliament decided in 1824 to abolish the public granary system.[17] From the mid-1820s grain policies were restricted to loans or support in kind to distressed regions to meet immediate needs. These activities declined over the years and came to a halt in the 1860s. In principle, these advances were supposed to be repaid, although the government was reasonably generous in extending the period of repayment and in the implied interest rates charged. There was an unsuccessful attempt at reviving a system of local co-operative granaries in the early 1830s, this venture will be discussed in detail below because the hostile reception it got reveals an ideological turn away from traditional grain market management.

The gradualism, the inconsistencies and the slow pace of Swedish reforms were replicated in continental Europe with the exception of Tuscany. In Tuscany the reforms in 1767–75 were more radical and consistent than elsewhere in this period, and they were consequently praised in the *Ephémérides du citoyen*, which fretted, and with reason, at the frailty of French reforms. International trade in grain without the customary restrictions was permitted. The reforms have been seen as the work of Pietro Leopoldo, prince of Tuscany, who became Leopold II of the Habsburg monarchy on the death of his brother, the equally francophile Joseph II. There is now evidence that the reform plans predated Pietro Leopoldo's taking power in 1765. Tuscany could boast an indigenous liberal intellectual tradition, as represented by Sallustio Bandini writing in the 1730s, and carried over to the decades of reform by Pompeo Neri. Neri not only published Bandini but also played an important role in the

---

[16] The new policy direction was announced in several government papers in the period 1835–45, see especially *Kungl. Majts. Nådiga proposition . . . angående medel för undsättningar vid inträffade svårare missväxter*, Stockholm, 1834 and *Kungl. Majts. Nådiga proposition . . . angående åtgärderna till behöfvandes undsättning i missväxtår*, Stockholm, 1841.

[17] See R. Adamson, 'Statlig spannmålspolitik i övergången mellan merkantilism och liberalism 1810 – 1825', in J. Myrdal (ed.), *Statlig jordbrukpolitik under 200 år*, Stockholm: Nordiska Muséet, 1991.

design of the dismantlement of the *Abbondanza,* the Tuscan system of grain market management.[18] The liberalism of Bandini had nothing to do with Physiocratic ideas since his work preceded them; like the Physiocrats, he owed an intellectual debt to the pioneer French liberal writer Boisguilbert (see chapter 1) without having the latter's power of persuasion. Bandini was in a sense a bridge between Boisguilbert and Richard Cobden, the nineteenth-century anti-corn law campaigner who held Bandini in high esteem.[19] Like Chydenius, Bandini voiced the concern of a neglected region. His case for liberal reforms was made from the perspective of *La Maremma*, the coastal region southwest of Siena, where he happened to be a land-owner. Rich in agricultural possibilities, its development was subject to dictates from Florence. In Bandini's view, arbitrary controls on external trade depressed prices and restricted potential output in the Maremma.

Why was reform comparatively easy to complete in Tuscany? The reforms were much delayed in other parts of Italy, both in the Habsburg Lombardy, discussed below, and in southern Italy's *Regno di Napoli*.[20] Perhaps Tuscany had an advantage in a comparatively good market performance in the terms defined in chapter 5. As shown there, well established trading networks gave eighteenth-century Tuscan markets such as Pisa and Siena the lowest price volatility of all the European markets investigated. Were Tuscans more inclined towards reform, because they had prior experience of well functioning markets? We can only guess, but it follows from the general thrust of our argument that good market performance helps to broaden the support for reforms.

France: the fraility of reform

Nowhere is the precarious balance between enlightened reform and initial popular defiance better illustrated than by the fate of reform in France. The swings from reform to counter-reform were frequent until the early nineteenth century and the food riot was a constraint on liberal reforms. It is true that bureaucratic inertia and sabotage from vested interests in the traditional machinery of grain policy administration played a role in the early years. More important, however, was the unfortunate timing of reforms, which more than once coincided with severe subsistence crises that would have threatened the political order under

---

[18] See M. Mirri, *La lotta politica in Toscana intorno alle 'riforme annonarie'*, Pisa: Pacini, 1972, pp. 17–19.

[19] Cf. the Connena Bonelli edition of S. Bandini's *Discorso Sopra la Maremma di Siena*, Florence: Leo S. Olschki Editore, 1968, p. 214.

[20] P. Macry, *Mercato e societá nel Regno di Napoli. Commercio del grano e politica economica del '700*, Naples: Guida Editori, 1974, chapter 6.

any circumstances. Attempts at reform in the mid-1760s, and again in the 1770s, were partly aborted owing to poor harvests, and the next wave of reform had to wait the outbreak of the French Revolution. It was not long-lived, either;[21] during the radicalisation of the revolution price controls were introduced, and customary interventions in grain trade became the order of the day. With Napoleon the tide turned again, and a gradual liberalisation took place. Attentive to the moods of the population Napoleon succeeded in isolating the most radical revolutionary groups, who wanted a permanent return to old-style regulation.[22] There was also an increased reliance on selective means. Soup kitchens served *Rumfort*, a vegetable soup, and the police did not hesitate to repress rioters. The policy was thus one of carrot and stick.[23] However, not even Napoleon was immune to popular agitation. Although he had publicly mocked the inefficiency of politically imposed maximum prices in the 1790s, he found himself re-introducing similar legislation during the 1812 famine. The return to traditional methods of market management did not secure the availability of grain in the areas most in need, however. Since it was left to the regional councils to determine maximum prices, they did so in a 'beggar-thy-neighbour' way so as to retain local grain or attract it from regions which were less shrewd. This unsuccessful intervention was the last large-scale revival of old practices on a national scale. The return to liberal policies became irreversible during the Restoration monarchy.

An important shift in policy occurred in France as in other countries when external trade became subject only to a sliding-scale tariff, with high import duties when the internal price was low, and high export duties when the internal price was high. The purpose was to insulate the French market from extreme external price shocks, but also to fix French prices at a level above the world market. This represented a policy more in tune with the landed interest, and such legislation remained in force, with minor modifications, until repeal of the corn laws in the mid-nineteenth century.

Two latecomers: the Habsburg monarchy and Prussia

While early French reforms vacillated owing to popular opposition and bureaucratic inertia, a hesitant mood reigned in the Habsburg monarchy,

---

[21] See P. Binet, *La réglementation du marché du blé en France au XVIIIe siècle et à l'époque contemporaine*, Paris: Librarie sociale et économique, 1939.

[22] See R. Monnier, 'De l'an II à l'an IX, les derniers sans-culottes', in J. Nicolas, *Mouvements populaires et conscience sociale, XVIe–XIXe siècles*, Paris: Maloine, 1985, pp. 591–602.

[23] G. Lavalley, *Napoleon et la disette de 1812: A propos d'une émeute aux Halles de Caen*, Caen 1896.

despite the presence of able and outspoken free traders in the entourage of Joseph II. Joseph's own views were rather eclectic and his choice of counsellors somewhat erratic. When he finally employed the reformer count Karl von Zinzendorf it was only when Joseph Necker, who had repealed Turgot's grain policies in the 1770s, turned down a job offer. Von Zinzendorf had travelled widely throughout the monarchy, and came under the influence of radicals in the *Caffè* group in Milan before he visited the Physiocratic *salons* in Paris.[24] Reforms were piecemeal, with some progress being made in the heartland. Not only was breakthrough in the Habsburg empire rather late, but its timing was unlucky, coming just before severe disturbances in harvests and in international trade in the late 1780s. As a result, this first liberal experiment was short-lived. There were regional differences, though. A stronger liberal spirit prevailed in the Habsburg Low Countries, given their long-standing involvement in the international grain trade, and this encouraged local political pressures for free trade.[25] The wavering mood in Vienna was reinforced by local opposition in Austrian Lombardy, even though Milan also had a vital group of enlightened intellectuals active in reform politics, such as Pietro Verri and Cesare Beccaria. Count Kaunitz, who headed the Italian office in Vienna, was also a reformer with Physiocratic links and hoped to make Lombardy a testing ground for free trade. Several reforms were drafted but abandoned before being enacted because of unfavourable harvests or local opposition from the Milanese oligarchy. In the end, reforms in Lombardy had to wait until Vienna finally decided on free trade in the entire empire, just a decade before the Napoleonic invasion brought further reforms.[26]

The slow start and hesitancy of the Habsburg reform movement may have simply been a reflection of the weakness of the liberals within the élite. Given the fact that in this period reforms did not appeal to a stable consensus, this proved to be a decisive defect. When Leopold II – alias Pietro Leopoldo of the Tuscan reforms, and by any standard the most reform-minded of Maria Theresa's sons – succeeded Joseph II, contemporaries were surprised and some were disappointed by his moderation and

[24] See H.P. Liebel-Weckowics, 'Count Karl v.Zinzendorf and the liberal revolt against Joseph II's economic reforms, 1783–1790', in H.V. Wehler (ed.), *Sozialgeschichte Heute, Festschrift für Hans Rosenberg zum 70.Geburtstag*, Göttingen: Vandenhoeck & Ruprecht, 1974, pp. 69–85.

[25] See H. van Houtte, *Histoire économique de la Belgique à la fin du ancien régime*, Ghent: 1922, and chapter 5 in W.A. Davies, *Joseph II: An Imperial Reformer for the Austrian Netherlands*, The Hague: Martinus Nijhoff, 1974.

[26] A.I. Grab, *La politica del pane. Le riforme annonarie in Lombardia nell'età Teresiana e Giuseppina*, Milan: F. Angeli, 1986, and 'The politics of subsistence: the liberalization of grain commerce in Austrian Lombardy under Enlightened Despotism', *Journal of Modern History* 57, 1985, pp. 185–210.

retreat from previous commitments. Yet his behaviour might simply reflect the fact that he was isolated, not only politically but also intellectually.[27]

Prussia was also a late starter in the movement towards grain market deregulation. Once there, in the second decade of the nineteenth century, there was less ambiguity. Grain market liberalisation was only a part of a general move towards economic deregulation and did not precede it as in many other nations. When the sweeping new legislation which aimed at *Gewerbefreiheit* was put into force, the momentum of a liberalism with a Physiocratic imprint was long gone and had been replaced by the teachings of Adam Smith. The favourable reception of Adam Smith in the German university world was astonishing given the institutional strength of Cameralism, the German version of Mercantilism. But it helped to forge an intelligentsia that resisted calls for a return to the old order in the turbulent years to come.[28] Smith's teachings flourished in several universities in the late eighteenth century, most notably in Göttingen and Köningsberg, and to some extent in Halle.[29] Since public servants were recruited from the universities, Smith's disciples were to be found at all levels in the early nineteenth-century state administration, and most importantly at the top. The architects of German liberalisation, Stein and Hardenberg, both had an intimate direct knowledge of and admiration for Adam Smith's work. The need for reform had been highlighted by Prussia's humiliating defeat by France, but it was an enlightened bureaucracy rather than a despot that seized the initiative. The pressing need to cut costs was an important impetus for reform. 'Zahlen! Zahlen! Das ist das Lied des Kaisers', as Hardenberg – one of the architects behind the reforms – confessed to his diary. But to some extent the weakness of Frederick William III gave the bureaucracy an independence to implement policies they believed necessary for the modernisation of Prussia.[30]

---

[27] N. White, *Serf, Seigneur, and Sovereign: Agrarian Reform in 18th Century Bohemia*, Minneapolis: University of Minnesota Press, 1966, pp. 158–9.

[28] They were by no means insensitive to the hardships they saw and some of them revised their doctrines accordingly. During the 1816–17 famines Julius Soden, an outspoken liberal academic, was quick to recognise the harvest failures as the basic reason for the increase in prices, but he came out in favour of a re-establishment of public granaries. In his view, the violent price increase was also due to the fact that granaries had ceased to play a role they previously had in smoothing price movements. See *Die Theurung im Jahr 1816. Versuch einer Darstellung der Quellen dieser Theurung und der ohnfehlbaren Mittel, deren Wiedererscheinung auf immer zu verhüten*, Leipzig, 1817.

[29] See W. Treue, 'Adam Smith in Deutschland, zum Problem des Politischen professors zwischen 1776 und 1810' in W. Conze, (ed.), *Deutschland und Europa. Festschrift für Hans Rothfels*, Düsseldorf: Droste Verlag, 1951, pp. 101–33.

[30] There is a large literature on the Prussian 'mandarins' that cannot be reviewed here. A few relevant studies related to the theme in this chapter can be mentioned however: I. Mieck, *Preussische Gewerbepolitik in Berlin 1806–1844*, Berlin: W. de Gruyter, 1965 and B. Vogel, *Allgemeine Gewerbefreiheit*, Göttingen: Vandenhoeck & Ruprecht, 1983.

The abolition of the guilds came comparatively early, and market principles governing behaviour and prices were resisted by the representatives of the old order, often supported by local administrations – for example, the Berlin *Magistrat*. By and large the political homogeneity of the central administration stymied attempts to reintroduce old regulations.[31] However, even though the guilds were deprived of their formal privileges, they remained strong, though not in all areas: industrial milling arrived before the first industrial bakery in Berlin, the latter not until the mid-nineteenth century. In the international grain trade quantitative restrictions were replaced by tariffs in 1818, three years before the *échelle mobile* tariff was introduced in France. Germany later followed French swings between free trade and mildly protectionist tariffs in the closing decades of the nineteenth century. However, the return to protectionism in some European countries did not imply a return to the old policies of grain market management. The new protectionism of the late nineteenth century was not aimed at establishing price *stability*, but with increasing the *level* of prices.

The changing mood of bureaucracies and their subjects

The basic problem that reformers faced was that the predicted and promised decline in price volatility as a consequence of the deregulation of grain markets did not materialise until well into the nineteenth century when cheaper transport stimulated the integration of markets. As long as prices fluctuated violently, the reforms were at risk. By the first quarter of the nineteenth century the most critical moment for grain market liberalisation had passed in the sense that the core elements in the reforms were not repealed, not even temporarily. The popular demands for a reversal of policies had not ceased, but governments were now ideologically determined not to give in, and had the strength to resist. During the *ancien régime* rulers defaulted in one or both respects. The free internal market was established, literally, with recourse to the forces of order as much as with ideological persuasion. With the wave of international trade liberalisation in the mid-nineteenth century, which presupposed a more robust international order, the long transition from quantitative ad hoc restrictions to free trade, so typical of the international disorder of the *ancien régime*, was completed. There were still occasions when governments were forced by acute subsistence crises to take extraordinary action to secure the supply of food, but the times of systematic intervention in grain markets were gone. There were stations of this change. Bureaucracies,

<hr>

[31] R.K. Oselleck, *Preussen zwischen Reform und Revolution*, Stuttgart: E. Klett Verlag, 1966.

both central and local, increasingly converted to a liberal ideology and then pursued it conscientiously and *furthermore* the ultimate popular demand for radical intervention, often expressed in the food riot, waned. Liberal views were diffused to a wider audience, both socially and geographically, in the sense that the new ideas were not restricted to metropolitan élites. This change in the public mind was a slow process, which can be traced back to the end of the old order. A new and more understanding view of the corn merchants appears in the pamphlet literature; often the victims of public scorn, they were now praised for their accomplishments 'fetching Corn from the Place where it is in the greatest Plenty, and carrying it to that place which stands most in need of it'. There was also much more self-esteem: 'We Corn-factors will dig, and bring Corn out of holes before a Want shall happen', an English pamphleteer writes referring to the Mediterranean habit of underground storage.[32] At the outset, this was a dissident voice: the traditional animosity against market principles did not disappear lightly. It no longer remained unchallenged, however, and in due course it became the dominant view.

The campaign for a free market in early nineteenth-century France and Sweden

Let us first focus on the changing attitude and role of bureaucracies. This entails a close reading of documents which refer to critical moments in the transition to a market economy for grain – in 1812 and 1816–17 in France, and the early 1830s in Sweden. In the first wave of reforms in the 1760s, reformers, particularly in France, bitterly complained about the sabotage against the reforms undertaken by hostile local authorities and an indifferent central government. But things were very different in the early nineteenth century. In 1812 and 1816–17 France was the centre of two major subsistence crises which during the old regime would have unleashed a whole series of governmental regulations. The successive governments reacted very differently, and this time the intense correspondence between local and central government reveals a decisive shift in economic ideology. In May 1812 Napoleon introduced, perhaps more out of desperation than conviction, a series of tight regulatory initiatives, which signalled a return to traditional policies. Although free internal circulation of grain was defended in principle, local *préfets* and mayors were supposed to be informed about transports out of their *département*, and they also obtained the legal means to make requisitions and impose maximum prices. Local officials were also instructed to make a census of

---

[32] Anon., *Sentiments of a corn-factor on the present situation of the corn trade*, London, 1758, p. 11.

all available grain. The reaction from the *préfets* to this initiative varied between reluctant loyalty to outright defiance, with the majority coming closer to defiance.

Finding little enthusiasm or support for the measures undertaken, the Ministry of the Interior distributed a questionnaire, a reflection perhaps of the anxious mood in Paris, in which the *préfets* were asked to respond to a set of questions about the need for action, resultant improvements in supply, if any, and potential counter-productive effects of the measures undertaken.[33] Very few responding *préfets* showed enthusiasm for, or even signs of understanding, the sudden return to the old order. In fact the only unreserved support, but with a suspiciously subservient tone, came from the occupied Italian province of *Appenines*. Further to the south in the occupied Tuscan province *Ombrone* – a place with a tradition of free trade in grain since Pietro Leopoldo's days and the home of the liberal pioneer Sallustio Bandini – the opposite position was taken, and *con brio*. This was also closer to the typical response. In summary, the replies suggested that the measures introduced brought no observed improvement in supply; on the contrary, the effects – if any – were counter-productive. The supply to markets dried up on the very day of the publication of the new regulations, the *préfet* in *Haute-Loire* complained. Most mayors defied the order to carry out a census of available grain but the reasons given differed. In some cases it was reported that since the region was a deficit region grain was always lacking before harvest, and hence it would be meaningless to undertake a census at the time (May) the instructions to do so were issued. Others argued that since producers would suspect that a census might constitute the informational basis for future expropriations they would rather hide, and consequently withdraw, their grain from the open market. Besides, the scope for cheating was too great to make a census meaningful since quite a few of the mayors responsible for the practical execution of the census were themselves farmers.[34]

The *préfets* were no strangers to how markets worked, although some were more cunning than others. There were consequently two main reactions to the instructions on a maximum local price. Those who set the price below the prevailing market price found their markets deserted and complained to Paris about the higher price permitted in other regions. Nantes on the Atlantic coast, for example, which depended on grain supplied from regions along the Loire, got its price wrong. Consequently its regular supply dried up because of the 'beggar-thy-neighbour' policies of other regions. In *Haute-Loire* – usually a source of supply for Nantes – the

[33] The relevant documents and the correspondence are found in Archives Nationales, Paris, boxes F11 700–F 11 725.
[34] See the *Loiret* dossier in F 11 712 (16 July 1812), date of letter in parentheses.

préfet was quite explicit about the mechanisms at work. He admitted when writing to Paris that no attempt had been made to keep prices down, because it would jeopardise internal supply.[35] The unfortunate regions which persisted in their attempts to regulate prices at below market level had to rely on requisitions, but quite a few found such measures '*embarrassante pour l'administration*', and resorted to competitive price maxima to attract grain from law-abiding *départements*.[36] The apparent indifference on the part of the central authorities towards the open or poorly disguised defiance from the regional authorities contrasted distinctively with the way things were handled in the next subsistence crisis, in 1816–17, which was as severe as the preceding one. By then Napoleon and his policies were history. Louis XVIII presided over a law and order government, whose reigning ideology was that of the primacy of the market and the free circulation of grain. Tensions began to mount after the harvest in 1816, but the government made it clear by means of a *circulaire* in November that no mass intimidation of merchants, attempts at halting inter-regional transport, or *taxation populaire* (a practice whereby the crowd imposes a price on merchants or farmers under threat) would be tolerated. It made clear that the forces of order would be used with determination and that any sign of weakness or vacillation must be avoided. By and large local authorities complied, some more enthusiastically than others, of course.[37] The *préfet* of *Aube* revealed that the establishment of an orderly market economy need not always be a peaceful and harmonious process: '*L'autorité militaire et l'administration marchent d'un pas égal pour protéger la libre circulation des grains*', he reported proudly.[38] Such reactions can be interpreted as the instinctive empathy of the local representative for law and order. But there was more to it than that. In 1816–17 local authorities were expected to obey and not to give in to any sort of local opposition, be it popular unrest or disloyalty on the part of the local administration. The *Ministère de la Police Générale* in Paris reacted immediately to the smallest sign of defiance on the part of the local powers. In some cases they had reason to do so because local authorities returned to traditional habits of regulation and requisitions. But such cases were exceptional and severely reproached by Paris. The *préfet* of *Aude* offers a

---

[35] While part of the new regulation was followed, the price maximum was not, or as the *préfet* puts it with a surprising but revealing verbal twist: that part had been executed 'beaucoup moins ou pour mieux dire ne l'a pas été'. *Haute-Loire* dossier F 11 712 (12 September 1812).

[36] See the letters from the *préfets* in *Alpes-Maritimes* and *Alpes Basses*, which both explain the motives for their fixing prices at a competitive level. F 11 706 (24 December 1812) and (28 July 1812), respectively.

[37] The relevant documentation on the 1816–17 crisis is in the Archives Nationales, Paris, boxes F 11 723–F 11 735.   [38] See the *Aube* dossier in F 11 723 (6 October 1816).

rare example of an official who openly expressed sympathies for old policies, and Paris urgently dispatched a condemnation of this ideological
disobedience. A return to the methods of 1812 was out of the question.
These policies not only proved to be impractical and useless, they had
been a failure in that very *département* that year, and they were also an
indefensible infringement of private property rights. In short, the
Ministry offered troops for repression and lectures in political economy.[39]

There were several riots in this period and the Ministry in Paris followed the judicial processes closely, pointing out over and over again that
fermeté was needed. If the desired determination was lacking or if leniency
characterised the handling of the suspects, Paris did not take long to
intervene.[40] But the Ministry did not restrict its attention to cases of
obvious mismanagement, laxity or weakness. It also reacted to the slight-
est sign of ideological impurity or signs of a lack of understanding of the
principles of a market economy. When a *préfet* wrote that the markets
were calm and adequately supplied '*de confiance*', the Ministry's reaction
was a barely disguised allegation that some sort of administrative pressure
was involved to help supply the markets. Before giving the *préfet* a chance
to reply, the Ministry proceeded to affirm that such political pressures
were against the principles of a free market.[41] While repression of the
riots and the determined persecution of the leaders constituted one pillar
in the new policy, the other was an effort to popularise the ideology of the
market. On several occasions these two aims had to be reconciled because
lower ranks of the forces of order were susceptible to '*erreurs populaires*',
and spontaneously sided with the insurgents. They consequently had to
be educated and convinced about the merits of the new ideology.[42]

In Sweden, where public granaries continued to play a role, the 1820s
saw an increased hostility to state involvement in the grain trade. That the
shift in opinion was not limited to the metropolitan élite was revealed by
discussion regarding the future of the local granaries. These local granaries constituted a type of voluntary savings bank, where the savings were in
grain rather than in cash, and helped subscribing peasants evade high real
interest rates when they faced temporary shortages during the harvest
year. All transactions were made in terms of grain and the interest rate
was fairly low, although it was a little higher for non-members.[43] A

---

[39] See the *Aude* dossier in F 11 725.
[40] See, for example, the Loire-et-Cher dossier in F 11 727.
[41] This revealing correspondence between 28 December 1816 and 18 January 1817 is in
the *Haute-Garonne* dossier, F 11 727.
[42] See, for example, the instructions from the Ministry of War in the F 11 206 dossier to the
préfet in Lille, in northern France, who was struggling to gain control over the soldiers, 1
December 1816.
[43] The economic rationale of this institution is discussed in chapter 2 above.

government proposal to make these institutions compulsory was circulated among regional assemblies which were asked to spell out their opinions. The government proposal got some support, but in general the responses from regional officials and representatives suggest that a new mood was in the process of penetrating the country. Liberal convictions and the belief in market principles were now supported by the educated classes. The clergy, officers and regional government officials displayed an elementary capacity for liberal economic reasoning, especially if they were from regions which were involved in the grain trade. In the end, needless to say, the government's proposal came to nothing. That increased trade was more likely to produce price stability than public granaries was a central tenet of the new ideology.[44] The discussions in the 1820s paved the way for an entirely new way of addressing the subsistence problem. In the decades that followed, public works emerged as an alternative to traditional market regulation.

The decline of the food riot

Even though the documents referred to above indicate a geographical and social diffusion of the new ideas, they do not tell us much about the opinions of ordinary men and women, and there is no easy way of finding out about them. If we want to interpret the changing mood of the common people we are probably best served by studying their actions, in which case the food riot stands out as an adequate index of popular sentiment. The food riot expressed in a desperate way the disrespect for property rights and the blind forces of the market. Ideas of fairness and the right to be adequately fed were central beliefs; political pressures, pillage, or imposed 'fair' prices, were the means towards these ends. As late as the 1840s rioters all over Europe called for the return of the old regulations, but with little success. However, the threat of riots was long a constraint for the liberalisation of grain markets and helps explain its slow pace. Nonetheless, the evolution of the incidence of food riots suggests a lengthy process of popular acceptance of deregulation. Popular revolts and food riot were an almost permanent feature of European history up till the mid-nineteenth century, but their incidence varied. A combination of increasing prices and price volatility proved to be the most certain indication of their resurgence. Periods of rioting also coincided with regulatory responses. One such period was the late sixteenth century, which witnessed the codification of rules prescribing market transparency in the Tudor *Book of Order*; the early decades of the seventeenth century were

---

[44] See 'Handlingar rörande inrättandet av sockenmagasiner, Kungliga remisser', Riksarkivet (National Archives, Stockholm), series D: aa.

also turbulent. The latter half of the seventeenth century, with the exception of the 1690s and the first half or two-thirds of the eighteenth century, depending on what country one investigates, were comparatively calm. The latter half of the eighteenth century and early parts of the nineteenth century, a period encompassing the first phase of liberal reform, contained the most turbulent years. Yet by 1850 the food riot as an endemic social phenomenon had vanished.[45] There were isolated outbursts of social agitation, but liberal convictions were now stronger and a combination of poor relief and the forces of law and order halted a return to the old situation.

The underlying long-run structural forces explaining the disappearance of food rioting must also be emphasised. The detailed account of improved market performance given in chapter 5 corroborated the intuition of Turgot, Herbert and other early French liberals that market integration would diminish price volatility. Not until the nineteenth century can one speak of well integrated markets, however. Before that it was a case of regional but little national or international integration. 'Integration' here means that pairs of markets pass cointegration tests. Furthermore the speed of adjustment back to equilibrium price ratios between markets after shocks increased considerably during that century and, finally, price volatility measured as the standard deviation of the residual of the best predictive model declined.[46] By the second half of the nineteenth century price volatility had fallen to about one-third of the level attained in the sixteenth century. More importantly it was considerably lower than in Cologne, the 'role model' of successful grain market regulation. Alone among major European cities, Cologne never experienced a food riot in the seventeenth and eighteenth centuries.[47]

There was a simultaneous economic and social differentiation of the population: an increase in the size of the middle classes and the evolution of groups of relatively well paid workers who spent a declining proportion of their income on food at a time when the number of substitute foods (notably maize and potatoes) increased. For the poorer half of the popu-

[45] The chronology of food rioting in Europe is well researched, and there is no need to be more specific here. See A. Charlesworth, *An Atlas of Rural Protest in Britain 1548–1900*, London: Croom Helm, 1983; C.B. Bouton, *The Flour War, Gender, Class and Community in Late Ancien Régime French Society*, University Park: Pennsylvania State University Press, 1993; L.B. Tilly, 'The decline and disappearance of the classical food riot in France', *Working Paper*, 147, New School of Social Research, 1992.

[46] The best predictive model was either a 'pure' random walk with seasonal dummies or a model with a short autoregressive structure, often just one lag.

[47] See D. Ebeling, 'Versorgungskrisen und Versorgungspolitik während der Zweiten Hälfte des 16.Jahrhunderts in Köln', *Zeitschrift für Agrargeschichte und Agrarsoziologie*, 27 (1), 1979, pp. 32–59.

lation the budget share spent on grain (and food and drink based on grain) declined from a pre-industrial level around 50–75 per cent to 15–30 per cent by the end of the nineteenth century. Price volatility affecting grain was therefore no longer a severe threat to the maintenance of a customary standard of living. The 'Engel effect' – i.e. the decreasing proportion of income spent on food – was partly reinforced by the international integration of grain markets. Reduced transport costs brought cheap grain from Russia and the New World to Europe, contributing to a prolonged decline in food prices and an increase in real wages. At first glance, a decline in price volatility to a third of its previous level might seem modest. However, when combined with the declining share of grain in consumption, it makes a great difference. A measure of the combined 'impact' would involve comparing the residual standard deviation of price volatility multiplied by the share of grain in consumption at two points in time. Such a measure is meaningful because when the price elasticity of demand for grain is low a price increase would significantly affect the customary consumption pattern, in the sense that grain consumption would necessarily have a 'crowding-out' effect on other items in the diet. The higher the share of income spent on grain, the higher the price volatility and the more inelastic demand, the more important this effect. Our results from chapter 5 suggest that the share of grain in consumption was around 25 per cent and the residual variation 4 per cent by the second half of the nineteenth century, down from 65 and 11 per cent, respectively, during the *ancien régime*. Thus the implied change in the 'impact', measured as suggested above, is a sevenfold decrease (0.65 times 0.11/0.25 times 0.04 = 7.15).

The Continent in the English mirror

Poverty did not disappear. Yet social differentiation and rising real wages in the second half of the nineteenth century opened the way for *selective* rather than *general* policies, since rising prices no longer threatened the entire population, or even a major part of it. A pan-European drift towards free trade inspired by the repeal of Corn laws in the United Kingdom helped to secure the secular rise in real wages, so that the proportion of population in need during a subsistence crisis dwindled to 10–20 per cent. Entitlement protection for those most at risk by means of social policy and insurance then developed as a more adequate policy response. And the fact that agitation around grain market regulation had disappeared by the middle of the nineteenth century as the new social policies developed was not accidental. Social policy stressed income support rather than market management, and thereby marked a shift in the political priorities of governments, trade unions and political parties. It is true that liberals were worried about the adverse effects on effort from poor relief, but they showed great ingenuity in making relief conditional on good behaviour. In Sweden, for example, economic support was from early on tied to temporary employment in infrastructure projects such as road construction.

These new institutions were more efficient and more reliable than the poor relief of earlier epochs, which was organised by private and religious charities. England pioneered a fairly comprehensive system of poor relief financed by property taxes rather than voluntary contributions from the wealthy, and there is no clear sign that taxation crowded-out private donations. Although English poor relief pre-dated the Industrial Revolution, an obvious interpretation would be to see it as another sign of the modernity of the first industrialising nation. Peter Solar has suggested that the English poor relief actually paved the way for economic development by inviting the poor not to hang on to tiny plots of land but to seek employment knowing that if they failed temporarily to do so they still had some entitlement protection.[48] The paradoxical implication of this is that poor relief helped labour markets to work more smoothly. Did it also help in the liberalisation of commodity markets? The peculiarity of the English experience is the *timing*: efficient poor relief *and* grain market liberalisation come at about the same time *and* almost a century earlier than on the Continent. E.P.Thompson explicitly linked the early decline in grain market regulation in England to the late seventeenth-century development of poor relief. Its provision offered 'an institutional safety-net'.[49] The net failed to catch many who needed help, but it compared favourably to the systems in the rest of Europe at a time when traditional market regulation still prevailed. England took the lead in targeting those in need and gave them some entitlement support; not surprisingly, poor relief spending reached an all-time high during the Napoleonic wars, as a response to high grain prices. From the first half of the nineteenth century onwards, in the wake of the dismantling of market regulation, continental Europe followed the English example by introducing tax-financed poor relief. Public spending on poor relief had converged to a rate of about 1 per cent of national income by the latter half of the nineteenth century: a modest accomplishment by modern standards, but a substantial improvement compared to the charities-based systems practised during the *ancien régime*.

[48] P.M. Solar, 'Poor relief and English economic development before the industrial revolution', *Economic History Review*, 48 (1), 1995, pp. 1–22.
[49] E.P. Thompson, *Customs in Common*, Harmondsworth: Penguin Books, 1993, pp. 299–300.

The triumph of economic liberalism presupposed not only an improvement in living standards and market performance that would give credibility to the affirmations of liberal ideology as to the advantages of markets over government, but also new ways for governments to rectify market outcomes.

Sources

UNPUBLISHED SOURCES

Archivio di Stato di Pisa, *Opera del Duomo*, Files no. 989–1009; referred to in this book as the Malanima manuscript. *See below* under Pisa
Archives Nationales, Paris F 11 200–F 11 206, F 11 700–F 11 725
Riksarkivet, Stockholm, series D: aa, Handlingar rörande inrättandet av socken-magasiner. Kungliga remisser

PUBLISHED SOURCES

DESCRIPTION OF THE DATA SET

The price data are homogeneous in the sense that they are all *market prices* based on price series which have been collected by officials and entered into records of market exchanges of wholesale or semi-wholesale markets, the so-called *Marktprotokolle* (Vienna), *Fruchtpreisbücher* (Cologne), *Termatieboeken* (Brussels), *Donderdaghs Prothocol* (Ruremonde) or *mercuriales* (France and French-speaking Belgium). The London prices are an exception to this rule, *see* below. In published sources, prices are either monthly averages, or average price at a particular day each month, usually the first market day of each month. The purpose of recording grain prices, a task in most cases undertaken by city authorities, was to form a basis for price and weight controls of bread – the assize of bread – and to intervene in grain markets to stabilise prices by selling or buying of stocks and to regulate trade. Prices, if not otherwise specified, are nominal prices expressed in the prevailing unit of account in the area.

There is also a problem of missing data. Incomplete series have been completed by a method described in the appendix to chapter 5 (p. 114). Single price series have been converted to logarithms and, if possible, to uniform units of account. When this is not possible, as in the nineteenth-century Vienna series, the linkage between series with different units of account have been arranged in the following way. The first observation in the new series has been simulated on the basis of the preceding series. That simulated value forms the index base for the new series, with the first observation taking the simulated value, and subsequent observations indexed on the first observation.

Brussels (Bruxelles), Belgium, 1568–1696 and 1728–94, 1800–1902
Wheat and rye
C. Verlinden (ed.), *Dokumenten voor de geschiedenis van prijzen en lonen in*

156

Vlanderen en Brabant, vol. 1, Bruges: De Tempel, 1959. J. Craeybeck was responsible for the collection of the *ancien régime* data; description of the source, pp. 481–5; tables, pp. 486–501. Prices are based on the first market day of each month. Units of account: Stuivers per sester.

For 1800–1902, C. Verlinden (ed.), *Dokumenten voor de geschiedenis van prijzen en lonen in Vlanderen en Brabant,* vol. 3, Bruges: De Tempel, 1972. C. Vandenbroeke was responsible for the collection of the data; description of the data set, pp. 289–96. Price quotations date from the first market day of each month. Prices and volumes have been converted to the following uniform units of account: Francs per hectolitre.

Bruges, Belgium, 1796–1914
Wheat and rye
C. Verlinden (ed.), *Dokumenten voor de geschiedenis van prijzen en lonen in Vlanderen en Brabant,* vol. 4, Bruges: De Tempel, 1973.
W. Vanderpijen was responsible for the collection of the data, which reports price on the first market day of each month; description of the data set pp. 167–76. Prices and volumes have been converted to the following uniform units of account: Francs per hectolitre.

Cologne (Köln), Germany, 1531–1797
Wheat and rye
D. Ebeling and F. Irzigler, *Getreideumsatz, Getreide- und Brotpreise in Köln 1368–1797,* vol. 65, Cologne: Mitteilungen aus dem Stadtarchiv von Köln, 1976; description of sources, pp. xxi–xxx. Monthly averages based on weekly averages. Monthly tables, pp. 530–663. Units of account: Albus per Kölner Maltern.

France, various cities, 1825–1913
About 50 French cities, completed by S. Drame *et al., Un siècle de commerce du blé en France 1825–1913,* Paris: Economica, 1991; description of the data, pp. 99–103. For most of the period one price (the first market day) per month (two records per month in 1825–1913). Units of account: Francs per hectolitre.

France, yields of wheat, 1825–69.
Yields in hl per ha, nine regions
Ministère de l'Agriculture et du Commerce, Direction de l'Agriculture, Bureau des Subsistances, *Récoltes des céréales et des pommes de terre de 1815 à 1876,* Paris, 1878.

London, England, 1683–1799 and 1845–72
Wheat
W. Beveridge, *Prices and Wages in England from the Twelfth to the Nineteenth Century,* vol. 1, London, Frank Cass 1965.
Description of the source, pp. 535–9.
This is a navy victualling source, and therefore not necessarily comparable with the *'mercuriale'*-based series.
The 'London' series for 1845–72 are *Banker's Gazette* prices extracted from *The Economist.* I am grateful to Jan Tore Klovland, Norwegian School of Economics

and Business Administration, who kindly permitted me to use a data set he had prepared.

Paris, France, 1520–1698
Wheat
M. Baulant and J. Meuvret, *Prix des céréales extraits de la mercuriale de Paris*, Paris: Ecole Pratique des Hautes Etudes, 1960.
Units of account: Livres tournois per Paris-setier.

Pisa, Italy, 1549–1818
Wheat, rye, barley, oil and beans
Unpublished manuscript; Professor Paolo Malanima, Pisa University, has been kind enough to let me use the data. Price quotations relate to the first market day of each month.
Units of account: Lire per sacco.

Ruremonde, The Netherlands, 1599–1796
Wheat and rye
J. Ruwet et al., *Marché des céréales à Ruremonde, Luxembourg, Namur et Diest aux XVIIe et XVIIIe siècles*, Leuven: Presse de l'Université de Louvain, 1966.
Description of sources, the so-called Donderdaghs Prothocol, pp. 13–24; tables, pp. 49–90. Prices are from the first market day of each month.
Units of account: Gulden per malder.

Siena, Italy, 1546–1765
Wheat
Giuseppe Parenti, *Prezzi e mercato del grano a Siena 1546–1765*, Florence: C.Cya, 1942. Description of the sources, pp. 19–32; table in appendix. Monthly averages based on weekly prices. Prices have been transformed to lire per sacco.
Units of account: Soldi per staio senese.

Toulouse, France, 1486–1913
Wheat
Series based on '*mercuriale*' sources first published by G. and G. Freche, *Les prix des grains, des vins et des légumes à Toulouse*, Paris: Presses Universitaires de France, 1967.
This source uses different units of account per setier (Toulouse) in different periods but the series has been transformed to Francs per hectolitre.

Utrecht, The Netherlands, 1534–1690
Wheat and rye
J. A. Sillem, *Tabellen van marktprijzen van granen te Utrecht in de jaaren 1393 tot 1644*, Verhandlingen der Koninklijke Akademie van Wetenschappen te Amsterdam, New Series, vol. III, no. 4. This material was later completed by N. W. Posthumus, *Inquiry into the History of Prices in Holland*, vol. 2, Leiden: International Scientific Committee on Price History, 1964, pp. 399–434. Accounting principles changed in the eighteenth century and I have therefore not used the whole series.
Units of account: Stuivers per modius.

Wien (Vienna), Austria, 1692–1910
Wheat, rye and barley
A.F. Pribram, *Materialen zur Geschichte der Preise und Löhne in Österreich*, vol. 1,
Vienna: Carl Überreuters Verlag 1938.
Description of the sources, pp. 193–8; tables pp. 386–402. Monthly averages have
been estimated from a large number of recorded transactions during each month.
Units of account: Kreuzern per Wiener- or Land-Metzen. Frequent changes in
accounting units.

Bibliography

CONTEMPORARY POLITICAL ECONOMY, 1690–1850

JOURNALS, C.1760–C.1770

Ephémérides du citoyen (EdC), *Gazette du Commerce* (GdC), *Journal de l'Agriculture, du Commerce et des Finances* (JdA), *Journal Économique* (JE)

PUBLISHED LISTS OF BOOKS AUCTIONED PUBLICLY, AVAILABLE BUT UNREGISTERED AT THE ROYAL LIBRARY (KB) IN STOCKHOLM

Förteckning på en samling af medicinska, oeconomiska och diverse andra böcker, Stockholm, 1765
Förteckning på en samling af wackra och wälconditionerede böcker, mest om handel, Stockholm, 1765
Förteckning på en samling af wäl conditionerade fransyska, ängelska och andre böcker, Stockholm, 1765

PAMPHLETS

Abbé Baudeau, N. (1768). *De l'entière et parfaite liberté de commerce des bleds,* EdC, 1768: I
Abeille, L.-P. (1768). *Faits qui ont influencé sur la cherté des grains en France & Angleterre,* also in JE, July and August 1768.
Anon. (1757a). *A compendium of the corn trade,* London.
    (1757b). *Considerations on the present dearness of corn,* London.
    (1758). *Sentiments of a corn-factor on the present situation of the corn trade,* London.
    (1766a). *A letter from Richard in the Country to Dick in the City on the Subject of Publick Granaries,* Dublin.
    (1766b). *An essay to state some arguments relative to Publick granaries,* Dublin.
    (1767). *An appeal to the public: or consideration on the dearness of corn,* London.
    (1770). *Considerations on the exportation of corn,* London.
Bandini, S.(1968). *Discorso Sopra la Maremma di Siena,* ed. L.C. Bonelli, Florence: Leo S. Olschki Editore
Boisguilbert, P., (1696). *Le detail de la France, ou la France ruinée sous la règne de Louis XIV,* Cologne

Browne, S. (1765). *The laws against ingrossing, forestalling, regrating and monopolizing*, London

Carleson, C. (1759). *Tal om spannemålsbristens afhjelpande*, Stockholm

Chydenius, A.(1765a) *Den nationale vinsten*, Stockholm

(1765b). *Källan till rikets wanmagt*, Stockholm

(1765c). *Wederläggning af de skäl hvarmed man söker bestrida Öster- och Wästerbotniska samt Wästernorrländiske städerne fri seglation*, Stockholm

(1772). *Tal hållet vid vår allernådigste konungs, konung Gustav III's höga kröning*, Stockholm

Davenant, C. (1699). *An essay upon the probable methods of making people gainers in the balance of trade*, London

Delamare, N. (1710). *Traité de la police*, vol. 2, Paris: P. Cot

Dickson, A. (1773). *An essay on the causes of the present high prices of provisions*, London

Dupont de Nemours, P.S. (1764). *De l'exportation et de l'importation des grains*, Paris

(1770). *Observations sur les effets de la liberté du commerce des grains*, EdC, 1770: VI

Galiani, F. (1770). *Dialogues sur la commerce des blés*, London

Herbert, C.-J. (1755). *Essai sur la police générale des grains, sur leurs prix et sur les effets de l'agriculture*, Berlin

(1759). *Observations sur la liberté du commerce des grains*, Amsterdam

Kryger, J.F. (1755). *Tanker om Swenske fabriquerne*, Stockholm

(1769). *Landtbrukets hjelp genom en fri spannemålshandel*, Stockholm

Kungl. Majts. Nådiga proposition till rikets ständer, angående medel för undsättningar vid inträffade svårare missväxter, 23 September 1834, Stockholm 1834

Kungl. Majts Nådiga proposition till rikets ständer, angående åtgärderna till behöfvandes undsättning i missväxtår, 24 February 1834, Stockholm 1841

le Mercier de la Rivière, J.H. (1767). *L'ordre naturel et essentiel des sociétés politiques*, Paris

Necker, J. (1775). *Sur la législation et le commerce des grains*, Paris

Quesnay, F. (1757). *Grains*, in Diderot, D. et al., *Encyclopédie*, vol. 7, Paris

Récoltes des céréales et des pommes de terre de 1815 à 1876, Paris, 1878

Schröder, E. (1792). *Tal on nyttan av en utvidgad handel med inrikes spannmål*, Stockholm

Smith, A. (1776). *An inquiry into the nature and causes of the wealth of nations*, London

Smith, C. (1758). *A short essay on the corn trade and the corn laws*, London

(1766). *Three tracts on the Corn Trade*, London

Soden, J. (1817). *Die Theurung im Jahr 1816. Versuch einer Darstellung der Quellen dieser Theurung und der ohnfehlbaren Mittel, deren Wiedererscheinung auf immer zu verhüten*, Leipzig

Turgot, A.R.J. (1913–23).*Oeuvres de Turgot et documents le concernant*, ed. G. Schelle, vols. 1–5, Paris: F.Alcan

Verri, P. (1962). *Riflessioni sulle Leggi vincolanti principalmente nel commercio de'-grani* (1769, 1797), in S. Romagnoli (ed.), *Illuministi settentrionali*, Milan: Rizzoli

Whitworth, C. (ed.) (1771). *The Political and Commercial Works of Charles D'Avenant*, vol. 2, London
Young, A. (1775). *Political arithmetic*, London

REFERENCES

Adamson, R. (1991). 'Statens spannmålspolitik i övergången mellan merkantilism och liberalism 1818–1825', in J. Myrdal (ed.), *Statens jordbrukspolitik under 200 år*, Stockholm Nordiska muséet
Ahlström, G. (1993). 'Swedish economic thought in the eighteenth century', in L. Jonung (ed.), *Swedish Economic Thought, Explorations and Advances*, London: Routledge, 1–15
Alter, G. and J.C. Riley (1989). 'Fraility, sickness and death: models of morbidity in historical populations', *Population Studies*, 43, 25–46
Anderson, T.W. (1994). *The Statistical Analysis of Time Series*, New York: Wiley Classical Library
Appelby, A.B. (1979). 'Grain prices and subsistence in England and France 1590–1740', *Journal of Economic History*, 39, 865–87
Ardeni, P.G. (1989). 'Does the law of one price really hold for commodity prices?, *American Journal of Agricultural Economics*, 71(3), 661–9
Aymard, M. (1966). *Venise, Raguse et le commerce du blé pendant la seconde moitié du XVIe siècle*, Paris: Les Editions de l'Ecole des Hautes Etudes en Sciences Sociales
Åmark, K. (1915). *Spannmålshandel och spannmålspolitik i Sverige 1719–1830*, Stockholm: I. Marcus Boktryckeri
Balani, D. (1987). *Il vicario tra città e stato. L'ordine publico e l'annona nella Torino del Settecento*, Turin: Deputazione subalpina de storia patria
Barnes, D.G. (1930). *A History of the English Corn Laws from 1660 to 1846*, London: Routledge
Basini, G.L. (1960). *L'uomo e il pane. Risorse, consumi e carenze alimentari della populazione modenese nel Cinque e Seicento*, Milan: A. Giuffrè
Baulant, M. and J. Meuvret (1960). *Prix des céréales extraits de la mercuriale de Paris*, Paris: Ecole des Hautes Etudes
Bengtsson, T. and R. Ohlsson (1985). 'The standard of living and mortality response in different ages', *European Journal of Population*, 1
Beveridge, W. (1929). 'A statistical crime of the seventeenth century', *Journal of Economic and Business History*, 1, 503–33.
  (1965). *Prices and wages in England from the Twelfth to the Nineteenth Century*, vol. 1, London: Frank Cass
Binet, P. (1939). *La réglementation de marché du blé en France au XVIIIe siècle et à l'époque contemporaine*, Paris: Librarie sociale et économique
Blanc, H. (1939). *La Chambre des Blés de Genève*, Geneva: Georg & Cie SA
Bohstedt, J. (1983). *Riots and Community Politics in England and Wales*, Cambridge, Mass: Harvard University Press
Bouton, C.B. (1993). *The Flour War, Gender, Class and Community in Late Ancien Régime French Society*, University Park: Pennsylvania State University Press
Bowden, P. (1967). 'Statistical appendix', in J. Thirsk, (ed.), *The Agrarian History of England and Wales*, vol.4, Cambridge: Cambridge University Press, 814–70

Britnell, R.H. (1993). *The Commercialisation of English Society 1000–1500*, Cambridge: Cambridge University Press

Broadberry, S.N. and N. F. R. Crafts (eds.) (1992). *Britain in the International Economy*, Cambridge: Cambridge University Press, 1992.

Charlesworth, A. (1983). *An Atlas of Rural Protest in Britain 1548–1900*, London: Croom Helm

Chartres, J. (1990), 'The marketing of agricultural produce, 1640–1750' in J. Chartres (ed.), *Agricultural Markets and Trade 1500–1750*, vol. 4 in J. Thirsk (general ed.), *Chapters from the Agrarian History of England and Wales, 1500–1750*, Cambridge: Cambridge University Press, 160–255

Craeybeck, J. (1958). Brod en levensstandard. Kritische nota betreffende de prijs van het brood te Antwerpen en te Brussel in 17e en de 18e eeuw', *Cahiers d'Histoire des Prix*, 3, 133–62

Dal Pane, L. (1932). *La questione del commercio dei grani nel Settocento in Italia*, vol. 1, Milan: F.lli Tampieri

Davies, W.A. (1974). *Joseph II: An Imperial Reformer for the Austrian Netherlands*, The Hague: Martinus Nijhoff

Drame, S. *et al.* (1989). *Un siècle de commerce du blé en France 1825–1913*, Paris: Economica

Drèze, J. and A. Sen (1989). *Hunger and Public Action*, Oxford: Clarendon Press

Early Malnutrition and Mental Development (1974). XII Symposia of the Swedish Nutrition Foundation, Uppsala: Almqvist & Wiksell

Ebeling, D. (1979). 'Versorgungskrisen und Versorgungspolitik während der Zweiten Hälfte des 16. Jahrhunderts in Köln', *Zeitschrift für Agrargeschichte und Agrarsoziologie*, 27 (1), 32–59

Ebeling, D. and F. Irzingler (1977). *Getreideumsatz, Getreide- und Brotpreise in Köln, 1368–1797*, Vienna: Bohlau Verlag

Ejrnæs M. and K.G. Persson (1999). 'Grain storage in early modern Europe', *Journal of Economic History*, 59 (3)

Engle, R.F. and C.W.J. Granger (eds.) (1991). *Long-run Economic Relationships. Readings in cointegration*, Oxford: Oxford University Press

Everitt, A. (1990). 'The marketing of agricultural produce, 1500–1640', in J. Chartres (ed.), *Agricultural Markets and Trade 1500–1750*, vol.4 in J. Thirsk (general ed.), *Chapters from the Agrarian History of England and Wales, 1500–1750*, Cambridge: Cambridge University Press, 15–141

Fahrmeir, L. and G. Tutz (1994). *Multivariate Statistical Modelling Based on Generalised Linear Models*, Berlin: Springer Verlag

Flinn, M. (ed.) *Proceedings of the Seventh International Economic History Congress*, Edinburgh: Edinburgh University Press

Fogel, R. (1989). 'Second thoughts on the European escape from hunger: famines, price elasticities, entitlement, chronic malnutrition and mortality rates', *NBER Working Papers on Historical Factors and Long Run Growth*, 1
(1992). 'Second thoughts on the European escape from hunger: famines, chronic malnutrition, and mortality rates', in S.R. Osmani (ed.), *Nutrition and Poverty*, Oxford: Clarendon Press, 243–86

Franz, G. (1960). 'Die Geschichte des deutschen Lebensmittelhandels', in G. Franz *et al.* (eds.), *Der deutsche Landwarenhandel*, Hanover: Strothe

Freche, G. and G. Freche (1967). *Les prix des grains des vins et des legumes à Toulouse*, Paris: Presses Universitaires de France

Froot, K.A., M. Kim and K. Rogoff (1995). 'The law of one price over 700 years', *NBER Working Paper*, 5132

Galassi, F. (1992). 'Was feudalism inevitable? A critique of Gunnar Persson', *Scandinavian Economic History Review*, 40 (2), 34–43

Galloway, P.R. (1985). 'Annual variations in death by age, deaths by cause, prices, and weather in London 1670–1830', *Population Studies*, 39, 487–505

   (1988). 'Basic patterns in annual variations in fertility, nuptuality, mortality and prices in pre-industrial Europe', *Population Studies*, 42, 275–304

Garnsey, P. (1988). *Famine and Food Supply in the Graeco-Roman world: Response to Risk and Crisis*, Cambridge: Cambridge University Press

Gibson, A.J.G. and T.C. Smout (1995a). *Prices, Food and Wages in Scotland 1550–1780*, Cambridge: Cambridge University Press

   (1995b). 'Regional prices and market regions: the evolution of the early modern Scottish grain market', *Economic History Review*, 48 (2), 258–82

Gomez, V. and A. Maravall (1994). *TRAMO, Time Series Regression with ARIMA Noise, Missing Observations and Outliers*, Manual, European University Institute, Florence, mimeo

Goodwin, B.K. (1992). ' Multivariate cointegration test and the law of one price in international wheat markets', *Review of Agricultural Economics*, 14 (1), 117–24

Grab, A.I. (1985). 'The politics of subsistence: the liberalization of grain commerce in Austrian Lombardy under Enlightened Despotism', *Journal of Modern History*, 57, 185–210

   (1986). *La politica del pane. Le riforme annonarie in Lombardia nell'età Teresiana e Giuseppina*, Milan: F. Angeli

Granger, C.W.J. and C.M. Elliot (1967). 'A fresh look at wheat prices and markets in the 18th century', *Economic History Review*, 20 (2), 257–65

Grantham, G. (1989). 'Jean Meuvret and the subsistence problem in Early Modern France', *Journal of Economic History*, 49 (1), 43–72.

Green, W.H. (1993). *Econometric Analysis*, 2nd edn., Englewood Cliffs: Prentice-Hall International

Halfpenny, P. (1981). 'Two-variable and three-variable functional explanations', *Philosophy of Social Science*, 11, 27–32

Hansen, H. and K. Juselius (1995). 'CATS in RATS, cointegration analysis of time series', Institute of Economics, University of Copenhagen, mimeo

Harley, Knick C. (1992). 'The world food economy and pre-World War I Argentina', in S.N. Broadberry and W.F.R. Grafts (eds.), *Britain in the International Economy*, Cambridge: Cambridge University Press, 244–68

Hatanaka, M. (1994). *Time-series based econometrics*, *Advanced Texts in Econometrics*, Oxford: Oxford University Press

Hecksher, E. (1943). 'Fysiokratismens ekonomiska inflytande i Sverige', *Lychnos*, 1–20

Herlitz, L. (1974). *Fysiokratismen i svensk tappning*, Gothenburg: Meddelanden från Ekonomisk historiska institutionen vid Göteborgs universitet

Hertner, P. (1978). 'L'approvisionnement des villes et la politique des prix alimentaires des administrations municipales aux 17e et 18e siècles', in M. Flinn (ed.), *Proceedings of the Seventh International Economic History Congress*, Edinburgh: Edinburgh University Press, 347–59

Herzog, A. (1909). *Die Lebensmittelpolitik der Stadt Strassburg im Mittelalter*, Berlin: W. Rothschild

Hillebrand, H. (1923). 'Die Getreidepolitik und Brotversorgung der Reichsstadt Aachen', *Zeitschrift des Aachener Geschichtsvereins*, 45, 1–66

Hori, T. (1984). 'La crise alimentaire de 1853 à 1856 et la Caisse de la Boulangerie de Paris', *Revue Historique*, 552, 375–401

Hoskins, W.G. (1964). 'Harvest fluctuations and English economic history, 1480–1690', *Agricultural History Review*, 12 (1), 28–46

(1968). 'Harvest fluctuations and English economic history, 1620–1759', *Agricultural History Review*, 6 (1), 15–31

van Houtte, H. (1922). *Histoire économique de la Belgique à la fin du ancien régime*, Ghent

Jevons, S. (1879). *Theory of Political Economy*, London, Macmillan

Johansen, H.C. (1969). 'Staten som kornhandler, 1783–88', in *Erhvervshistorisk årbog 1969*, Aarhus: Universitetsforlaget, 62–82

Johansen, S. (1995). *Likelihood-based Inference in Cointegrated Vector Autoregressive Models*, Oxford: Oxford University Press

Johnston, J. (1994). *Econometric Methods*, Singapore: McGraw-Hill International

Jörberg, L. (1972). *A History of Prices in Sweden*, 2 vols., Lund: C.W.K. Gleerup

Kaplan, S. (1976). *Bread, Politics and Political Economy in the Reign of Louis XV*, 2 vols., The Hague: Martinus Nijhoff

(1984). *Provisioning Paris, Merchants and Millers in the Grain and Flour Trade in the Eighteenth Century*, Ithaca: Cornell University Press

(1996). *The Bakers of Paris and the Bread Question, 1700–1775*, London: Duke University Press

Larrère, C. (1992). *L'invention de l'économie au XVIIIe siècle. Du droit naturel à la physiocratie*, Paris: Presses Universitaires de France

Lavalley, G. (1896). *Napoleon et la disette de 1812: A propos d'une émeute aux Halles de Caen*, Caen

Lee, R. (1981). 'Short-term variations in vital rates, prices, and weather' in E.A. Wrigley and R. Schofield, *The Population History of England 1541–1871: A Reconstruction*, London: Edward Arnold

Liebel-Weckowics, H. P. (1974). 'Count Karl v. Zinzendorf and the liberal revolt against Joseph II's economic reforms, 1783–1790', in H.V. Wehler (ed.), *Sozialgeschichte Heute, Festschift für Hans Rosenberg zum 70. Geburtstag*, Göttingen: Vandenhoeck & Ruprecht, 69–85

Lunn, P.G. (1991). 'Nutrition, immunity and infection', in R. Schofield, D. Reher and A. Bideau (eds.), *The Decline of Mortality in Europe*, Oxford: Clarendon Press, 131–45

Macry, P. (1974). *Mercato e società nel Regno di Napoli. Commercio del grano e politica economica del '700*, Naples: Guida Editori

Mattozzi I. *et al.* (1983). 'Il politico e il pane a Venezia, 1570–1650: calmieri e governo della sussistenza', *Società e Storia*, 20, 271–303

McCloskey, D.N. and J. Nash (1984). 'Corn at an interest: the extent and cost of grain storage in Medieval England', *American Economic Review*, 74 (1) (March), 174–87

Meuvret, J. (1977). *Le problème des subsistances à l'époque Louis XIV. La production des céréales dans la France du XVIIe et du XVIIIe siècle*, Paris: Mouton

(1988). *Le problème des subsistances à l'époque Louis XIV. Le commerce des grains et la conjoncture*, 2 vols., Paris: Editions de l'Ecole des Hautes Etudes en Sciences Sociales

Mieck I. (1965). *Preussische Gewerbepolitik in Berlin 1806–1844*, Berlin: W. de Gruyter

Miller, J.A. (1995). *The Stealth State: Supplying Cities in Early Nineteenth Century France*, Department of History, Emory University, mimeo

Mirri, M. (1972). *La lotta politica in Toscana intorno alle 'riforme annonarie'*, Pisa: Pacini

Mitchell, B.R. (1992). *International Historical Statistics, Europe*, 3rd edn, London: Macmillan

Mizon, G.E. (1991). 'Modelling relative price variability and aggregated inflation in the United Kingdom', *Scandinavian Journal of Economics*, 93 (2), 189–211

Mokyr, J. and R. Stein (1994). *Science, Health and Household Technology: The Effect of the Pasteur Revolution on Consumer Demand in the UK 1850–1941*, National Bureau of Economic Research, mimeographed conference report

Monnier, R. (1985). 'De l'an II à l'an IX, les derniers sans-culottes', in J. Nicolas *Mouvements populaires et conscience sociale, XVIe–XIXe siècles*, Paris: Maloine

Myrdal, G. (1933). *The Cost of Living in Sweden, 1830–1930*, London: P.S.King

Myrdal, J. (ed.) (1991). *Statlig jordbrukpolitik under 200 år*, Stockholm, Nordiska Muséet

Naudé, W. (1901). *Die Getreidehandelspolitik und Kriegsmagazinverwaltung Brandenburg-Preussens bis 1740*, Berlin: Acta Borussia

Naudé, W. and U. Stalwiet (1910). *Die Getreidehandelspolitik und Kriegsmagazinverwaltung Preussens 1740–1756*, Berlin: Acta Borussia

Newbery, N.M.G. and J.E. Stiglitz *The Theory of Commodity Price Stabilization. A Study in the Economics of Risk*, Oxford: Clarendon Press

Nielsen, R. (1997). 'Storage and English government intervention in early modern grain markets', *Journal of Economic History*, 57 (1), 1–33

Ó Gráda, C. (1999). *Black '47 and Beyond: The Great Irish Famine in History, Economy and Memory*, Princeton: Princeton University Press

Olofsson, J. (1996). *Arbetslöshetsfrågan i historisk belysning. En diskussion om arbetslöshet och social politik i Sverige 1830–1920*, Lund: Lund University Press

Olsen, G. (1942–4). 'Studier' i Danmarks Kornavl og Kornhandelspolitik i Tiden 1610–60', *Historisk Tidsskrift*

Oncken, A. (ed.), (1888). *Ouevres économiques et philosophiques de F. Quesnay*, Paris: J. Peelman

Oselleck, R.K. (1966). *Preussen zwischen Reform und Revolution*, Stuttgart: E. Klett Verlag

Osmani, S.R. (ed.) (1992). *Nutrition and Poverty*, London: Clarendon Press

Outhwaite, R.B. (1981). 'Dearth and government intervention in English grain markets, 1590–1700', *Economic History Review*, 34, 389–406

Parenti, G. (1942). *Prezzi e mercato del grano a Siena 1546–1765*, Florence: C. Cya

Persson, K.G. (1988). *Pre-Industrial Economic Growth. Social Organization and Technological Progress in Europe*, Oxford: Basil Blackwell

(1991). 'Was feudalism inevitable?', *Scandinavian Economic History Review*, 39 (1), 68–76

(1996). 'The seven lean years, elasticity traps, and intervention in grain markets in pre- industrial Europe', *Economic History Review*, 49, 692–714

(1999). 'Grain storage', see under Ejrnœs and Persson

Peyer, H.C. (1949). *Zur Getreidepolitik Oberitalienischer Städte im 13.Jahrhundert*, Vienna: Universum Verlag

Pietrzik, K. (ed.) (1991). *Modern Lifestyles, Lower Energy Intake and Micronutrient Status*, Berlin: Springer Verlags

Piuz, A.M. and D. Zumkeller (1981). 'Stocaggio dei grani e sistema annonario in Ginerva nel secolo *XVIII*', *Quaderni Storici*, 46, 168–91

Posthumus, N.W. (1964). *Inquiry into the History of Prices in Holland*, vol. 2, Leiden: International Scientific Committee on Price History, 399–434 (completion of Sillem's material)

Pribram, A.F. (1938). *Materialen zur Geschichte der Preise und Löhne in Österreich*, Vienna: Carl Überreuters Verlag

Pult Quaglia, A.M. (1990). *Per provvedere ai popoli. Il sistema annonario nella Toscana dei Medici*, Florence: Olschki Editore

Rambaud, A. (1911). *La chambre d'abondance de la ville de Lyon 1643–1777*, Lyons

Ravallion, M. (1988). *Markets and Famines*, Oxford: Clarendon Press

   (1997). 'Famines and economics', *Journal of Economic Literature*, 35 (3) (September)1205–42

Revel, J. (1992). 'Le grain de Rome et la crise de l'annone dans la seconde moitié du XVIIIe siècle', *Mélanges de l'Ecole francaise de Rome, Moyen Age-Temps Modernes*, 84 (1), 201–82

Rogers, Thorold (1908). *Six Centuries of Work and Wages*, London

Romani, M.A. (1975). *Nella spirale di una crisi. Popolazione, mercato e prezzi a Parma tra Cinque e Seicento*, Milan: A.Giuffrè

Rosenberg, N. and L. Birdzell (1986). *How the West Grew Rich*, New York: Basic Books

Rothkrug, L. (1965). *Opposition to Louis XIV The Political and Social Origins of the French Enlightenment*, Princeton: Princeton University Press

Rothschild, E. (1992). 'Commerce and the state: Turgot, Condorcet, and Smith', *Economic Journal*, 102, 197–210

Ruwet, J. et al. (1966). *Marché des Céréales à Ruremonde, Luxembourg, Namur et Diest aux XVIIe et XVIIIe siècles*, Leuven: Presse de Université de Louvain

Samuelson, P.A. (1957). 'Intertemporal price equilibrium: a prologue to the theory of speculation', *Weltwirtschaftliches Archiv*, 79, 181– 219

Schelle, G. (1913–23). '*Oeuvres de Turgot*, vols. 1–5, Paris: Felix Alcan

Schofield, R.S., D. Reher and A. Bideau (eds.) (1991) *The Decline of Mortality in Europe*, Oxford, Clarendon Press Cambridge: Cambridge University Press

Scholliers, E. (1960). *De levensstandard in de XVe en XVI eeuw te Antwerpen*, Antwerp: De Sikkel

Schumpeter, J. (1954). *History of Economic Analysis*, Oxford: Oxford University Press

Sen A. (1981). *Poverty and Famines: An Essay on Entitlement and Deprivation*, Oxford, Clarendon Press

   (1983). 'Poor relatively speaking', *Oxford Economic Papers*, 35, 153–69

   (1992). *Inequality Reexamined*, Cambridge, Mass.: Harvard University Press

Sillem, J.A. (n.d.). *Tabellen van markt-prijzen van granen te Utrecht in de Jaaren 1393 tot 1644, Verhandlungen der Koninklijke Academie van Wetenschappen te Amsterdam*, New Series. Vol. III, no. 4; see under Posthumous

Slicher van Bath, B.H. (1963). *The Agrarian History of Western Europe, AD 500–1850*, London: Edward Arnold

Solar, P.M. (1995). 'Poor relief and English economic development before the industrial revolution', *Economic History Review*, 48 (1), 1–22

Stoltz, P. (1977). *Basler Wirtschaft in vor- und frühindustrialer Zeit*, Basle: Schulthess Verlag

Stouff, L. (1970). *Ravitaillement et alimentation en Provence aux XIVe et XVe siècles*, Paris: Mouton

Symposia of the Swedish Nutrition Foundation XII (1974). *Early Malnutrion and Mental Development*, Uppsala: Almqvist & Wicksell

Thirsk, J. (general ed.) (1990). *Chapters from the Agrarian History of England and Wales, 1500–1750*, vol. 4, Cambridge: Cambridge University Press

Thompson, E.P. (1971). 'The moral economy of the English crowd in the eighteenth century', *Past and Present*, 51

(1993). *Customs in Common*, Harmondsworth: Penguin Books, originally published by Merlin Press (1991)

Thurow, L.C. (1971). 'The income distribution as pure public good', *Quarterly Journal of Economics*, 85, 327–36

Tilly, L.B. (1971). 'The food riot as a form of political conflict in France', *Journal of Interdisciplinary History*, 2, 184–200

(1992).'The decline and disappearance of the classical food riot in France', *Working Paper*, 147, New School of Social Research

Tits-Dieuaide, M.-J. (1975). *La formation des prix céréaliers en Brabant et en Flandre au XIVe siècle*, Brussels: L'Edition de l'Université de Bruxelles

Treue, W. (1951). 'Adam Smith in Deutschland, zum Problem des Politischen Professors zwischen 1776 und 1810', in W. Conze (ed.), *Deutschland und Europa. Festschrift für Hans Rothfels*, Düsseldorf: Droste Verlag

Usher, A.P. (1973). *The History of the Grain Trade in France 1400–1710*, 1913; reprint New York: Octagon Books (1973)

Vandenbroeke, C. (1975). 'Agriculture et alimentation', *Centre Belge d'histoire rurale*, 49

Verlinden, C. (ed.) (1959). *Dokumenten voor de Geschiedenis van prijzen en lohen in Vlanderen en Brabant*, vol. 1, Bruges: De Tempel

Verlinden, C. (ed.) (1972). *Dokumenten voor de Geschiedenis van prijzen en lohen in Vlanderen en Brabant*, vol. 3, Bruges: De Tempel

Verlinden, C. (ed.) (1973). *Dokumenten voor de Geschiedenis van prijzen en lohen in Vlanderen en Brabant*, vol. 4, Bruges: De Tempel

Vogel, B. (1983). *Allgemeine Gewerbefreiheit*, Göttingen: Vandenhoeck & Ruprecht

Walter, J. and R.S. Schofield (eds.) (1989). *Famine, Disease and the Social Order in Early Modern Society*, Cambridge: Cambridge University Press

Walter, J. and K. Wrightson (1976). 'Dearth and the social order in early modern England', *Past and Present*, 71, 22–42

Watson, R.R. (ed.) (1984). *Nutrition, Disease Resistance and Immune Function*, New York: M. Decker

Wehler, H.V. (1974). 'Sozialgeschichte Heute', *Festschrift für Hans Rosenberg zum 70. Geburtstag*, Göttingen: Vandenhoeck & Ruprecht

Weir D. (1989). 'Markets and mortality in France 1600–1789', in J. Walter and R. Schofield (eds.), *Famine, Disease and Crisis Mortality in Early Modern Society*, Cambridge: Cambridge University Press

White, N. (1996). *Serf, Seigneur, and Sovereign: Agrarian Reform in 18th Century Bohemia*, Minneapolis: University of Minnesota Press

Will, P.-E. and R.B. Wong (1991). *Nourish the People: The State Civilian Granary*

System in China 1650–1850, Ann Arbor: Center for Chinese Studies, The University of Michigan

Winnick, M. (1976). *Malnutrition and Brain Development*, New York: Oxford University Press

Wrigley, E.A (1987). *People, Cities and Wealth*, Oxford: Basil Blackwell

Wrigley, E.A and R.S. Schofield (1981). *The Population History of England 1541–1871: A Reconstruction*, London: Edward Arnold

Index

References are to Europe unless otherwise stated.

Abbé Baudeau N., 4, 8, 11
Abbé Terray, 13
Abeille, L.-P., 7
Adamson R., 141
agriculture
  distressed state , 7, 11–3, 30
  investments, 18–21, 28
  profits, 15–7
Ahlström G., 139
Åmark K., 74, 138, 140
Aristotle, 106
Arras, 94–6
assize of bread, 78–81
Austria see Habsburg monarchy
autharchy, 84–5 see also trade
Aymard M., 77

Balani, D., 81
Baltic area, 8, 67, 99, 111
Bandini S., 3, 11,141–2, 148
bargaining, 1, 85
Barnes D.G., 73
Basini G.L., 79
Beccaria, C., 144
Bengtsson T., 34
Beveridge, W., 56
Binet P., 143
Blanc H., 83
Bohstedt J., 41
Boisguilbert P., 2–3
Book of Order, 57, 62, 75–6, 89, 151
Bordeaux, 54, 102–3
bounty on grain exports, 12, 85
Bouton C.B., 152
Britnell, R.H., 56, 75
Browne S., 10, 75
Brussels, 78, 101, 112

Caffé group, 144
Carleson, C., 111
Carlos III, 136
carry-over of grain see storage
Charlesworth A., 152

Charlemagne, 1
Chartres, J., 47, 73, 75–6, 87
Chydenius A., 137, 139
cointegration, 96–7, 122–30
Colbert J.B., 1,3
Cologne, 3, 68–71, 78–81, 88–9, 99,
  111–2
collusion see market power
consumption of grain (food), 2, 24–31,
  63–4, 81
  and diversification, 20, 29
  and survival chances, 31–3
consumer protection, 5, 24
Copenhagen, 85
Craeybeck J., 79
credit market imperfections 25, 30, 70;
  sockenmagasin, 30–1
crisis mortality, 33–5, 86

Dal Pane, L., 74
Davenant C., 8,10, 48–52,106
Davies W.A., 144
Danzig, 84
Delamare N., 1,75
Denmark, 85
Diderot, D., 50
Dickson A., 10,76
distribution of income (property, wealth),
  23, 72, 74, 80–1, 133
doings and beings, 23, 32 see also Sen A.
Drame S., 34
Drèze J., 7, 23
Dupont de Nemours P.S., 4–5, 13

Ebeling, D., 80, 152
efficiency in markets for grain, 4, 41, 72,
  74, 86–7, 91– 93
elasticity
  demand, 8, 14, 17, 25, 48–54
  income, 8
élite, 4,7
  governing (ruling) 75, 151 ;
Elliot C.M., 105

England, 54,104–5
    economic thought and subsistence
        policy 1– 2, 10–2, 75, 90, 153–4
    grain prices 50–2, 55– 62
    see also Book of Order and moral
        economy
Engle, R.F., 94
entitlement protection, 7,
    49–50,90,135,141,153
equilibrium error correction see price
    adjustment
external effects of price stabilisation, 71–4,
    77
Everitt A., 75,86–7

Flinn, M., 76
Florence, 3
food riot, 40–1, 132, 152
Fogel R. W., 49–54, 64
France
    depressed state of agriculture, 11, 17
    economic thought 1–8, 12, 136
    grain market policy 1, 5–6, 21, 50–2,
        142–3, 147–9
    mortality 34–7
Franz G., 74
Frederick the Great, 1, 82
Frederick William III, 136, 145
free trade, 2, 4, 8–9, 137–8 see also trade
French revolution, 6, 83, 113
functional explanation of institutional
    change, 132–6

Galassi, F., 133
Galiani F., 4, 6
Galloway P.R., 33–4
Garnsey P., 8
Geneva, 83
Germany see Prussia,
Gibson A.J.G., 78, 105
Grab A.I., 144
grain price see price
Granger C.W. J., 105
Granger R.F., 99
Grantham G., 93
Great Irish Famine, 31
Gustavus III, 136–7, 139

Habsburg monarchy, 131
    economic thought 136
    grain market policy, 102, 143–4
    see also Joseph II and Leopold II
Halfpenny, P., 134
harvest, 11, 13–8
    aggregate versus local shocks, 8, 16–7
    magnitude of failure 47–54, 62–4

health production function, 32–9, 42–7
Hecksher E.,138
Herbert C.-J., 3–5, 9, 106
Herlitz L., 3, 139
Hertner P., 76
Herzog A., 74
Hillebrand H., 81
Holland see The Netherlands
Hori T., 138
Hoskins W.G., 49, 56–7

income effect, 27–9
integrated market see market integration
insider information, 22, 74–5 see also
    market power
intertemporal redistribution see storage
inventory adjustment see storage
investments see agriculture
Irzigler, F., 80
Italy see Tuscany and Habsburg monarchy

Jevons, S., 49
Johansen H.C., 77
Joseph II, 136, 144
Jörberg L.,61, 91

Kaplan, S., 1, 6, 68, 73, 75, 87
Kaunitz, Count, 144
King G., 48–9
Kryger J.F., 10–1, 139

labour supply see wages
Lavalley, G., 143
law of one price, 9, 91–6 see also
    cointegration
Lee R., 33, 64
Leopold II, 136, 141
liberalism, 3–5, 131–2, 135, 139–40,
    146–7
Liebel-Weckowics H. P., 144
Limoges, 5–6
London, 83–4, 88–9, 101, 104, 112
Lyons, 102–5, 112

Macry, P., 142
Malanima, P., 66
malnutrition, 38–40
Maremma, 3, 11, 42
market failure see efficiency of markets for
    grain
market integration
    and consumption , 29–31
    and endemicisation, 39
    and price stability, 7–9, 65–6, 92–3
    and profits in agriculture, 13–17, 20
    and transport costs, 65–7, 95

market leadership, 98–9, 101, 103
market power, 47, 68– 70, 73, 75
Marseille, 102
Mattozzi I., 78
McCloskey D.N., 68–71
Mercantilism, 11–2, 145
Mercier de la Rivière J.H., 4, 137
Meuvret J., 6, 75, 93
Mieck I., 145
Milan, 10
Mirri M., 142
Mokyr J., 35
Molière, 4
Monnier R., 143
moral economy, 23, 41–2
Myrdal G., 62
Myrdal J., 141

Napoleon, 143, 147, 149
Nash, J., 68–71
Naudé W., 74, 82, 84
Necker J., 6
Netherlands, The, 8, 100
Nielsen R., 55–4, 60–2
Normandy, 3

Ó Gráda, C., 31
Olofsson J., 138
Olsen G., 64, 85
Ohlsson R., 34
Oselleck R.K., 146
Osmani S.R., 49
Outhwaite R.B., 84

Paris, 3, 21, 98–9
Peyer, H.C., 74
Physiocrats see Dupont de Nemours,
    Quesnay, Turgot
Physciocratic school, 2–14, 136–7, 139
Pietro Leopoldo see Leopold II
Pisa, 29, 66–71, 88–9, 94–6, 98–100,
    104–5, 110, 112
Piuz A.M., 83
Plato, 4
poor relief, 90, 153–4
Pribam A.F., 66
price
    adjustment 92–4, 98–105
    bubble, 9, 82
    consequences of free trade, 2–4, 7–8,
        100–1
    convergence, 91–2
    equlibrium see law of one price
    maximum 143, 147–8
    modelling, 57–62, 66, 107–9
    seasonality, 67–72

volatility, 1, 3, 7–10, 13, 18, 106–13,
    153
prisoner's dilemma, 85
Prussia, 83–5, 145–6
public granaries see storage
public works, 141
Pult Quaglia A.M., 74

Quesnay, F., 4, 11, 13–4, 50–2

Rambaud, A., 83
Ravallion,M., 9, 31, 33, 42, 82, 106
returns from storage see storage
Revel J., 81
Rogers T., 49, 68
Romani M.A., 85
Rothkrug L., 3–4
Rouen, 94–6, 102–5, 112
Ruremonde, 89, 100, 105

Samuelelson, P.A., 67–8
Savary, J., 68
Schelle G., 13
Schofield R.S., 33–4, 64, 72
Scholliers, E., 81
Schröder, E., 140
Schumpeter J., 5
Scotland, 78–9, 104–5
Sen A., 7, 23, 50
Siena, 3, 68–71, 94–6, 98–9
sliding scale see tariffs
Smith A., 8, 24, 145
Smith C., 2, 10, 76
Smout T.C.
social gains see external effects
Solar P.M., 154
Spain, 136 see also Carlos III
Stalwiet U., 82
Stein R., 35
Stockholm, 10, 139
storage (of grain), 9, 67, 81–4
    extent, 50, 53–4
    price stabilising effects, 10, 47, 65, 68
    profitability, 55, 58–60, 69–71, 88
    public vs. private, 86–90
    rule of thumb, 60–1, 71, 88
Stouff L., 77
social gain see external effects
substitution effect, 27–9
Sweden 61, 136, 138–40

tariffs 56, 140, 146
taxations populaires, 12, 149
Thompson, E.P., 41–2, 154
Thurow L.C., 72
Tilly L.B., 93, 152

Tits-Dieuaide M-J., 73
Toulouse, 88–9, 98–104, 107, 112
trade, 3, 65, 84–5, 91 *see also* free trade
transport cost *see* market integration
Turgot A.R.J., 4–6, 9–11, 13–7, 20–2,
   51–2, 106, 138
Tuscany 3, 8, 11, 21, 98, 136, 141–2

uncertainty, 11, 18, 69–70
Usher, A.P., 73
Utrecht, 112

Vandenbroeke, C., 85
Venice, 78
Verri P., 10–1

Vienna, 66–7, 88–9, 100–2, 112–3
Vogel B., 145

weak exogeneity *see* market leadership
Weir, D., 34
White N., 145
Will P.-E., 134
Wong R. B., 134
Wrigley E.A., 33–4, 49, 55–6, 64

Young, A., 10–12

Zinzendorff, K. von, 114
Zumkeller D., 83